Poetry is no longer a frightening monster lurking in the academic darkness, waiting to leap out and trap the poor, unsuspecting reader. Poetry is an art, and so it communicates. There are high poems and low poems, sad and happy poems, poems that tell a story and poems that sing for the sheer love of singing. And though there are cultures which have no prose, there has never been a culture that did not have poetry. It may not be natural to teach it in schools, but it has always been supremely natural to sing it.

Which is why people go on writing poems, and why people go on reading them.
                                                    —from *How to Read a Poem*

Burton Raffel, author of four books of poetry and of studies of the poets Robert Lowell, T. S. Eliot, and Ezra Pound, has also published nearly twenty volumes of poetry in translation. He is professor of English at the University of Denver.

HOW TO READ
A
POEM

BURTON RAFFEL

A MERIDIAN BOOK

NEW AMERICAN LIBRARY

TIMES MIRROR

NEW YORK AND SCARBOROUGH, ONTARIO

Copyright © 1984 by Burton Raffel

MERIDIAN TRADEMARK REG. U.S. PAT. OFF. AND FOREIGN COUNTRIES
REGISTERED TRADEMARK—MARCA REGISTRADA
HECHO EN HARRISONBURG, VA., U.S.A.

SIGNET, SIGNET CLASSIC, MENTOR, PLUME, MERIDIAN AND NAL
BOOKS are published *in the United States* by New American Library,
1633 Broadway, New York, New York 10019, *in Canada* by The
New American Library of Canada Limited, 81 Mack Avenue,
Scarborough, Ontario M1L 1M8

PERMISSIONS AND ACKNOWLEDGMENTS

Chairil Anwar, "In Vain," from THE COMPLETE POETRY AND
PROSE OF CHAIRIL ANWAR, © 1962, 1963, 1964, 1968, 1970 by
The Research Foundation of State University of New York.
Reprinted by permission of Burton Raffel.

Douglas Asper, "You close your eyes for a moment," "Housecat,"
"One," and "Coccidiodmycosis," reprinted by permission of Douglas
Asper.

John Berryman, "Dream Song #77," from 77 DREAM SONGS,
copyright © 1959, 1962, 1963, 1964 by John Berryman. Reprinted by
permission of Farrar, Straus and Giroux, Inc.

Gwendolyn Brooks, "my dreams, my works, must wait till after hell,"
from THE WORLD OF GWENDOLYN BROOKS, Copyright 1945
by Gwendolyn Brooks Blakely. Reprinted by permission of Harper &
Row, Publishers, Inc.

Caedmon, "Caedmon's Hymn," and anonymous, "The Moon and the
Sun," from POEMS FROM THE OLD ENGLISH, translated by
Burton Raffel, © 1960, 1964 by University of Nebraska Press.
Reprinted by permission of Burton Raffel.

Catullus, poem #58, from CATULLUS, THE COMPLETE
POETRY, translated by F. O. Copley, Copyright © by The
University of Michigan 1957. Reprinted by permission of The
University of Michigan Press.

C. P. Cavafy, "The City," from THE COMPLETE POEMS OF
CAVAFY, translated by Rae Dalven, copyright © 1948, 1949, 1959,
1961 by Rae Dalven. Reprinted by permission of Harcourt Brace
Jovanovich, Inc.

The following pages constitute an extension of the copyright page.

Library of Congress Cataloging in Publication Data

Raffel, Burton.
  How to read a poem.

  Bibliography: p.
  Includes index.
  1. Poetics. 2. English poetry—Explication. 3. American poetry—
Explication. 4. English poetry. 5. American poetry. I. Title.
PN1042.R228 1984   808.1   83-21978
ISBN 0-452-00682-1

First Printing, April, 1984

1 2 3 4 5 6 7 8 9

PRINTED IN THE UNITED STATES OF AMERICA

CONTENTS

1
WHAT POETRY MEANS

DEFINITIONS TELL US a lot less than demonstrations. Most of this book is demonstration—poems and commentary on poems. But here is a reasonable working definition of poetry:

> *Poetry is a disciplined, compact verbal utterance, in some more or less musical mode, dealing with aspects of internal or external reality in some meaningful way.*

Instead of analyzing or elaborating on the definition, let us test it— demonstrate its workability or unworkability—against one of the hardest cases I know of, Lewis Carroll's "Jabberwocky":

'Twas brillig, and the slithy toves
    Did gyre and gimble in the wabe:
All mimsy were the borogroves,
    And the mome raths outgrabe.

5 "Beware the Jabberwock, my son!
    The jaws that bite, the claws that catch!
Beware the Jubjub bird, and shun
    The frumious Bandersnatch!"

He took his vorpal sword in hand:
10   Long time the manxome foe he sought—

So rested he by the Tumtum tree,
    And stood awhile in thought.

And, as in uffish thought he stood,
    The Jabberwock, with eyes of flame,
15 Came whiffling through the tulgey wood,
    And burbled as it came!

One, two! One, two! And through and through
    The vorpal blade went snicker-snack!
He left it dead, and with its head
20   He went galumphing back.

"And hast thou slain the Jabberwock?
    Come to my arms, my beamish boy!
O frabjous day! Callooh! Callay!"
    He chortled in his joy.

25 'Twas brillig, and the slithy toves
    Did gyre and gimble in the wabe:
All mimsy were the borogroves,
    And the mome raths outgrabe.

Any definition that excluded "Jabberwocky," that said it could not be a poem, would pretty clearly be a defective definition.

But what does it *mean*? In part, surely, it is sheer nonsense. The poet has invented many of the key words—but not entirely out of whole cloth. "Brillig," for example, is sufficiently close to "brilliant" to make at least a bit of sense. No one knows what a "tove" might be, but "slithy" is close enough to words like "slither" and "slimy" to convey at least some bits of meaning. "Gyre" and "gimble," too, resemble (though they appear to be verbs) the noun "gyre," meaning movement in a ring or circle, and the verb "gambol." And can anyone doubt that to be "frumious" is bad, whatever else it may (or may not) mean? Or that "frabjous" is just as plainly good?

And in part "Jabberwocky" is not nonsense, but parody, good chortling fun at the expense of a large number of wearisome poems about heroes and heroics. Carroll published *Through the Looking Glass*, in which "Jabberwocky" appears, in 1872; almost twenty years earlier Tennyson had published his "Charge of the Light Brigade," a set of stirring stanzas celebrating the heroism of six hundred British soldiers, charging to certain death but obeying orders nonetheless. Similar celebrations of military exploits were common in Victorian England. And although we do not know precisely what Carroll himself thought "Jabberwocky" meant, we do know that he was a gentle eccentric, fond of little girls and mathematical puzzles, and not in the least disposed to epic gestures or martial displays. So, though the "meaning" is not precise or certain, still it is there; "Jabberwocky" has it, just as it has all the other elements of a poem. It is delightfully musical, it handles formal patterns (stanzas, meter, rhyme, even internal rhyme) with grace and ease, it even tells a sort of story. It has a beginning, a middle, and an end—and how much more can we ask?

There is rather less "meaning," in the strict sense, in the lovely drunken parody of a nursery rhyme known to everyone:

> Starkle, starkle, little twink,
> What the hell you are, you think?
> Up there anyhow?

This is not Shakespeare, but it is clearly poetry. So too is the verse sung by every American schoolchild to the universally familiar John Philip Sousa marching tune: "Be kind to your web-footed friend,/ For a duck may be somebody's mother;/ She lives in the field and the swamp,/ Where it's always cold and damp./ You may think that this is the end./ Well it is." Poetry is not a frumious monster, lurking in the academic darkness, ready, willing, and able to leap out and trap the poor unsuspecting student. There is high poetry and there is low poetry; there is sad poetry and there is happy poetry; there is poetry that tells a story and poetry that sings for the sheer love of singing. And though there are cultures, current as well as historical, which have no prose, because they have no writing method to write prose in, there has never been a culture, anywhere on the earth, that did not have poetry. It may not be natural to teach it in schools, but it has always been supremely natural to sing it.

Which is why people go on writing it.

And why people go on reading it.

Poetic meaning is like and yet unlike ordinary meaning, just as poetry is both like and unlike ordinary speech or ordinary writing in prose forms. There are aspects of a poem which we can understand much as we understand a request for a loan or a declaration that it is raining. There are other aspects of a poem which must be approached somewhat differently. The key, of course, is learning when we are dealing with might be called literal meaning, and when we are dealing with what might be called nonliteral meaning. When a poet writes "It is raining," that is unmistakably literal: the statement is factual, it is not in any sense figurative or metaphorical. To adhere thus strictly to the natural meaning of words is by definition to be literal. But if the poet writes "It is raining in my heart," he is being anything but factual. He does not *really* mean what the words in their natural meaning might convey. Instead, he is being figurative or metaphorical; he is using natural or literal meaning in order to convey nonliteral or metaphorical meaning. "It is raining" means, in short, exactly what it says: there is rain falling. "It is raining in my heart" means "I am sad"—for how could it literally rain inside someone's heart, when as we all know it rains in the external world only? It is impossible for "It is raining in my heart" to be literal, because it is factually impossible.

Figurative, metaphorical language is, of course, neither limited to nor original with poetry. Each of us uses figurative expressions all the time, in our everyday lives (which is in good part why we can recognize them in poetry). "Kill the bum," we shout at an umpire, but we neither mean that the man is literally a bum (a vagrant, a hobo) nor that we propose literally that he be killed. We are using nonliteral, figurative language, because it is both more vivid and also more powerful than literal language would be. "I disagree with you, Mr. Umpire" or "You're quite wrong" simply doesn't do the trick. When we use the figurative expression "That kills me," no one thinks we're speaking literally—and everyone understands what we mean. Nonliteral language, though we tend to take it so much for granted that we hardly know we are using it, is thus a basic feature of everyone's linguistic usage.

And in our everyday language, as in poetry, the literal and the nonliteral are frequently so mixed together that no one either could or would want to separate them. "Let's play tennis, and I'll beat you to a bloody pulp." The literal invitation to play tennis (factual, possible) is tied to a nonliteral (nonfactual) assertion about the conclusion of that game. But what is literal and what is not can shift, depending on context. When the heavyweight champion literally beats someone to a bloody pulp, and TV and newspaper photographers document the fact that such a beating did actually occur, what is in one context a nonliteral, figurative expression has been transformed into a literal one. To understand the inevitable interweaving of these different contexts, these different approaches to reality, is to take the first and perhaps the largest step toward understanding poetry.

> I'm going out to clean the pasture spring;
> I'll only stop to rake the leaves away
> (And wait to watch the water clear, I may):
> I sha'n't be gone long. —You come too.
>
> 5 I'm going out to fetch the little calf
> That's standing by the mother. It's so young
> It totters when she licks it with her tongue.
> I sha'n't be gone long. —You come too.
>
> (ROBERT FROST, "The Pasture")

This is a lovely poem; it plainly means something, and it is plainly both earnest and emotional about whatever that something is. But since the poem is neither completely literal nor completely nonliteral, its meaning is inseparable both from what is literally conveyed and from what is nonliterally conveyed. Its meaning is an interwoven composite of both the literal and the nonliteral components of the poem. It works subtly but not mysteriously; untangling what the poet has so delicately put together is neither injurious to nor a betrayal of the poem.

The first of the poem's two stanzas starts with an assertion that, given the lack of context, seems conclusively literal: "I'm going out to clean the pasture spring." This would seem to be a farmer's comment, to his wife or to someone else in his household. He continues: "I'll only stop to rake the leaves away." This too seems literal (factual, possible), though the slightly unusual emphasis on "only" also seems to point to a problem, an uncertainty of some sort. Has this particular farmer been unusually lazy about cleaning the pasture spring in the past? Or is there some other explanation for the slightly defensive quality of "only"? Or is that quality not defensive but something else? Barely two lines into the poem, we lack sufficient context to be sure.

The parenthetical third line, however, gives us a good deal of significant information, useful for answering the sorts of questions raised by line 2. A typical farmer is concerned with the results of farming, not with lying about "to watch the water clear." Our hypothetical farmer, accordingly, is revealing himself as a very different person from the sort we had assumed him to be. Whether he is or is not a farmer, he is not a typical one. It is significant, too, that he is not entirely sure what he will or will not do, once he gets out of doors: "And wait to watch the water clear, *I may*" (italics added). And the poem continues, in line 4, with yet more indications that what seems wholly literal at first sight is distinctly less than that upon closer examination. There are two parts to line 4, separated by both a period and a dash. The first part says "I sha'n't be gone long." By itself, this would be very literal indeed. But it is joined to a second part, which suddenly issues an invitation to the person being addressed: "You come too." If the apparently literal assertions are in truth literal, this invitation does not belong in the poem. If, that is, the speaker is literally explaining his imminent absence, on matters of business, why does he invite the person being addressed, abruptly, to join him? But we have already noted, beginning in line 2, that what seems literal is increasingly likely to be nonliteral here. Taken together with the invitation of line 4, these indications begin to point toward a meaning which is above and beyond the literal meanings of the words employed. If we were to try to formulate that nonliteral meaning, even before looking carefully at the rest of the poem, we might think in terms of fellowship and of affection, both linked to the simple, pastoral environment in which the two parties appear to be living. There certainly seems to be some value, some importance, to literally straightforward actions (cleaning a pool, raking leaves, watching water clear) which transcends their literal meaning.

Stanza two confirms the tentative formulation, for the tone of affective simplicity is continued and intensified. Significantly, too, the poem's focus shifts away from inanimate things, and the speaker's reactions thereto, to very animate things indeed, specifically to a mother cow and its relatively new calf. Animal affection, thus lovingly portrayed, is a large step toward human affection, which to be sure it closely resembles. Literally, we are being shown a mother cow caring for its young. Again, the poem transcends the literal, suggesting by this point that what the speaker is "going out" to do is neither so straightforward nor so simple as his words at first indicated. The repeated invitation—"You come too"—stresses the importance to the speaker of the other person's company. Not so that the pasture spring might be more efficiently cleaned, or the leaves more thoroughly raked away, and certainly not so that he might the better bring home "the little calf/ That's standing by the mother." No: the other person, and that other person's company, is important for the nonliteral reasons suggested (but not literally stated) earlier in the poem. Fellowship and affection, like our cry at the umpire, take on power and vividness when thus suggestively rather than literally presented. Indeed, is it possible to present fellowship and affection as well in literal terms as it is to present them in nonliteral ways? Robert Frost's "The Pasture," considered in that light, is a superlative intermixing of literal and nonliteral because, in a word, it almost has to be such a mixture in order to convey the sorts of things the poet wants to convey—not farming lessons, or meteorological ones, but comments on the value and importance of (a) the rural environment as opposed to the urban one, and (b) the fellowship and affection which, he indicates, flourish quite as well (and perhaps even better?) in that environment as do crops and herds.

> Now's the time for mirth and play.
> Saturday's an holiday;
> Praise to heav'n unceasing yield,
> I've found a lark's nest in the field.
>
> 5 A lark's nest, then your play-mate begs
> You'd spare herself and speckled eggs;
> Soon she shall ascend and sing
> Your praises to th'eternal King.
>
> (CHRISTOPHER SMART, "For Saturday," Hymn XXXIII
> of *Hymns for the Amusement of Children*)

Frost's apparent straightforwardness turns out to be distinctly complex. Christopher Smart's apparently literal lines (until he reaches the theological suggestion in the poem's last two lines) remain determinedly literal. This is not, that is, the subtle, complex simplicity of an adult mind, but a simplicity much more baldly childlike. The primitive excitement of a child who has found a bird's nest with an egg in it is literally and only that, a child's immense but unquestioning excitement. It is wonderfully accurate: no adult would find a bird's nest of such intense excitement, and no adult would link endless praise of heaven with a bird's nest. The sermonizing conclusion assures us that an adult and not a child, after all, has written the poem. But there is no need to probe for higher associations, or to hunt for higher and more complex meanings, in the earlier lines. There aren't any: what you see is what you get, neither more nor less.

Epigram, Engraved on the Collar of a Dog Which I Gave to His Royal Highness

I am his Highness' Dog at *Kew*;
Pray tell me Sir, whose Dog are you?

(ALEXANDER POPE)

(Kew was a famous botanical garden near London.) In these two lines, by a contemporary of Smart, we are right back in the mixed world of literal and nonliteral. On the one hand, this inscription for a canine collar is plainly about four-footed dogs. On the other hand, "dog" being—in British usage—a word of contempt for a person of lower social standing, the second line of the little poem forces us to think also in two-footed terms. Pope is unambiguously adult. We can enjoy his poem all the more once we accept its two levels of meaning as existing simultaneously, each working with the other, each acquiring poetic strength from the other, but neither totally independent of the other. The poet's delicate craft has woven the two strands into this indissolubly complex little entity: we need to understand, not to try to favor one level over another. The joy as well as the art of reading a poem as it is meant to be read, in short, is to learn to accept what the poet has given us.

I Remember When

my father climbed the western mountain.
Every day he chopped more
of its peak off so we could have more
daylight to grow our food in, and when he'd
5 chopped deep enough that in midsummer we had
sun for an extra minute, which
is, of course, an exaggeration, he
knew he had done something real, and called us
to watch the sun settle
10 in the chink and disappear.

Next day the sun had moved, but he kept digging
the same dent, wanting one day a year.
One day, he told us, the mountain would be
chopped in two and there would be
15 one complete day
hours longer than there'd ever been.

People in the town called him "Father" too.
Some volunteered to help, but no,
it was his, his dent and his light; they were lucky
20 he was willing to share. At night there were new stars.

—When he hit a spring and the water gushed out
a waterfall, flooding the valley, the town,
to form a beautiful lake, deep,
cold, and full of fish found
25 nowhere else, the animals that lived
wild on his mountain rejoiced and grew
wilder, more passionate. They rejoiced!
We still do.

(MICHAEL HETTICH)

Who could possibly take this literally? Where has there ever been a
man successfully chopping off the peak of a mountain, to let in more
light? This "is, of course, an exaggeration," the poem itself assures us.
"At night there were new stars"; there were "fish found nowhere else."
Were there? Literally, no, of course not: this "is, of course, an exagger-
ation." But what is the poem all about, what does it mean, if on the one
hand it tells us fabulous lies, and on the other hand it calmly assures us
that none of it is "true"? Take the poem as it presents itself to us,
however, accept what it gives—and what it tells—us, and this apparent
difficulty turns out to be neither difficulty nor conflict. The poet is
writing about his father: a child sees his father as impossibly large,
powerful, ambitious, potent. A child is notoriously unable to stick to
or to finish anything: the sight of his father determinedly, doggedly
working away at whatever impossible task is inevitably awe-inspiring.
The child also sees adult determination as somehow ridiculous, too,
stubborn, unnecessary: why struggle so hard, the child wonders, in a
world where everything comes to you anyway, precisely because you

are a child? And yet there is enormous admiration in the carefully drawn picture, rising to the almost sacerdotal creation of "a beautiful lake, deep, cold, and full of fish found nowhere else." The animals rejoiced, "and grew wilder, more passionate. They rejoiced!" the poet repeats emphatically, still wonderingly—and then, in the lovely swift modulation of the final line, we pass at once from animals to human-kind: "We still do." We here pass, equally deftly, from a kind of historical present to a distinctly backward-looking memorialization. The title (which is also the poem's first line) has suggested but never fully explained this memorialization: "I Remember When . . ." In the brief final line, the suggestion is (like a suspended musical chord) resolved, and the poet's retrospective portrait of his father is neatly completed.

Of course, this too is "an exaggeration." How can we assume, reading a poem full of seemingly literal details, but set in an unmistak-able framework of nonliteral meaning, that the "father" of the poem is in fact the literal father of the poet himself? The answer is that we cannot, though for the sake of convenience I have, to this point, been making what I know to be an invalid assumption. Just as the poet is not his poem, so too the poet in his poem is not himself, but a quasi-fictional creature we call the "persona" (Latin for "person") of the poem. That is, in the imaginative, artificial creation which a poem inevitably must be, the poet assumes, for as long as the writing of the poem lasts, a persona (a "mask," the great poet William Butler Yeats called it) which he treats as his own. He knows it is a fictive construct; we ought to know it too—though it can sometimes be hard to separate what we know of a particular poet, a particular event, a particular poem, from the only partially literal world of the poem's meaning. Consider, in this light, two poems by Robert Browning, most famous for his dramatic monologues—poems very much like small plays, spoken by a single character. First, "Home-Thoughts, from Abroad":

Oh, to be in England
Now that April's there,
And whoever wakes in England
Sees, some morning, unaware,
5   That the lowest boughs and the brushwood sheaf
Round the elm-tree bole are in tiny leaf,

While the chaffinch sings on the orchard bough
In England—now!

And after April, when May follows,
10 And the whitethroat builds, and all the swallows!
Hark, where my blossomed pear-tree in the hedge
Leans to the field and scatters on the clover
Blossoms and dewdrops—at the bent spray's edge—
That's the wise thrush; he sings every song twice over,
15 Lest you should think he never could recapture
The first fine careless rapture!
And though the fields look rough with hoary dew
All will be gay when noontide wakes anew
The buttercups, the little children's dower
20 —Far brighter than this gaudy melon-flower!

Once we know that Browning spent much of his life abroad—in Italy for the most part—it becomes evident that whatever separation there is between the poet himself and the persona of this poem, it is at most a very small one. The longing recollection of England's birds, and England's flowers, and all the glories of the English spring, is deeply and personally felt, as is the sudden unfavorable comparison of English glories to "this gaudy melon-flower," one, we are to suppose, which he is at that moment contemplating in his far-off exile. We may not share his affection for England, or indeed for birds and flowers generally; perhaps only an Englishman, and a nineteenth-century Englishman at that, could feel precisely as Browning says he feels. But we need to be neither English nor nature worshipers to *understand* the power and the poignance of his yearning for his homeland: "Oh, to be in England/ Now that April's there!"

But Browning was a dramatic poet—that is, one who specialized in poems which create both a dramatic situation and, to express it, an imagined speaker. Consider the distance between Robert Browning, British Victorian poet, and the sixteenth-century Duke of Ferrara (a portrait drawn from life: Alfonso II d'Este, Duke of Ferrara, married his first wife in 1558, when she was only fourteen years old, and she died suspiciously three years later), who is imagined to speak the poem "My Last Duchess":

That's my last duchess painted on the wall,
Looking as if she were alive. I call
That piece a wonder, now: Frà Pandolf's hands
Worked busily a day, and there she stands.
5   Will't please you sit and look at her? I said
"Frà Pandolf" by design, for never read
Strangers like you that pictured countenance,
The depth and passion of its earnest glance,
But to myself they turned (since none puts by
10 The curtain I have drawn for you, but I)
And seemed as if they would ask me, if they durst,
How such a glance came there; so, not the first
Are you to turn and ask thus. Sir, 'twas not
Her husband's presence only, called that spot
15 Of joy into the Duchess' cheek: perhaps
Frà Pandolf chanced to say "Her mantle laps
"Over my lady's wrist too much," or "Paint
"Must never hope to reproduce the faint
"Half-flush that dies along her throat": such stuff
20 Was courtesy, she thought, and cause enough
For calling up that spot of joy. She had
A heart—how shall I say?—too soon made glad,
Too easily impressed; she liked whate'er
She looked on, and her looks went everywhere.
25 Sir, 'twas all one! My favor at her breast,
The dropping of the daylight in the West,
The bough of cherries some officious fool
Broke in the orchard for her, the white mule
She rode with round the terrace—all and each
30 Would draw from her alike the approving speech,
Or blush, at least. She thanked men—good! but thanked
Somehow—I know not how—as if she ranked
My gift of a nine-hundred-years-old name
With anybody's gift. Who'd stoop to blame
35 This sort of trifling? Even had you skill
In speech—which I have not—to make your will
Quite clear to such an one, and say, "Just this
"Or that in you disgusts me; here you miss,
"Or there exceed the mark"—and if she let

40 Herself be lessoned so, nor plainly set
   Her wits to yours, forsooth, and made excuse,
   —E'en then would be some stooping; and I choose
   Never to stoop. Oh sir, she smiled, no doubt,
   Whene'er I passed her; but who passed without
45 Much the same smile? This grew; I gave commands;
   Then all smiles stopped together. There she stands
   As if alive. Will't please you rise? We'll meet
   The company below, then. I repeat,
   The Count your master's known munificence
50 Is ample warrant that no just pretense
   Of mine for dowry will be disallowed;
   Though his fair daughter's self, as I avowed
   At starting, is my object. Nay, we'll go
   Together down, sir. Notice Neptune, though,
55 Taming a sea-horse, thought a rarity,
   Which Claus of Innsbruck cast in bronze for me!

The basic situation is historical, though the names of the two artists—
Frà Pandolf and Claus of Innsbruck—are fictitious. But this is poetry,
not history. "My Last Duchess" is a chilling self-portrait, as if from the
very mouth of the arrogant, selfish, cold-blooded aristocratic monster
who is made to speak it. His first wife, plainly, was an enthusiastic
young thing, and the Duke bitterly resented her familiarity, especially,
with men of lesser rank than that conveyed by his "nine-hundred-years-
old name." Nor would he tell her how she offended him: "I choose
never to stoop." He issues "commands"; the young wife is murdered—
and now, we suddenly learn, he is in fact arranging for her successor,
and is indeed explaining the whole ghastly tale to the marriage emis-
sary of his prospective second wife. Blandly, he tells it exactly as it
happened, quite certain that he is in no way at fault. He goes on to
speak of the dowry he will expect, lying smoothly as he assures the
emissary that the girl herself, "as I avowed at starting, is my object."
The emissary appears to be so nauseated that he wants to escape from
the monstrous presence of the Duke; the Duke, however, is blandly
insistent that "we'll go together down, sir." And as they descend, the
Duke goes on to point out yet another of his art treasures (in addition,
that is, to the lovely portrait of his first wife, so beautifully painted that
the girl looks "as if she were alive. I call that piece a wonder, now"), a

Neptune "which Claus of Innsbruck cast *for me!*" (italics added). His blandly selfish approach to everything, his supreme and chillingly invulnerable egotism, is thus vividly highlighted. *He* is the point of reference for everything.

There is no doubt of the persona, in this second Browning poem: it is the imagined character of the Duke of Ferrara. Only careless reading could confuse the monstrous duke with the poet who describes him; nor do we assume that a sixteenth-century Italian nobleman with little "skill in speech" has taken the trouble to record his brief dialogue with the marriage emissary. Again, there are historical facts underlying the poem; to this extent it is a literal rendering of something that might well have happened. But history can take us only a small way. No one knows what happened to the first Duchess; no one who may have been there when a marriage emissary spoke with the Duke has ever left a record; indeed, there is no reason to think that Frà Pandolf's portrait exists, or existed, any more than did the painter himself. The imagined character portrait is revoltingly strong, and arguably accurate, but it is not, in the historical sense, *real*, any more than the imagined characters of a story or a novel are real. The psychology is appallingly possible: monsters like the Duke have certainly existed, in the sixteenth century and in our own time as well. But the poem is a fictive construct, given a semblance of literal truth but not aiming at literalness. Browning is not writing history, but poetry. He did not confuse the two genres; neither should we.

> She dwelt among the untrodden ways
>   Beside the springs of Dove.
> A Maid whom there were none to praise
>   And very few to love.
>
> 5 A violet by a mossy stone
>   Half hidden from the eye!
> —Fair as a star, when only one
>   Is shining in the sky.
>
> She lived unknown, and few could know
> 10   When Lucy ceased to be;
> But she is in her grave, and, oh,
>   The difference to me!
>
>   (WILLIAM WORDSWORTH)

This may sound like a griefstricken lover's deeply felt, deeply personal memorial to his dead love. It may seem, that is, perfectly simple and straightforward, a literal (albeit musical) expression of realistic sorrow. It is in fact nothing of the sort. Not only has no one ever been able to identify "Lucy," who is even more completely the poet's creation than is the Duke of Ferrara in Browning's poem, but there are many indications in the poem itself to clue us in to the totally fictive nature of the experience, and of the girl, and of the love affair. "The untrodden ways," in line 1, is generalized and therefore vague, but that is the poem's beginning, and specificity is not perhaps to be expected. But in line 2 we hear that she lived "beside the springs of Dove"—and while Americans may not know it, Englishmen are well aware that there are a fair number of English streams named Dove. Which is intended? Or all? Or none, since *nothing* solid is meant? There is no resolution of these matters in the next two lines, where we learn that the girl was unmarried ("a Maid"), that no one praised her (why? we may wonder), and that almost no one loved her (why?). The avoidance of particularity begins to seem pronounced, by this point, and surely deliberate. If she deserves celebration, exactly why did no one praise her? What had she done, who was she? And why were there a "few," but only a few, who loved her? If Wordsworth had wanted us to know, he would have told us—but stanza two, instead, offers us more and more generalized assertions, even more generalized, now, because highly metaphorical. She was a flower, and fair, growing in an unlikely spot ("a violet by a mossy stone"), but not easily seen. Again, we are not told why, as metaphor is piled on metaphor (note the dash which precedes line 7, as if to say: Here comes yet another way of looking at it). She was explicitly fair, as a gleaming star is fair, and even fairer, for she glowed like the sky when only a single star is shining there. And that is in fact the end of the "description" and account, for the third and final stanza returns to memorialization of the dead girl. No one much knew her, or about her, and almost no one knew when she was dead. The last two lines of the poem, beautifully cadenced (the hesitating rhythm at the end of line 11 is extremely deft), purport to be personal. The girl is indisputably dead, "and, oh, the difference to me!" But if the girl and her surroundings and everything about her are vague, stylized, why should we assume that the persona of the poem is any more real? (We must *not* assume the persona of the poem is anything but a persona, an imaginative projection. The persona of this poem is emphatically not the poet himself.) That is, this is a poem about love and about loss—but not about a specific love and a specific loss. There need be no autobiography in a poem; there need be no true particularity; there need be nothing we could possibly call history. Neither poetry nor any other art requires any of those things. A poem, in other words, can be about emotions without being about people actually having those emotions.

The Young Housewife

At ten A.M. the young housewife
moves about in negligee behind
the wooden walls of her husband's house.
I pass solitary in my car.

5   Then again she comes to the curb
to call the ice-man, fish-man, and stands
shy, uncorseted, tucking in
stray ends of hair, and I compare her
to a fallen leaf.

10 The noiseless wheels of my car
rush with a crackling sound over
dried leaves as I bow and pass smiling.

(WILLIAM CARLOS WILLIAMS)

Williams was a doctor; he frequently (even mostly) wrote about real events and real people. And yet, much as Wordsworth did, here he generalizes the "young housewife" into any and all young housewives, three quarters of a century ago, confined "behind the wooden walls of [their] husband's house," "shy" when out in public, nervously "tucking in stray ends of hair." The passing poet-doctor, "solitary in my car," compares her to that wispy, essentially helpless and un-self-motivated common object, "a fallen leaf." He bows and smiles, passing by—but the otherwise "noiseless wheels of my car," as he glides by, "rush with a crackling sound over dried leaves." There are dead leaves in the road-way, the car crackles them into powder—but the woman too has just been explicitly compared to one of those same leaves. There is a subdued but clearly sensual power in both the act and the sound; so too there is an unspoken but plainly perceived sexual tension between the confined young woman and the "solitary" man going past her house. Nothing is likely to happen between them. After all, the man is not her husband, and he is sufficiently formal and proper to "bow." But he also is sufficiently aware of the dry social comedy, quite as dry as the crunching leaves, to smile, too. Williams has curiously generalized himself, as well, making what Henry James used to call a *ficelle* (a device, a literary tool) of the narrating presence in the poem. Williams in a sense hides himself behind a kind of literary pose, or persona: it is exactly what Yeats meant by the word "mask."

It is not a new procedure; poets have always employed one form or another of mask. Emily Dickinson, who literally hid herself, and her face, hid too in her verse. For all its power and sweep, it is no guide whatever to her autobiography:

> I heard a Fly buzz—when I died—
> The Stillness in the Room
> Was like the Stillness in the Air—
> Between the Heaves of Storm—
>
> 5 The Eyes around—had wrung them dry—
> And breaths were gathering firm
> For that last Onset—when the King
> Be witnessed—in the Room—
>
> I willed my Keepsakes—Signed away
> 10 What portion of me be
> Assignable—and then it was
> There interposed a Fly—
>
> With Blue—uncertain stumbling Buzz—
> Between the light—and me—
> 15 And then the Windows failed—and then
> I could not see to see—

The intense, focused particularity of the first half of the poem's opening line, "I heard a Fly buzz," is at once revealed to be not a literal particularity, for "when I died" cannot, of course, be literal. The poet's imaginative projection focuses both on small details and on large, obviously generalized metaphors. "The Stillness in the Room/ Was like the Stillness in the Air—/ Between the Heaves of Storm" is indeed richly metaphorical, and in more ways than one. A New England poet naturally writes of the stillness between the batterings of a storm, but the "storm" is also implicitly analogized to life itself, and the "heaves" to the "storms" of human existence. The dry eyes, wrung dry because of a plethora of tears, and the breaths "gathering firm" in that expectation of imminent death, are finely realized detail work, but the notion of God's appearance in the death chamber, at the moment of death, is of course visionary—real vision, to the pious mind, but visionary all the same. The giving away of earthly belongings is handled first realistically—"I willed my Keepsakes"—and then, without a pause, metaphorically—"[I] signed away/ What portion of me be/ Assignable," a careful evocation of a legalistic process which has no realistic relevance. When the fly of the poem's first line reappears, suddenly, in line 12, the two strands—small details and impressive metaphors—fuse grandly into one. The straightforward "buzz" of that opening line has now become something (an "uncertain stumbling" something) that "interposed . . . Between the light—and me." That is, the specific detail of light in the room has been delicately expanded to include the light of life itself. When therefore "the Windows failed" and "I could not see to see," the imagined darkness is both a detail and death itself.

Imaginative projection, forceful, poignant, compelling, cannot disguise the deeply deceptive—and deliberately deceptive—familiarity of the poem. Emily Dickinson has resolved to tell you a great deal about what she wants to tell you, and nothing whatever about herself, in any personal, intimate sense. We learn an immense amount about her hope for heavenly peace; we learn of her cheerful surrender of life and possessions; but we learn not a thing about her character except, in the least definable of ways, some characteristics of what might be called her "sensibility." She plainly sees the world, alive and dead, in vivid terms. Her observational acuity is of a high order, embracing high stillness and the low buzzings of an insect. She lets us see something of the others in the death chamber ("The Eyes around") but not a thing that is personal in the imaginatively dying poetic persona she has "interposed" between her reader and herself.

The Garden

Like a skein of loose silk blown against a wall
She walks by the railing of a path in Kensington Gardens,
And she is dying piece-meal
               of a sort of emotional anemia.

5 And round about there is a rabble
of the filthy, sturdy, unkillable infants of the very poor.
They shall inherit the earth.

In her is the end of breeding.
Her boredom is exquisite and excessive.
10 She would like some one to speak to her,
And is almost afraid that I
               will commit that indiscretion.

(EZRA POUND)

The presence of any persona at all is, in a way, half accidental in this biting poem. The woman is an overbred, aristocratic narcissist, "the end of breeding" in the sense of "end" as terminus, finish. She pretends to a boredom which is patently false, "exquisite," yes, but also "excessive." The "sort of emotional anemia" of which she is "dying piece-meal" is obviously abhorrent to the poet, who carefully compares her preciosity and lack of vitality to "the filthy, sturdy, unkillable infants of the very poor," who will in no uncertain terms, says the poem, "inherit the earth" that she and those like her have owned and manipulated and dominated, in the historical past. We learn the poet's views, that is, but what do we learn of the persona's personality? Remarkably little, if anything: the woman "would like some one to speak to her," a statement that has to do solely and exclusively with the woman herself, and "[she] is almost afraid that I/ will commit that indiscretion." The "I" is at best tangential; it tells us, and intends to tell us, nothing about the poet who lies behind that convenient first-person pronoun. It is the poet, yes, but it reveals nothing personal about him.

Poets can, to be sure, reveal a great deal about themselves, if and when they choose to, and this is especially true of twentieth-century poets. In our own time, all art sometimes verges on the almost-too-personal, the intimate, the "confessional."

In Vain (Sia-sia)

The last time you came
You brought flowers,
Red roses, white jasmine,
Blood and Holiness,
5   And spread them in front of me
With a wondering look: for you.

We were stunned
And asked each other: what's this?
Love? Neither of us understood.

10   That day we were together.
We did not touch.

But oh my heart that will not give itself!
Break, you bastard, ripped by your loneliness!

(Chairil Anwar, translated from the Indonesian by BURTON RAFFEL)

The Indonesian poet was not quite twenty-one when he wrote this poem, which helps explain something of the context. It seems apparent on even a first reading that the "you" is female, and represents a real person, and that the "me" is male and is indeed the poet himself. The realistic details of the first two strophes (lines 1–9) culminate in the psychological realism of lines 10 and 11: "We did not touch." There are larger and more symbolic associations to line 4, "Blood and Holiness," but the overall tone is indeed literal. Even the final two lines, in which the poet-persona both acknowledges and condemns his inability to give himself, have a vividly personal, confessional tone. Anwar was much concerned with mirrors, in all his work; everything that is known of his brief, intense life suggests that the mirror-portrait of the poem is precise and exact. This is what I am, who I am, says the poet, take it or leave it. And precisely because his personality is strikingly powerful, and his honesty is scrupulous, the poem moves us, and the poet's strategy succeeds.

In the next poem, the title of which is also meant to be read as the first line, the poet takes a different approach to personal material, turning it into an analysis which is no less self-critical than is Anwar's, but which is a great deal more positive, even rhapsodic:

You close your eyes for a moment

and you're there, screened-in on the porch,
you and the grandfolks watching red-streaked
rhubarb ripen: they tell you this is you,
the pushing up and out of the earth to some
5   purpose, some beauty: you believe what
they say, you smell it in their pores,
taste it when you kiss them, the old earth
they're part of like memories that should ripen
and never fall, but they do, and now
10   they're half in the ground: then a door shuts
and the lids of your eyes snap open, you're back,
but still in the earth looking up you see them
poised with clippers over the rhubarb, it's you,
it's always been you, now the red-whiskey nose,
15   the mind a screen sifter for eyes ugly
with ruptured veins, pushing, forty years,
and still pushing.

(DOUGLAS ASPER)

Starting with what seems to be a perfectly straightforward childhood
scene, a child and his grandparents watching "red-streaked/ rhubarb
ripen," the poem moves swiftly into a larger statement. Child-growing
and rhubarb-growing are morally and esthetically comparable, even in
a sense identical, say the old people, and "you believe what/ they say."
There is a deft (and again very swift) elegy to the wise grandparents,
who are part of "the old earth . . . like memories that should ripen and
never fall . . ." This is beautifully managed: the comparison between
child-ripening and rhubarb-ripening has now been extended to include
the grandparents—and then, immediately, for this is a poem that
pivots and wheels with continuous speed, the poet takes the compari-
son away again. They ought not to fall, "but they do, and now/ they're
half in the ground . . ." Note how deliberately and delicately evasive
this is: not simply, flatly, "in the ground," but "*half* in the ground"
(italics added). We are dealing, after all, with a personal poem that is
also something of a dream poem: use of the indeterminate "half" pre-
serves that mixture of present and past, of here-and-now and forever

gone. "A door shuts," probably both literally and figuratively, and the persona's eyes "snap open"; he is "back" and yet somehow still remembering, still seeing "them/ poised with clippers over the rhubarb." Except that now, with the perspective of years and greater wisdom, the persona knows that what he really sees, recalling his grandparents, is himself in them. Nor does he like what he sees, what has been kept from him by the "screen sifter" of his mind, namely "eyes ugly/ with ruptured veins, pushing, forty years,/ and still pushing." This is no less vividly personal than the Anwar poem, but its tone and the after-echoes of its neatly structured "message" are as deeply different as are the personalities of the two poets, the first an Oriental and a perpetual rebel, the second an American of great thoughtfulness (who once considered the ministry, as Anwar could not possibly have done).

Nor is deeply personal poetry reserved for contemporary poets alone: it has been an essential part of poetry for centuries, though at different times and in different places poets have "confessed" to different things. Here is the greatest of the Russian poets, Alexander Pushkin, compressing into a lyric of eight lines an intensity of personal passion that no poet has ever surpassed and few have equalled:

I Loved You

I loved—maybe I love you,
Still, but forget
This love that pressed
At you—no tears, just laugh.
5   I loved you in silence, hopeless,
True, jealous, and afraid—I loved you,
Oh how I loved you! May God give you
A lover like me again, some day.

(translated by BURTON RAFFEL and ALLA BURAGO)

Written roughly a century and a half ago, this is a stark, poignant poem, far more ambivalent, far more two-sided than it may at first seem. "I loved you," declares the title, and though this is largely echoed in the first line, it is also partly denied: "Maybe I love you, still." The denial is then denied, in its turn: "but forget/ this love that pressed/ at you." The past tense of the verb, "pressed," suggests the past tense of the initial statement—a past love, not a present one. But the first part of the phrase just quoted, "but forget this love," also manages to suggest a present tense, and an enduring love. "No tears, just laugh," urges the persona. But how entirely does he mean what he says? When he speaks of the character of his love, his praise could not be more glowing: "I loved you in silence, hopeless,/ True, jealous, and afraid . . . Oh how I loved you!" It hardly sounds like a dead love. And even the final assertion, "May God give you/ a lover like me again, some day," does not preclude the possibility of this lover-to-come being in fact the persona. Whether that may or may not come to pass, however, the praise of his own capacity for "true" love becomes so very powerful, in these final words, that all the disclaimers in the world could not convince us of the persona's neutrality—or of his own forgiveness, his own ability to forget. The two-sidedness of love itself is thus beautifully mirrored in the poem's brilliant dualities.

Almost three thousand years ago, the Greek poet Sappho wrote:

Pain penetrates

Me drop
by drop

(translated from the Greek by MARY BARNARD)

Could anything be more intense, and more personal, and more powerfully moving than this ancient fragment? No confession could be more open or more revealing: clearly, there are no barriers to the inner intimacies which poetry is capable of displaying.

There is much, much more to reading a poem—much more than I have yet discussed—just as there is more to learning how to truly hear a Beethoven quartet, or how to really see a painting by Rembrandt or by Picasso. Poetry's boundaries are man's boundaries, neither more nor less: different people, living in different times, in different cultures, employing different languages and also employing different poetic techniques, write different poems. I would argue that Shakespeare is the greatest poet the world has ever seen, in any language and in any period. But we cannot automatically use Shakespeare as our standard, in learning to read the poetry of different times and places and languages.

> With a lantern,
> Someone walking in the night,
> Through the plum trees.

This is a Japanese *haiku*, a seventeen-syllable form in the original language. (The author is Meisetsu, the translation is by R. H. Blyth.) This Englished version has fifteen syllables—and that fact is no more significant than the fact that, in this translation, this little poem has no rhyme and, in traditional terms, no meter. Much more to the point, this *haiku*—like most things in Japanese art and Japanese culture— works as much with what is not in the poem as it does with what is there. The details are sensual, immediate: the light of the solitary lantern in the darkness, "someone" unnamed carrying it "in the night," and—the farthest thing from accidental—walking "through the plum trees." We know that plum trees (and cherry trees) flower beautifully; we know that romantic souls cherish their beauty. What then is the lantern-bearer up to? All the associations of the poem point to a zealous worshiper of beauty, though whether or not a lover, whether or not sad or happy, we are not told. The omission is deliberate: the meaning of the poem is in the emotion it evokes, the sense of someone so in love with beauty that he (or she) cannot forgo it, even when darkness falls and covers beauty away. This is as perfectly Japanese a poem as one is likely ever to find—but despite the differences in approach, and in ultimate meaning, the poem is readily comprehensible to any human being anywhere.

Not surprisingly, the Chinese approach to poetry distinctly resembles, though it is not the same as, the Japanese approach (which in fact is much influenced by the Chinese).

Parting Gift

> Much love
>   —why did it seem no love at all?
> Over the last bottle, nothing;
>   could not rouse a smile

5   The candle
                gracious enough to regret our parting
      made tears for us
                Dawn came in a while

(Du Mu, translated by C. H. KWOCK and VINCENT MCHUGH)

Once again, there is quite as much left unsaid as there is actually said. There is no way of knowing why the lovers are parting, or even whether they are parting voluntarily or are being forced to separate. It is suggested that they are too afflicted, or perhaps too worn out, to shed tears, and equally unable to laugh or joke with one another ("could not rouse a smile"). But we cannot be sure—and that is part and parcel of the poem's approach. What we are to know is the emptiness of the loveless present as compared to the love-full past, in which there was "much love," but viewed from that loveless present it necessarily appears to the lovers, sadly, bewilderingly, as "no love at all." In most poems, the coming of dawn is a good sign, the reappearance of light, and day, and life. In this poem, dawn is the equivalent—never precisely stated but nevertheless clear—of the dreaded moment of final, irreversible parting. The deliberate imprecision of the final three words, "in a while," is thus perfectly characteristic of everything that has come before.

The great Irish poet William Butler Yeats illustrates how much there is in common, as between West and East, in the evoking of emotion in verse:

Politics

"In our time the destiny of man presents its meaning in political terms."
—Thomas Mann

      How can I, that girl standing there,
      My attention fix
      On Roman or on Russian
      Or on Spanish politics?
5   Yet here's a traveled man that knows

What he talks about,
And there's a politician
That has read and thought,
And maybe what they say is true
10 Of war and war's alarms,
But O that I were young again
And held her in my arms!

This poem fixes the contrast of present and past quite as vividly and poignantly as does the Chinese poem by Du Mu. Yeats is more ironic: the rather pompous epigraph, taken from the German novelist Thomas Mann, helps establish the ironic tone. But the poem is so tightly focused that despite our knowledge that "war and war's alarms" were indeed serious at the time (just before the outbreak of World War II), all we too can see and think of is "that girl standing there." There is more of what we are pleased to think of as "personality" in the Yeats poem, but it hardly warrants the description "confessional." The stance taken is simply too generalized, too universally human, for the reader to worry about merely personal matters.

The Passionate Shepherd to His Love

Come live with me, and be my love,
And we will all the pleasures prove°
That valleys, groves, hills and fields,
Woods, or steepy mountain yields.

5 And we will sit upon the rocks,
Seeing the shepherds feed their flocks
By shallow rivers, to whose falls
Melodious birds sing madrigals.

And I will make thee beds of roses,
10 And a thousand fragrant posies,°
A cap of flowers, and a kirtle,°
Embroidered all with leaves of myrtle.

---

2 **prove** test, experience   10 **posies** bouquets, and also collections of poetic gems   11 **kirtle** skirt

A gown made of the finest wool,
Which from our pretty lambs we pull,
15 Fair lined slippers for the cold,
With buckles of the purest gold.

A belt of straw and ivy buds,
With coral clasps and amber studs,
And if these pleasures may thee move
20 Come live with me and be my love.

The shepherds' swains° shall dance and sing
For thy delight each May morning.
If these delights thy mind may move
Then live with me, and be my love.

(CHRISTOPHER MARLOWE)

The English of this poem is faintly unfamiliar, as is its literary style. Marlowe died in 1593. But there is no mistaking the meaning of the poem: "Come live with me, and be my love," it says directly and literally (in one sense), and offers the inducements appropriate to the invitation. But is this any more personal than the Yeats poem, or than the Japanese and Chinese poems? Rather less personal, in point of fact—for there is even less necessity to think of this shepherd as a particular individual than there is to think of the sad lover, in Du Mu's poem, as an individual, or than there is to think of aging, lustful William Butler Yeats, trying to fix his wandering mind on serious international issues while staring bug-eyed at a beautiful girl. There is no direct echo of Christopher Marlowe, either as man or as poet, in the poem. What seems to be literal is, on further examination, straightforward but not particularized. This could, and was meant to be, any lover appealing to any woman.

The House Was Quiet and the World Was Calm

The house was quiet and the world was calm.
The reader became the book; and summer night

---

21 **swains** sweethearts, lovers

Was like the conscious being of the book.
The house was quiet and the world was calm.

5   The words were spoken as if there was no book,
Except that the reader leaned above the page,

Wanted to lean, wanted much most to be
The scholar to whom his book is true, to whom

The summer night is like a perfection of thought.
10   The house was quiet because it had to be.

The quiet was part of the meaning, part of the mind:
The access of perfection to the page.

And the world was calm. The truth in a calm world,
In which there is no other meaning, itself

15   Is calm, itself is summer and night, itself
Is the reader leaning late and reading there.

(WALLACE STEVENS)

This is clearly a different kind of poetry and, the poem being quite typical of his work, clearly also a different kind of poet. The intensity here is what Stevens himself, in line 11, calls "part of the mind." The drama, the tension, occurs in mental images—into which are woven, because this is a poet who never forgets that the mind operates in a physical world, images of that concurrent physical existence. I do not know of another poet who could have written: "The summer night is like *a perfection of thought*" (italics added). The furniture of the poem is extremely spare: a house, a book, the reader of the book, and some-where beyond them a summer night and the world in general. That is indeed all—but Stevens moves back and forth between mind and matter, interlacing the mental and the physical. "The reader became the book," we learn. It is emphatically not literal, but in a psychological sense it is highly realistic: intent reading is personal absorption. (As it is, too, with music, "heard so deeply," in T. S. Eliot's words, "that it is not heard at all, but you are the music while the music lasts.") Stevens crosses back and forth: "the summer night was like the conscious being of the book"; "the words were spoken as if there was no book"; "the summer night is like a perfection of thought"; "the quiet was part of the

meaning"; and finally reaches the assertion, in lines 14–16, that the
world "itself is calm, itself is summer and night, itself is the reader. . . ."

To understand how deeply Stevens believes in this interpenetration
of mind and matter, it is helpful to consider yet another poem, "The
Snow Man":

> One must have a mind of winter
> To regard the frost and the boughs
> Of the pine-trees crusted with snow;
>
> And have been cold a long time
> 5   To behold the junipers shagged with ice,
> The spruces rough in the distant glitter
>
> Of the January sun; and not to think
> Of any misery in the sound of the wind,
> In the sound of a few leaves,
>
> 10   Which is the sound of the land
> Full of the same wind
> That is blowing in the same bare place
>
> For the listener, who listens in the snow,
> And, nothing himself, beholds
> 15   Nothing that is not there and the nothing that is.

"The Snow Man" can seem forbidding, even impenetrable, until and
unless we realize that Stevens is neither playing with words nor trying
to deceive. This is not a game: he passionately believes that there is no
fundamental distinction between mind and spirit, and that therefore
the one can and must be comprehensible in terms of the other. He sees,
in short, a *psychology* in this understanding of how the world, the
flesh, and the spirit are entirely and inevitably unitary, inseparable. In
"The Snow Man" it is the psychology of the snow man himself (or
*it*self) that is being probed. The "mind of winter" is of course exactly
what a snow man possesses. The snow man has been "cold a long
time"—and only a man of snow, as opposed to a man of flesh and
bone, would not "think of any misery in the sound of the wind," for
what does cold wind matter to a creature made of frozen water (snow)?
The "listener," in line 13, is again the snow man, who is "nothing
himself" because he has been heaped together out of inert snow. And

this creature of nothingness "beholds nothing that is not there": he sees, that is, what he sees, and no more, being neither capable nor concerned with anything more (as a man of flesh and bone would be). And since winter is a time of emptiness and death, when neither animal nor human much ventures abroad, all that there is to see is snow, and wind, and more snow, and more wind—or, in short, "nothing," which is exactly what the snow man sees: "the nothing that is [there]."

How can this be anything but a complex verbal game? How can it be serious when, under analysis, it turns out not to be saying anything profound and impressive? (Recall "Jabberwocky.") We need to understand, says Stevens, just what we are, and also what we are not. We need to understand our place in a world which is of us, just as we are of it (the summer night, the book, the reader, the world). If we do not believe any longer in the comforting assertions of religion, if we believe that mind and matter and everything else are one and the same— chemical, physical, unitary—then understanding the inner meanings, the psychology, of that very twentieth-century belief is terribly important. (See, in the supplement to this chapter, Stevens' great poem "Sunday Morning," which deals with exactly these subjects.) There is more, however, to Stevens' meaning. If we are no longer supported by religious belief, he seems over and over to be saying, at least we can enjoy trying to comprehend what we do have. He relishes the play of the mind, the very effort to understand. We cannot know the biographical side of the man from reading the poet, in this case. But we just as surely learn an immense amount about the man's attitudes and emotions, as well as a good deal about the suppleness of his mind. Stevens has sometimes been called abstract, but that is an extreme judgment. He is passionately involved; his beliefs and his attempts to probe the psychological dimensions of those beliefs pour out of poem after poem. What may seem, at first, an impenetrable verbal (or intellectual) screen is on closer reading nothing of the sort. Once we learn how to read the poems that Stevens has actually written, once we learn to take them as what they in truth are, there is a throbbing excitement in his work. And he means it to be there, he intends us to find what he has put on the page for our pleasure and our enlightenment. That is, in some ultimate sense, what all poetry is up to, and (again) why poets write it and, for all of recorded history, readers have continued to read it.

The point is not that the reader of poetry needs to be a reader, also, of critical histories, or of poets' biographies, but only that poetry proceeds out of and addresses the concerns of human experience. There is no such thing, in that sense, as a "pure" poet, a poet who writes without connection to his actual experience in his actual time and his actual place.

> In vain, in vain—the all-composing Hour
> Resistless falls: The Muse obeys the Power.
> She comes! she comes! the sable Throne behold
> Of *Night* Primaeval, and of *Chaos* old!
> 5 Before her, *Fancy's* gilded clouds decay,
> And all its varying Rainbows die away.
> *Wit* shoots in vain its momentary fires,
> The meteor drops, and in a flash expires.
> . . . .
> Thus at her felt approach, and secret might,
> 10 *Art* after *Art* goes out, and all is night.
> See skulking *Truth* to her old Cavern fled,
> Mountains of Casuistry° heaped o'er her head!
> *Philosophy*, that leaned on Heav'n before,
> Shrinks to her second cause, and is no more.
> 15 *Physic* of *Metaphysic* begs defence,
> And *Metaphysic* calls for aid on *Sense*!
> See *Mystery* to *Mathematics* fly!
> In vain! they gaze, turn giddy, rave, and die.
> *Religion* blushing veils her sacred fires,
> 20 And unawares *Morality* expires.
> Nor *public* flame, nor *private*, dares to shine;
> Nor *human* spark is left, nor Glimpse *divine*!
> Lo! thy dread Empire, CHAOS! is restored;
> Light dies before thy uncreating word:
> 25 Thy hand, great Anarch!° lets the curtain fall;
> And Universal Darkness buries All.

> (ALEXANDER POPE, conclusion to *The Dunciad*, Book IV)

---

12 **Casuistry** disingenuous or oversubtle reasoning   25 **Anarch** anarchist

Written about 1728, *The Dunciad* is a long, detailed, savage attack on bad writing and worse writers. (It is too long a poem to include here in its entirety.) In these final lines, Pope pretends that in spite of everything Dullness has been victorious—"She comes! she comes!"—and Fancy (meaning Imagination) dies, along with wit, and art, and virtually everything else worth caring (and fighting) about. These final lines of *The Dunciad* have such energy, such passion, and evoke so wild a scene of desperate fireworks leading to dismal darkness that it is sometimes hard to keep in mind their comparatively petty origin. Bad writing does matter, to be sure. Most people would agree that good writing is preferable to bad writing, and further would agree that society in general, and good writers in particular, benefit when writing is good rather than bad. But does a horror of bad writing really justify so intense, so dramatic a scene as Pope gives us?

The answer must be that the question is irrelevant. Pope wrote *The Dunciad*, and we did not. He established the standards from which he works and, using those standards, he has successfully evoked exactly the kind of apocalyptic scene he meant to evoke. Provided that a poet works honestly and deeply with the material he has chosen, it is simply not our business to attack him for choosing that material rather than something different.

And though we do not need to know the reasons for that choice, in Pope's case it may help to understand the point if I emphasize that he clearly had reasons, and reasons more than sufficiently persuasive to his own mind. His body had been deformed almost from birth; much of his life was necessarily spent with books. In addition, therefore, to the normal writer's loathing for meretricious hackwork, Pope had an inevitably greater absorption in the world of print. And he had an unusually thin skin—not perhaps unusual considering his personal circumstances, but unusual even among notoriously thin-skinned people like writers. He accordingly had vital personal reasons for hitting back at the many hack writers who, because of his prominence and because of his satirical bent and frequent attacks on others, had in their turn hit out at him. His own attacks were hard-hitting; theirs were at least as savage and, additionally, had the kind of dull brutality that frequently is the mark of the inferior mind. Pope's involvement was therefore passionate—and so too was the poetry of *The Dunciad*.

One of Pope's most fervent and outspoken admirers, George Gordon, Lord Byron, once scrawled on the back of the manuscript of canto one of *Don Juan* (his unfinished and completely delightful mock epic) the following brief stanza. It was written in pencil; many editions of *Don Juan* do not include it, since it uses the same form as the mock epic but is not really a part of that poem.

> I would to heaven that I were so much clay,
>> As I am blood, bone, marrow, passion, feeling—
> Because at least the past were passed away—
>> And for the future—(but I write this reeling,
> 5   Having got drunk exceedingly today,
>> So that I seem to stand upon the ceiling)
> I say—the future is a serious matter—
> And so—for God's sake—hock° and soda-water!

What does this marvelously wacky stanza *mean*? There are two deliberately opposed tones working here, the one apparently serious and sober and philosophical, the other inebriate and totally indifferent to philosophy and its stuffy questions about the future and the past. The inebriate tone ultimately prevails (no one knows if Byron was in fact drunk when he scribbled this stanza, but it is at least a good possibility). And the fact that drunkenness wins out is, I suppose, designed to say something, but surely nothing very precise, and certainly nothing in any way particularized. Does "Jabberwocky" mean more or less than this eight-line extravanganza? It is a close question; one could argue it either way.

And yet these are for me some of the most delightfully memorable lines in all English poetry. They have so intense a joy, so exuberant a vitality, so dashingly superconfident a technique, that I find them perpetually appealing. Indeed, one could even argue that these eight lines are a sort of little playlet—and since they are much better writing for the stage than anything Byron ever wrote in the dramatic form (and he wrote a lot in the dramatic form), the argument in that direction has its persuasive side. They are better dramatic writing simply because, as his letters and his whole biography demonstrate, this *is* the real man, Byron himself, and in his very best good-humored mode. (Like all professional wits, he had a vicious side, which does not show itself here.) People who knew and memorialized him describe him, with

---

8 **hock** white wine

virtual unanimity, as being exactly this sort of mercurial, charismatic, dazzling man. Writing to his poet friend Thomas Moore in 1817, Byron himself gives us a stunning revelation of his personality:

> Have you seen ——'s book of poesy? and, if you have seen it, are you not delighted with it? And have you—I really cannot go on. There is a pair of great black eyes looking over my shoulder, like the angel leaning over St. Matthew's, in the old frontispiece to the Evangelists—so that I must turn and answer them instead of you.

The letter ends at precisely that point; the lovemaking, with his young Italian mistress, plainly began immediately thereafter. A letter to that mistress, carefully written in English (which she could not read, as he well knew), and inscribed on the last page of a book which she owned, begins: "I have read this book in your garden—my love, you were absent, or else I could not have read it." And the letter continues with a very sober, very passionate declaration of his love for her, ending: "But all this is too late. I love you, and you love me [she was married]—at least, you *say so*, and *act* as if you *did* so, which last is a great consolation in all events. But *I* more than love you, and cannot cease to love you. Think of me, sometimes, when the Alps and the ocean divide us—but they never will, unless you *wish* it."

Men like Byron are extraordinary in any time, fascinating to know, important to understand. If a scribbled stanza can give us so vividly accurate a glimpse of such men, have we any right to complain (if anyone were so moved) that it does not give us more?

Poems Supplementary to Chapter 1

— 1 —

Deeply indebted to eighteenth-century philosophers like Locke and Rousseau, and himself the bellwether of the Romantic school of poets, Wordsworth here combines those strands of his thought with his very personal brand of pantheism. Line 7 is the heart of the poem.

> My heart leaps up when I behold
>   A rainbow in the sky;
> So was it when my life began;
> So is it now I am a man:
> 5   So be it when I shall grow old,
>   Or let me die!
> The Child is father of the Man;
> And I could wish my days to be
> Bound each to each by natural piety.

> (WILLIAM WORDSWORTH)

— 2 —

Pope's health was ruined, and his body badly bent out of shape, by a childhood illness: he could do little more about matters sexual than talk—and he talked about them often. Most of his poetry was written in couplet form, but not all. This bawdy rondeau, translated and adapted from the French, is a marvel of delicacy and wit.

> You know where you did despise
> (T'other day) my little eyes,
> Little legs, and little thighs,
> And some things of little size,
> 5   You know where.

You, 'tis true, have fine black eyes,
Taper legs, and tempting thighs,
Yet what more than all we prize
Is a thing of little size
10   You know where.

(ALEXANDER POPE, "Rondeau")

— 3 —

Part of a long cycle of lyric poems, *In Memoriam*, written in commemoration of the poet's dear friend Arthur Henry Hallam (1811–1833), this brief poem achieves remarkable intensity with simple, direct means. Note that, with only two exceptions, all the words used are of one or two syllables. Nor is the image material any more complex or elaborate: a house, a door, a street, rain—all things of the most common and everyday sort. The stark effect is beautifully sustained: the impact of the heavily alliterated final line is immense.

Dark house, by which once more I stand
    Here in the long unlovely street,
    Doors, where my heart was used to beat
So quickly, waiting for a hand,

5   A hand that can be clasp'd no more—
    Behold me, for I cannot sleep,
    And like a guilty thing I creep
At earliest morning to the door.

He is not here; but far away
10   The noise of life begins again,
    And ghastly thro' the drizzling rain
On the bald street breaks the blank day.

(ALFRED TENNYSON)

— 4 —

Of lower-middle-class origin, and in fact apprenticed to an apothecary (that is, a pharmacist), Keats acquired scattered learning in the traditional literary disciplines, but never learned Greek. This sonnet celebrates his discovery of the poetry of Homer, in the Elizabethan translation by George Chapman—and incidentally shows, by the historical error in the last four lines (it was Balboa and not Cortez who first saw the Pacific with European eyes), how spotty his learning was.

On First Looking into Chapman's° Homer

Much have I travelled in the realms of gold,
    And many goodly states and kingdoms seen;
    Round many western islands have I been
Which bards° in fealty to Apollo° hold.
5 Oft of one wide expanse had I been told
    That deep-browed Homer ruled as his demesne;°
    Yet did I never breathe its pure serene
Till I heard Chapman speak out loud and bold:
Then felt I like some watcher of the skies
10   When a new planet swims into his ken;
Or like stout Cortez when with eagle eyes
    He stared at the Pacific—and all his men
Looked at each other with a wild surmise—
    Silent, upon a peak in Darien.

(JOHN KEATS)

— 5 —

The keys to Wallace Stevens' "Sunday Morning," one of the very greatest poems of our century, are surprisingly simple. The first stanza

---

Chapman George Chapman, 1559?–1634?, British poet, dramatist, translator   **4 bards** poets; **Apollo** Greek god of (among other things) poetry   **6 demesne** estate (here pronounced "di-MEAN")

tells us both *who* the poem is concerned with, and *what* the poem is about. We are not told exactly how old the lady is, but from the nature of her concerns and from the contrast with the "maidens" (in line 74) we can assume that she is not young. Death is thus naturally on her mind, and all the religious questions associated with it. Her disposition is toward the naturalistic (lines 1–4), and this is sharply contrasted with the "ancient sacrifice" (line 5)—a significant way of describing the central event of Christianity. Everything else in the poem follows from this central opposition of natural/pagan and supernatural/Christian.

Sunday Morning

1.

Complacencies of the peignoir, and late
Coffee and oranges in a sunny chair,
And the green freedom of a cockatoo
Upon a rug mingle to dissipate
5   The holy hush of ancient sacrifice.
She dreams a little, and she feels the dark
Encroachment of that old catastrophe,
As a calm darkens among water-lights.
The pungent oranges and bright, green wings
10 Seem things in some procession of the dead,
Winding across wide water, without sound.
The day is like wide water, without sound,
Stilled for the passing of her dreaming feet
Over the seas, to silent Palestine,
15 Dominion of the blood and sepulchre.

2.

Why should she give her bounty to the dead?
What is divinity if it can come
Only in silent shadows and in dreams?
Shall she not find in comforts of the sun,
20 In pungent fruit and bright, green wings, or else
In any balm or beauty of the earth,
Things to be cherished like the thought of heaven?
Divinity must live within herself:
Passions of rain, or moods in falling snow;

25   Grievings in loneliness, or unsubdued
       Elations when the forest blooms; gusty
       Emotions on wet roads on autumn nights;
       All pleasures and all pains, remembering
       The bough of summer and the winter branch.
30   These are the measures destined for her soul.

      3.
       Jove in the clouds had his inhuman birth.
       No mother suckled him, no sweet land gave
       Large-mannered motions to his mythy mind
       He moved among us, as a muttering king,
35   Magnificent, would move among his hinds,°
       Until our blood, commingling,° virginal,
       With heaven, brought such requital to desire
       The very hinds discerned it, in a star.
       Shall our blood fail? Or shall it come to be
40   The blood of paradise? And shall the earth
       Seem all of paradise that we shall know?
       The sky will be much friendlier then than now,
       A part of labor and a part of pain,
       And next in glory to enduring love
45   Not this dividing and indifferent blue.

      4.
       She says, "I am content when wakened birds,
       Before they fly, test the reality
       Of misty fields, by their sweet questionings;
       But when the birds are gone, and their warm fields
50   Return no more, where, then, is paradise?"
       There is not any haunt of prophecy,
       Nor any old chimera of the grave,
       Neither the golden underground, nor isle
       Melodious, where spirits gat° them home,
55   Nor visionary south, nor cloudy palm
       Remote on heaven's hill, that has endured
       As April's green endures; or will endure

---

35 **hinds** peasants, field workers   36 **commingling** mingling together   54 **gat** got

Like her remembrance of awakened birds,
Or her desire for June and evening, tipped
60   By the consummation of the swallow's wings.

5.
She says, "But in contentment I still feel
The need of some imperishable bliss."
Death is the mother of beauty; hence from her,
Alone, shall come fulfillment to our dreams
65   And our desires. Although she strews the leaves
Of sure obliteration on our paths,
The path sick sorrow took, the many paths
Where triumph rang its brassy phrase, or love
Whispered a little out of tenderness,
70   She makes the willow shiver in the sun
For maidens who were wont to sit and gaze
Upon the grass, relinquished to their feet.
She causes boys to pile new plums and pears
On disregarded plate.° The maidens taste
75   And stray impassioned in the littering leaves.

6.
Is there no change of death in paradise?
Does ripe fruit never fall? Or do the boughs
Hang always heavy in that perfect sky,
Unchanging, yet so like our perishing earth
80   With rivers like our own that seek for seas
They never find, the same receding shores
That never touch with inarticulate pang?
Why set the pear upon those river-banks
Or spice the shores with odors of the plum?
85   Alas, that they should wear our colors there,
The silken weavings of our afternoons,
And pick the strings of our insipid lutes!
Death is the mother of beauty, mystical,
Within whose burning bosom we devise
90   Our earthly mothers waiting, sleeplessly.

---

74 **plate** household dishes

7.
Supple and turbulent, a ring of men
Shall chant in orgy on a summer morn
Their boisterous devotion to the sun,
Not as a god, but as a god might be,
95 Naked among them, like a savage source.
Their chant shall be a chant of paradise,
Out of their blood, returning to the sky;
And in their chant shall enter, voice by voice,
The windy lake wherein their lord delights,
100 The trees, like serafin, and echoing hills,
That choir among themselves long afterward.
They shall know well the heavenly fellowship
Of men that perish and of summer morn.
And whence they came and wither they shall go
105 The dew upon their feet shall manifest.

8.
She hears, upon that water without sound,
A voice that cries, "The tomb in Palestine
Is not the porch of spirits lingering.
It is the grave of Jesus, where he lay."
110 We live in an old chaos of the sun,
Or old dependency of day and night
Or island solitude, unsponsored, free,
Of that wide water, inescapable.
Deer walk upon our mountains, and the quail
115 Whistle about us their spontaneous cries;
Sweet berries ripen in the wilderness;
And, in the isolation of the sky,
At evening, casual flocks of pigeons make
Ambiguous undulations as they sink,
120 Downward to darkness, on extended wings.

(WALLACE STEVENS)

— 6 —

Genuinely and deeply religious, Herrick had not the slightest leaning toward either Puritanism or mysticism. His is a poetry of frank and completely open physicality.

Delight in Disorder

A sweet disorder in the dress
Kindles in clothes a wantonness;
A lawn° about the shoulders thrown
Into a fine distraction;
5 An erring lace, which here and there,
Enthralls the crimson stomacher:°
A cuff neglectful, and thereby
Ribbons to flow confusedly:
A winning wave (deserving note)
10 In the tempestuous petticoat:
A careless shoe-string, in whose tie
I see a wild civility:°
Do more bewitch me, than when art
Is too precise in every part.

(ROBERT HERRICK)

— 7 —

Most of Francis Sullivan's poems are religious—not surprising, since he is a Jesuit priest. But the religious content of the following poem is neither doctrinal nor overt. Rather, it inheres in the powerfully affirmative view which the poem underlines, using quiet but intense natural images. Sullivan's poetry demonstrates that love of beauty and deep religious feeling go easily hand-in-hand; his command of technique demonstrates that the modern religious poet need not be traditionalist or sentimental.

---

3 **lawn** shawl 6 **stomacher** bodicelike garment 12 **civility** politeness (here pronounced "si-VILL-i-tie")

Still Life

white and red
camellias
rot in a bowl,
as fruit,
5   but what they were
when ripe
and open
in clear water
cannot be annulled
10 even by their own
decay,
when they bend
too far back
and let go their hold
15 on their own pollen,
gold crumbs
stuck to small fingers
held up for
looks and licks
20 in the center of
a revelation of
what cannot be
annulled by rot,
if it has happened
25 once in a bowl
of clear water,
however soon
we put them in
the trash
30 to be a death
new camellias
cannot,
in their turn,
annul.

(FRANCIS SULLIVAN)

— 8 —

Carefully simple, even naive, the language of "Lion" deftly establishes
the nature of the "wild man" it celebrates, and also neatly contrasts
that simpleness with the immensely complex situation the man/lion is
in. And, simultaneously, the immensely complex situation *we* are in, as
we struggle to draw firm lines, to distinguish appearance from reality,
truth from Kafkaesque dreams.

Lion

Behind that door
in a white room we keep
a man who thinks
he is a lion.
5   You can see he's kept safe.
He thinks he's a lion!

Once he escaped
and ran through the city.
Disappeared.
10   Changed his name.
Actually this isn't him,
this is a lion.

And this is a picture
of the African plains.
15   We'll slip it beneath
his door now; he'll look at it
smiling, draw
an animal on it
and himself running
20   to catch it, slip
the picture back under
the door.

thus we study
the workings of his mind.

25   Today he's drawn
a bowl, that's a bowl

of soup, being carried
by a stick figure, a woman.

30 That's him smiling.
Notice the hair
is wild, that he wears
no shirt.
Each day the picture
is different, but he always
35 smiles. Tonight his dinner

is soup, of course,
and a woman, but what
do you think of his smile,
his naked chest, skinny
40 after months in the white room
but still wild—

What do you think
he looks like, who do you
think he is, who do you
45 think he thinks
he is, we are? These are some
of the questions we ask ourselves.
A wild man! A lion!

(MICHAEL HETTICH)

— 9 —

The key to "Hands" is lines 9–14. The poem becomes both less strange
and much easier to understand once we understand the ecological
perspective there established, and the urban/rural contrast delineated
in the second of the poem's four strophes.

Hands

Today thousands
of envelopes filled
with tiny hands
are passing through the mail.
5 It is a sunny

day and all
these small hands sweat
in their mailman's bags.
These are the hands
10 of the skunks, squirrels,
raccoons that have now
become so valued
for their strangeness, for their
resemblance to ours.

15 Deep in the woods
there are still small animals
with all four hands.
They hide well. And all
around the edges,
20 close to our houses,
many walk on stumps.
They don't walk far.

We feed them scraps
from our dinners, and they
25 grow fat and sleek.
They sleep without fear.

Their hands will last
forever now.

(MICHAEL HETTICH)

— 10 —

Poet, courtier, soldier, explorer, Sir Walter Ralegh had good reason
for the sour and cynical realism of this poem, written in reply to one by
Christopher Marlowe (see pages 26–27). Brilliant early successes were
followed by a series of personal disasters. Jailed three times, by both
Queen Elizabeth I and King James I, he spent 1603–1616 in the Tower
of London, charged with treason. Released so that he might make an
expedition to the New World in search of gold, he was rearrested and
executed in 1618, when that expedition too ended in failure.

The Nymph's Reply to the Shepherd

If all the world and love were young,
And truth in every shepherd's tongue,
These pretty pleasures might me move
To live with thee, and be thy love.

5   Time drives the flocks from field to fold,
While rivers rage, and rocks grow cold,
And Philomel° becometh dumb,
The rest complains of cares to come.

The flowers do fade, and wanton fields
10   To wayward winter reckoning yields,
A honey tongue, a heart of gall,
Is fancy's spring, but sorrow's fall.

Thy gowns, thy shoes, thy beds of roses,
Thy cap, thy kirtle, and thy posies
15   Soon break, soon wither, soon forgotten:
In folly ripe, in reason rotten.

Thy belt of straw and ivy buds,
Thy coral clasps and amber studs,
All these in me no means can move
20   To come to thee, and be thy love.

But could youth last, and love still breed,
Had joys no date, nor age no need,
Then these delights my mind might move
To live with thee, and be thy love.

(SIR WALTER RALEGH)

— 11 —

The comparison of helpless small animal and helpless human baby is one that everyone makes. But in this poem the poet infuses that comparison into a delicately drawn-out little drama, a hunt that is never fully pursued but which seems to hang over the first section of the

---

7 **Philomel** the nightingale

poem, much like the "autumn air" of which it speaks. And when the poem returns to the comparison between animal and baby, in the final lines, the notion of "tiny graves" gives an everyday linkage a very special poignancy.

Housecat

At summer's end, you still
remember what's missing:
a late night's cry like a baby's,
a wet nose tickling your ear, common things,
5   small doors that opened into his small pleasures.
Often you open one, hearing something,
feeling something familiar and alive
in the corners of the autumn air.

Weeks after he'd gone,
10 you open the last door. There at your feet
you find him, thin, hard,
fitted to earth like cement.
You lift him, enter a room filled
with crushed spines of leaves
15 and open mouths. For a moment,
your house breathes
with the chatter of tiny graves.

(DOUGLAS ASPER)

— 12 —

Poet and painter, Cummings was fiercely professional. He had no patience whatever with amateurs, and especially with drippily sentimental, self-indulgent amateurs. Cummings knew, however, how well artistic fakers often did, and was bitterly resentful of such unearned, undeserved success.

this young question mark man

question mark
who suffers from
indigestion question

5 mark is a remarkably
   charming person

   personally they tell

   me as for me
   i only knows that
10 as far as
   his picture goes

   he's a wet dream

   by Cézanne

       (e e cummings)

2

WHAT POETRY DOES: METAPHOR

METAPHOR IS NONLITERAL language, but it is both more and less than that. We have seen that poetry, and language generally, mixes literal and nonliteral expressions. But metaphor is a highly focused form of nonliteral language, the explication of one thing by a reference to something else. "The fullback went through the line like a tank." No one understands this to mean that the fullback weighed thirty or forty tons, was powered by a diesel motor, and boasted a large and deadly cannon. On the other hand, everyone understands that it is those *qualities* in a tank, as opposed to some less fearsome vehicle, that the comparison illuminates. In terms of football, that is, the fullback's rush was like the forward movement of a tank, considered in comparison to other vehicles. "He got there like a shot." Again, the metaphor compares man and bullet, not literally but figuratively, borrowing some of the bullet's qualities to explicate something about the man's speed.

Metaphor is a poetic device which sits at the center of most poetic expression, in virtually all languages and in almost all historical periods.

> Green grape, and you refused me.
>> Ripe grape, and you sent me packing.
>>> Must you deny me a bite of your raisin?

(Anonymous, translated from the Greek by DUDLEY FITTS)

The entire poem is built, plainly, on one basic metaphor. He knew her, says the poem, when she was young ("green grape"), and wanted her, and did not get her. He knew her when she had matured, had grown from a girl into a woman ("ripe grape"), and the story was still the same. Now she is old and withered ("raisin"), and he wants her still, and still she turns him down. Why, he asks? All he wants, by this point, is a "bite"—that is, he no longer wants or expects a lifetime (or indeed any significant time) of possession, but just to transiently enjoy a bit of what little is left to enjoy. A "raisin" is not much, he suggests; it is a dried and shrunken form of "grape." And all he wants is a "bite"—not the whole—of a "raisin." What is wrong with her, that she still turns him down?

The metaphor is tightly worked out; it expresses a number of things, all at the same time. First of all, the choice of an item of food as the metaphorical equivalent of his beloved expresses perfectly, and very naturally, her desirability. Lovers in fact frequently wish to eat their beloved, figuratively speaking: consummation of love is like consummation of hunger. (The feminist Margaret Atwood titled one of her novels *The Edible Woman*.) Parents too frequently play at "eating" their plump children: consumability is closely interwoven with love, and in all sorts of ways. That is, the metaphor is not simply striking, but also appropriate: "I love you so much I could eat you" makes sense, outside poetry or in it, but "I love you so much I could plant you like a tree" or "I love you so much I could plaster you like a wall" make no sense at all—and would therefore make bad metaphors. There has to be something already there, something connective of the two halves of the metaphorical equation, for the poet to have something on which he and his poem can build. The best metaphors start with that preexistent connection, and then extend it, use it to illuminate and underline aspects of the person or thing or condition being compared.

So in this little Greek poem the natural cycle of growth and decay, which grapes like all living things must go through, is pressed upon us. The "green grape" becomes inevitably a "ripe grape" and, finally, when old and moribund, a "raisin." So too do human beings, like the woman being addressed, go through their cycle of growth and decay: time is inexorable, death is unavoidable, dissolution is the end of all living things. The steady, heavy-footed march of time clomps through these lines like the pounding of a drum—and how much time is left, here at the end of those cycles of birth and decay? Quick, quick, before it's too late!

The choice of one single grape, furthermore, rather than a bunch of grapes, or a bushel of grapes, or any quantity greater than just one, also helps point the metaphor. For how valuable is one single grape, one single raisin? In cosmic terms, indeed, what the beloved has all these years refused him is utterly trivial, inconsequential—worth, says the metaphor without needing to say it, the ridiculous cost of one lousy grape, one lousy raisin. This too suggests, though it is not elaborated or even made entirely explicit, that while *he* has been perfectly reasonable, rational as well as long-suffering, *she* has been irrational, selfish, arrogant. (For an ancient Greek to insist that man is rational and admirable, while woman is irrational and of a distinctly inferior order of things, is as predictable as his arguing that a mule is stubborn or that birds have wings.) And as the rational party, the poem implies, he is of course able to appreciate and admire beauty, though the beautiful irrational party is apparently unable fully to understand what she possesses and, stupidly, refuses to make use of. She is even capable of going to her grave unwilling to use it—and how much stupider than that, the poem also implies, can one be?

Impressions: I

the sky a silver
dissonance by the correct
fingers of April
resolved

5   into a
clutter of trite jewels

now like a moth with stumbling

wings flutters and flops along the
grass collides with trees and
10   houses and finally
butts into the river

                  (e e cummings)

Instead of one central metaphor, extended and developed, this poem is built on three metaphors, consecutively presented. The sky is first seen in terms of a comparison to music: it is a "silver dissonance" (consonance=harmonious; dissonance=disharmonious). And if one knows music, one knows how to "resolve"—i.e., to oblige to go from dissonance to consonance—even a silvery dissonant chord.

But the comparison is richer than it looks, for music cannot literally be silvery or any other color or hue. There is a kind of synesthesia going on: that is, not only is the sky being compared to music, but to a metaphorical music which is partly musical and partly visual. This blending of sense images is one of the great opportunities, for a good poet (as it is one of the great dangers for the amateur). Cummings immediately uses it, indeed, to leap into his second comparison: the resolution, here, becomes linked to the visual rather than to the musical aspect of the metaphor, and the sky turns into "a clutter of trite jewels." (Note how the leap, in a poet as fond of spatial arrangement as Cummings is, is both verbal and literally spatial: after "resolved," in line 4, the poem has to fly over an empty space on the page, and lands, indeed, smack in the middle of line 5, the only indented line in the entire poem.) The first and second metaphors are linked doubly closely, for jewels in "a clutter" fit very neatly with music that is dissonant.

The third metaphor, which begins with line 7, is both the most animated and also the most elaborately developed. The sky now turns into a "moth with stumbling wings," bashing and bumping about, and finally—almost like a drunken calf or goat—butting into the river. How does Cummings fit this third metaphor to the other two? Very carefully: the dissonant sky, which has become a clutter of "trite" jewels, evolves naturally into a disorderly small flying animal. And the movement from "silver" in metaphor number one to "trite" in metaphor number two, similarly, evolves into sheer clumsiness and ineptitude. The night sky in spring ("April" tells us that this is spring; "silver" tells us that there is moonlight, as the "clutter of trite jewels" tells us that there are stars) is the subject of this "impression" poem—and the night sky ends in the river, appropriately, because that is where the moon ends, as night disappears and day resumes.

The basic metaphorical structure here is thousands of years old. In eighth- or ninth-century England, it was already so well understood a convention that poets could construct easily solvable riddles based on it.

The Moon and the Sun

I saw a silvery creature scurrying
Home, as lovely and light as heaven
Itself, running with stolen treasure
Between its horns. It hoped, by deceit
5   And daring and art, to set an arbor
There in that soaring castle. Then,
A shining creature, known to everyone
On earth, climbed the mountains and cliffs,
Rescued his prize, and drove the wily
10   Impostor back to darkness. It fled
To the west, swearing revenge. The morning
Dust scattered away, dew
Fell, and the night was gone. And no one
Knew where the soft-footed thief had vanished.

(Old English Riddle #29, translated by BURTON RAFFEL)

The poet's culture was more military than ours; he inevitably sees the contest between the moon and the sun in martial terms. But there is remarkably little difference between the metaphorical structure of his poem and that, eleven or twelve hundred years later, in Cummings' poem. There is no reason to think of any sort of direct influence: Cummings was a literate man, but hardly a medieval scholar, and he is probably unlikely ever to have run across the older poem. But who in a world of constantly interchanging light and darkness, the light dominated by the sun, the darkness dominated by the moon, is likely to need a literary source for such commonly perceived and understood matters?

The Sick Rose

O Rose, thou art sick.
The invisible worm

That flies in the night
In the howling storm

5   Has found out thy bed
Of crimson joy,
And his dark secret love
Does thy life destroy.

(WILLIAM BLAKE)

The poem has a botanical metaphor, it may at first seem. Roses are flowers, and flowers are subject to "worms" and other night-flying insect predators, which find their beds "of crimson joy" and "destroy" the flowers they "love." But there are puzzling aspects to the metaphor. We can understand why the worm is "invisible," for it flies at night. We can understand that, arguably, the worm is obliged to fly through a storm, even a "howling storm." But if that is the metaphor, then it is not in fact metaphorical at all, for it would be simply natural observation—and why include such a piece of gardening lore in a book portentously entitled *Songs of Experience*, which book is also the counterpart of an earlier book entitled, equally portentously, *Songs of Innocence*? And taken as a whole, there is an intensity to the "color words" (that is, the words of emotional strength) of the poem which suggests that gardening lore is not at issue at all. There is a similar intensity to many of the other poems in *Songs of Experience*, none of which are merely reporters' notes on the cultivation of flowers and trees and the like.

The poem is not as difficult as I have made it. In missing the first clue to the metaphor, quite deliberately, I have totally obscured the poet's purpose. For to what in human experience (*Songs of Experience*, remember, is the title of the book in which the poem appears) do we normally compare flowers? Women and girls—as the name Rose should at once tell us, if we are paying attention. The metaphorical comparison, then, is between a beautiful flower and a beautiful girl—and it is in no way esoteric or hard to follow. The rose is "sick": why? A "worm" has "found out thy bed/ Of crimson joy." And we suddenly perceive that "bed" is not *flower* bed at all, but *human* bed, as the very nature of metaphorical comparison requires. "Innocence" and "experience" take on a very different meaning, seen in such plainly sexual terms. So too do other aspects of the metaphor light up in different ways. The "worm" becomes—in the metaphor—something phallic. The "crimson joy" becomes—in the metaphor—a characteristic of female sexuality. And the fact that the worm is "invisible" indicates, in the terms suggested by the flower-girl metaphor, that the "worm" is a thought, an idea, rather than an actuality. It is his (the worm's) "dark secret love" which destroys her life. Why? Because instead of actual sexual experience she has only the false, hidden sexual experience of someone shut off—as in other poems Blake clearly protests—from the true, open experience of sex. In "The Garden of Love," he sees a newly built Chapel, "And the gates of this Chapel were shut,/ And 'Thou shalt not' writ over the door." There are "tomb-stones where *flowers* should be" (italics added) and "Priests in black gowns . . . binding with briars my joys & desires." It is the dead cold hand of religion, in Blake's view, which is responsible for the metaphorical "death" which, he argues, the denial of sexual experience amounts to.

"The Sick Rose" is immensely compressed; we need to turn, as I have done, to its companion poems in order to fully appreciate what Blake is up to. But the basic terms of the metaphor—the comparison between girl and flower, and between the predators which damage each—are neither difficult nor unnatural. They are, in fact, just as traditional and widely known as the sun and moon comparisons. Their expression, in Blake's poem, is not so full or admittedly so clear as in other poems—but the basic metaphorical structure remains powerfully simple and appropriate, as it must be for a poem to have deep and lasting effect.

To His Coy Mistress

Had we but world enough, and time,
This coyness, lady, were no crime.
We would sit down, and think which way
To walk, and pass our long love's day.
5 Thou by the Indian Ganges' side
Shouldst rubies find; I by the tide
Of Humber° should complain.° I would

---

7 **Humber** British river, flowing through the town where the poet lived; **complain** sing songs, write poems

Love you ten years before the flood,
And you should, if you please, refuse
10   Till the conversion of the Jews.°
My vegetable love should grow
Vaster than empires and more slow;
An hundred years should go to praise
Thine eyes, and on thy forehead gaze;
15   Two hundred to adore each breast,
But thirty thousand to the rest;
An age at least to every part,
And the last age should show your heart.
For, lady, you deserve this state,°
20   Nor would I love at lower rate.
       But at my back I always hear
Time's wingèd chariot hurrying near;
And yonder all before us lie
Deserts of vast eternity.
25   Thy beauty shall no more be found;
Nor, in the marble vault, shall sound
My echoing song; then worms shall try°
That long preserved virginity,
And your quaint honor turn to dust,
30   And into ashes all my lust:
The grave's a fine and private place,
But none, I think, do there embrace.
       Now therefore, while the youthful hue
Sits on thy skin like morning glow,
35   And while thy willing soul transpires°
At every pore with instant fires,
Now let us sport us while we may,
And now, like amorous birds of prey,
Rather at once our time devour
40   Than languish in his slow-chapped° power.
Let us roll all our strength and all
Our sweetness up into one ball,

---

10 **conversion of the Jews** the end of recorded time   19 **state** dignity   27 **try** test,
attempt   35 **transpires** breathes   40 **slow-chapped** slow-jawed (chaps—or chops—
meaning jaws).

And tear our pleasures with rough strife
Through the iron gates of life;
45 Thus, though we cannot make our sun
Stand still, yet we will make him run.

(ANDREW MARVELL)

Readers have been delighting in Marvell's dryly passionate, witty poem for more than three hundred years. There are all sorts of reasons for its justly deserved popularity, but one of them is surely the wonderfully apt, wonderfully clever metaphors which come streaming at us, one after the other. In drawing out "our long love's day," for example, Marvell reaches through time and space for the stuff of his comparisons. "Ten years before the flood," with its resounding echoes of the Biblical past, is followed by the end of all recorded time, again an image derived from religion, "the conversion of the Jews." Having swung from the beginning to the end of time, he then offers us a "vegetable love" growing—and note the deft synesthesia, as political and geographical elements are grafted onto the horticultural stem of the metaphor—"vaster than empires and more slow." When he turns away from this delightfully farfetched ideal lovemaking, the comparisons are similarly extravagant—and yet accurate, founded in everyone's and anyone's knowledge. "Time's wingèd chariot," one of the most memorable phrases in the poetry of our language, blasts us free of the "long love's day." And at once we are told of the "deserts of vast eternity" stretching before us: time, that is, not only races up behind us but, once having caught us, abandons us to the dried-out, passionless dust of "deserts." Again, Marvell pivots from one extreme to another, flashing both beginnings and ends on the page. No one can possibly enjoy "two hundred [years] to adore each breast" of his beloved; we die, and our beauty dies with us, and descends to the cold hardness of "the marble vault." Everything about us turns "to dust"—and so, in the poem's third section, Marvell evokes "morning glow" as a metaphor for his beloved's "youthful" vitality, and imagines "instant fires" breathing out of her "every pore." He has man and woman together turn on time "like amorous birds of prey," rather than as passive victims. "The iron gates of life" may indeed enclose us, he asserts, and we are sure to die in the end, but "though we cannot make our sun stand still," though we cannot stop time, we *can* make time flow delightfully by. "Yet we will make him run."

Suppose a man in mourning, and very specifically in mourning for a dearly beloved child, a boy for whom he had wanted and hoped many many wonderful things. Suppose that man a poet and suppose that he wrote, as indeed he did, this dirge for his son:

> Farewell, thou child of my right hand,° and joy;
> My sin was too much hope of thee, loved boy:
> Seven years thou wert lent to me, and I thee pay,
> Exacted by thy fate, on the just day.°
> 5 O could I lose all father now! for why
> Will man lament the state he should envy,
> To have so soon 'scaped world's and flesh's rage,
> And, if no other misery, yet age?
> Rest in soft peace, and asked, say "Here doth lie
> 10 Ben Jonson his best piece of poetry."
> For whose sake henceforth all his vows be such
> As what he loves may never like too much.

(BEN JONSON, "On My First Son")

Jonson's metaphors, typically, are more abstract than Andrew Marvell's. In lines 3 and 4, the basic comparison is monetary: the child has been "lent to me," and the debt can only be repaid "on the just [i.e., lawful, equitable, proper] day." The key metaphor, in lines 9 and 10, is poetic: this dead child, says the poet father, was in fact the best "piece of poetry" he had ever created. Much of the rest of the poem is not metaphorical—again, Jonson is typically fonder of statement than he is of metaphor. Much of the statement is religious in nature, appropriately for a mourning poem. In lines 1 and 2, the poet reproaches himself (but how seriously?) for the "sin" of too much affection for his child. In lines 4–8, the statement rests on the knowledge that the child is at peace in heaven, and has therefore escaped all worldly problems,

---

1 **child of my right hand** *ben yamin*, in Hebrew, means "son of my right hand," and the boy was named Benjamin   4 **the just day** the exact day; the boy died on his seventh birthday

and most especially that of having to grow old. And in the final two lines, the statement is simply a defensive disclaimer, a wistful proclamation that never again will he "like too much" what he loves. Jonson has woven his poem out of an alternation of statement and metaphor: each complements the other, each by varying the approach enlivens and heightens the other.

But there is more underlying the poignancy of the poem. A poet writes, as Ben Jonson most certainly wrote, with one eye pretty steadily on his fame in days to come. Most poets are ambitious; Jonson was unusually so. In that sense, then, his "best piece of poetry" matters a very great deal to him. And since a son, too, is a product intended for the future, and is at the same time himself that future, the loss suffered by the *man* is intensified by metaphorically terming it a loss for the *poet*. But there is a complex blending of persona and poet-father, here, for we are never permitted to forget that Jonson the poet is also Jonson the father, in mourning for the real loss of a real son. The metaphor thus becomes terribly real, almost in some way not a metaphor at all, but the simple aching truth. Finally, since Jonson is plainly very much alive, as he writes the poem, the assertion that the dead child was without any doubt his "best" poem—whether we fully credit that assertion or not—makes it impossible for Jonson the poet ever to attain so high a standard of achievement again. That is, the loss suffered by Jonson the father has, if we take him at his word, also injured Jonson the poet. It does not matter, ultimately, whether the assertion is accurate: what matters is that the poet makes it, and believes it. The assertion lends a haunting finality to *all* the assorted kinds of losses caused by the child's death. It imparts, as of course it is meant to do, a powerful sense of just how wondrous a child this was, in his grieving father's eyes.

My Maggie Machine

What a perfect machine
Of valves and springs
You are, my love,
Maggie, my love.
5   What things you can be
And do, so please
Feel free, my love,

To tell me if I fail
To wind you first
10 Or turn you, Maggie,
To off when out
Of use.

(ROBERT PAWLOWSKI)

Poetry celebrates, as well as mourns, and metaphors can bubble
and froth as well as weep. The poet is serious about his love for
Maggie, here: the way he uses her name three times (once, and with
heavy alliterative emphasis, in the poem's title) underlines that serious-
ness. But he is doubly playful, and wields the poem's central metaphor
—in truth, its only metaphor—as a device for lightening tone, and also
for turning a serious declaration of love into a teasing pretense. The
metaphor is announced in the first line, bluntly, with no attempt at
disguise: the woman is "a perfect machine." She has "valves" (devices
for opening and closing), she has "springs" (devices which impart mus-
cular tension and create movement, notably movement up and down).
The sexual character of the metaphor, as it is thus extended, is deli-
cately clear; it is also solidly founded in the appropriateness of the
metaphor in both sides of the comparison. "What things you can . . .
do," the poem quietly exults—and then, while preserving the appear-
ance of serious praise, the poem just as quietly shifts. "Please feel free"
has a dry quality; the notion of the woman needing to be wound up
before use ("to wind you *first*"; italics added) is softly mocking. It is not
nasty; it is, however, teasing—and the poem concludes, continuing in
this distancing, nicely arch manner, with the suggestion that when "out
of use" the woman may require the persona to turn her off. She is
plainly "my love," a fact insisted on three times, but she is just as plainly
someone with whom the persona coexists in a pleasantly ironic ten-
sion, pleasurable to both parties in the relationship. The first line of the
poem, accordingly, becomes considerably less unambiguous: the
woman may be "perfect," but she is also a love "machine."

It is important to emphasize, at this point, that there is no such
thing as a satisfactory prose paraphrase or analysis of a metaphor. No
critical analysis is ever the thing it analyzes; no paraphrase, no transla-
tion, is ever the thing paraphrased or translated. There is so much
localized, built-in, subtle information contained in a metaphor—

associative, rhythmical, shadings of meaning, degrees of linkage, and more—that analysis or paraphrase is in the end more a tourist guide-book than the thing being therein described. (That sentence, though prose, is itself founded in a metaphor—analysis or paraphrase as tour-ist guidebook rather than as the true equivalent of the thing being described.) Thus in the next poem, while the poet once again bluntly announces the metaphorical, nonliteral, unreal quality of his poem in the first line, and begins to suggest a controlling metaphor for the poem, in what follows he deliberately undercuts his own pronounce-ment. We watch the poem quickly taking on, and retaining, a chilling reality, knowing it has been declared nonreal but also knowing it to be totally possible, even if not literally actual.

Empire of Dreams

On the first page of my dreambook
It's always evening
In an occupied country.
Hour before the curfew.
5   A small provincial city.
The houses all dark.
The store-fronts gutted.

I am on a street corner
Where I shouldn't be.
10   Alone and coatless
I have gone out to look
For a black dog who answers to my whistle.
I have a kind of halloween mask
Which I am afraid to put on.

(CHARLES SIMIC)

Again, the metaphor is extended through the entire poem. But this time the shift in tone is delayed until the final two lines, and instead of lightening the poem it vastly darkens it. The "halloween mask" has wide-ranging associations with things secretive and dark, even witch-like; the fact that it is "a kind of" halloween mask, rather than any ordinary, straightforward halloween mask, makes it still more mysterious. The poet swiftly capitalizes on this sudden intensification of an already dark poem: the mask is something "which I am afraid to put on." The last line is deeply chilling, because in "an occupied" country, of course, everybody is always afraid, but also because—equally obviously—the halloween mask takes us back to the poem's first line (and its title), which announce this as a poem about dreams, not about literal reality. Just as in "My Maggie Machine," we can never be entirely sure just where the poet stands, as he addresses us. There is inevitably something that neither analysis nor any other kind of logical discussion can fully explain. The poem makes its own context, in the final analysis (another prose metaphor). The poem deals, ultimately, with what straightforward, nonmetaphorical language cannot truly get at. That is, each poem, if it is a good poem, creates a kind of small world of its own. We as readers of the poem are allowed to penetrate, to experience that small, different world. Straightforward ideas of the sort that are expressible in prose can and usually do emerge from that world, but the important fact is that we receive and we experience additional things as well, things not easily discussed in ordinary prose discourse.

Tribute to Kafka for Someone Taken

The party is going strong.
The doorbell rings. It's
for someone named me.
I'm coming. I take
5   a last drink, a last
puff on a cigarette,
a last kiss at a girl,
and step into the hall,
        bang,
10 shutting out the laughter. "Is
your name you?" "Yes."
"Well come along then."
"See here. See here. See here."

(ALAN DUGAN)

Apart from the literary reference (Kafka is known for two novels, *The Trial* and *The Castle*, in which the almost nameless central character—he is called "K."—is subjected to all sorts of utterly irrational arrests and harassments), this poem deals with virtually the same materials as "Empire of Dreams." But the localizations, the inner materials of the poem and the way in which the poem handles them, make the final effect totally different. There is one central metaphor, the unexpected arrest of someone for no known reason—but here that central metaphor *is* the poem. We may suspect this from the use of "someone" in the title: the deliberate nonspecificity is, however, not there conclusive. It becomes conclusive in line 3, where we learn that the bell tolls (or rings) for "someone named me."

In lines 4–8 the persona puts on a brave front, trying to act like the romantic heroes of traditional literature. But line 9 puts a stop to that, with a swift, solitary "bang." And then the laughter is shut out, and the suddenly helpless, hapless persona is confronted with a meaningless preliminary questioning—"Is your name you?"—and is at the end led away, stuttering protests that are also meaningless, as well as plainly ineffectual. The shift in tone at the end, from casual to bravado to helpless, stuttering fear, works on us quite differently than does the sudden mysterious darkening at the end of "Empire of Dreams."

A Poison Tree

I was angry with my friend:
I told my wrath, my wrath did end.
I was angry with my foe:
I told it not, my wrath did grow.

5   And I watered it in fears,
Night and morning with my tears;
And I sunned it with smiles,
And with soft deceitful wiles.

And it grew both day and night,
10   Till it bore an apple bright.
And my foe beheld it shine,
And he knew that it was mine,

And into my garden stole,
When the night had veiled the pole;
15 In the morning glad I see
My foe outstretched beneath the tree.

(WILLIAM BLAKE)

This controlling metaphor plainly anticipates the more exact and technically oriented formulations of Sigmund Freud. It is inner, irrational reality that the poem reveals. The language of comparison relates this inner world to the outer world of everyday reality, using the extended metaphor as its tool. But Blake is concerned with psychological states, rather than with the state of apple orchards or the preservation of private property rights in edible fruits generally.

Ozymandias°

I met a traveler from an antique land
Who said: Two vast and trunkless legs of stone
Stand in the desert. Near them, on the sand,
Half sunk, a shattered visage lies, whose frown,
5 And wrinkled lip, and sneer of cold command,
Tell that its sculptor well those passions read
Which yet survive, stamped on these lifeless things,
The hand that mocked them, and the heart that fed:
And on the pedestal these words appear:
10 "My name is Ozymandias, king of kings:
Look on my works, ye Mighty, and despair!"
Nothing beside remains. Round the decay
Of that colossal wreck, boundless and bare
The lone and level sands stretch far away.

(PERCY BYSSHE SHELLEY)

The statue can be considered real; the traveler may be considered real; the description may be considered accurate. But even without

---

Ozymandias Greek name of Ramses II, thirteenth century B.C., Egyptian pharaoh who is supposed, in fact, to have built a great statue of himself.

knowing Shelley's radical political beliefs, can any attentive reader really believe that this is a poem of art criticism, or of tourist appreciation? External, all-too-visible reality is here turned, in a powerfully evocative metaphor, into a representation of the consequences of tyranny, and of the psychological states that accompany it. The limitless, bare sands that "stretch far away" become the metaphorical products of a "sneer of cold command," a "wrinkled lip," a "frown."

The Hermit

With gravel glued together for arms and legs,
charcoal-blackened wood for feet,
hands,
the body a leather bolster,
5 head a hard ball—

      the withered dried up man who had
      eaten nothing but sweetened dew for 30 years
      knelt by the roadside.
      A robber attacked him from behind
10   cutting down the old man with his knife.
      He put on the old man's ragged robe
      and himself began to pray.
      "Lord, Lord, I have killed a good man
      gratuitously. What shall I do?"
15   But nothing happened.
      The old man's body began to rot.
      The robber sang and chanted.
      He forgot
      after some time
20   his origins.

(DIANE WAKOSKI)

The spatial division of the poem—five lines set at the normal margin, and fifteen lines indented—marks a time division in the events narrated. Lines 1–5 are a magical-sounding description of the almost entirely nonhuman creature the hermit has become, having (as we learn in line 7) "eaten nothing but sweetened dew for 30 years." His arms and legs are knobbly, thin, like "gravel glued together." His feet and his hands are black and dirty, like "charcoal-blackened wood." His body seems no more than a sort of leather pillow, his head only "a hard ball." He is precisely what line 6 calls him, a "withered dried up man."

These are all appropriate metaphors for the physical state of the holy man. But since the poem is not about the physical but about the spiritual state of being a hermit, the poet sets off these lines spatially and uses that spatial division to mark the end of the timeless, constant state of the old hermit and the beginning of the poem's narrative. And it is at this point that the central metaphor of the poem takes over, that metaphor being nothing less than the power which external events have over inner, psychological states. The hermit prays "by the roadside"; he is "attacked from behind" by a robber and killed. But in line 11, when the robber assumes the hermit's outer garb, his "ragged robe," he suddenly finds himself doing what the hermit had been doing: he "himself began to pray," says line 12. In lines 13 and 14, further, he asks for God's guidance—but in active terms, appropriate for a man still in part a robber, and not yet a contemplative, not yet a true hermit. Line 15 tells us that "nothing happened," except that, in line 16, "the old man's body began to rot." The body of the dead man is, however, far less important than his spiritual state, which in the rest of the poem so takes possession of the former robber that he "sang and chanted" and "after some time" is no longer a robber, but has himself become, like the man whose place he unwittingly took, a hermit.

It would take far more words for literal prose to accomplish what the metaphor here effects in barely twenty lines. And the fundamental truth of what the metaphor expresses—again, the power of external events over inner states—has often been demonstrated. After World War II, books were written to show that prisoners in Nazi concentration camps frequently tried to take on the traits of their captors. People who live together for a sufficiently long time begin, in many ways, to take on physical—i.e., external—resemblances. But all of these developments are marks of inner effects, and it is precisely those inner effects which "The Hermit" speaks to—and illuminates.

Gretel in Darkness

This is the world we wanted.
All who would have seen us dead
are dead. I hear the witch's cry

break in the moonlight through a sheet
5   of sugar: God rewards.
Her tongue shrivels into gas . . .

        Now, far from women's arms
and memory of women, in our father's hut
we sleep, are never hungry.
10   Why do I not forget?
My father bars the door, bars harm
from this house, and it is years.

No one remembers. Even you, my brother,
summer afternoons you look at me as though
15   you meant to leave,
as though it never happened.
But I killed for you. I see armed firs,
the spires of that gleaming kiln—

Nights I turn to you to hold me
20   but you are not there.
Am I alone? Spies
hiss in the stillness, Hansel,
we are there still and it is real, real,
that black forest and the fire in earnest.

(LOUISE GLÜCK)

Everyone knows the fairy tale of Hansel and Gretel, from which
this poem starts. That fairy tale is in a sense the poem's metaphor—for
what the poem reveals is that fairy tales are not make-believe, but
"real, real," at least in the psychological sense ("I killed for you"), at
least in the inner world of the poem itself. There is after-the-fact narra-
tive here, as well: no one likes to think of what happens after the final
tag line of "and they lived happily ever after." The poet has tried to
pierce through that obscuringly automatic phrase: "Why do I not
forget? . . . No one remembers." But although others act "as though it
never happened," as of course in literal truth it never did, "Gretel in
Darkness" works on the stark assumption that things have conse-
quences, often unperceivable consequences that inexorably require us
to face them and to deal with them. The final aspect of the metaphor,

"that black forest and the fire [that is] in earnest," expresses that inner meaning as I think no straightforward, literal formulation could possibly do.

Your Mother Sings

Your mother sings
an old song as she
hangs the wash. She looks around—

And when she is sure
5   no one is watching
(but you are watching) she lets the pigeons

she keeps at the bottom of her laundry basket
fly free—
Each has a note

10   in its beak. And now a pigeon
flies in your window, dies at your feet.
The note says: *I live alone, please*

come, please help me. But she doesn't live
alone, your mother
15   is downstairs now

moving pots and pans, starting
dinner, singing
a song she sang,

you imagine, when you couldn't sleep.
20   You hear her down there
singing. You see the pigeon on the floor.

(MICHAEL HETTICH)

Drawn half from fairy tale (though from no one fairy tale), drawn half from a careful blending of childhood memory and a present reality, the central metaphor of this poem expresses not one but two basic (and carefully unresolved) meanings. The good mother, singing "an old song as she hangs the wash," "singing a song she sang" in childhood "when you couldn't sleep," is both a captor of and someone who frees "the pigeons she keeps at the bottom of her laundry basket." The pigeons are both captives, in desperate need, and also tellers of untruths: "But she doesn't live alone." And yet the pigeon does fly, and does die, and "you see the pigeon on the floor." Again, though here in a singularly complex and delicate mixture, the metaphor seeks to probe profound inner realities, the love-hate ambiguities of the mother-child relationship. Those ambiguities, like the poem, are rarely if ever resolved. Even to approach, to half articulate them, is itself threatening, as indeed it is for the persona here. Perhaps only in the half-world, the never-never world if you will, of a poem can we safely approach, safely articulate what otherwise might more than threaten us—might actually destroy us, or at least the balance of our sanity.

Epitaph on Elizabeth, L.H.

Wouldst thou hear what man can say
In a little? Reader, stay.
Underneath this stone doth lie
As much beauty as could die;
5   Which in life did harbor give
To more virtue than doth live.
If at all she had a fault,
Leave it buried in this vault.
One name was Elizabeth;
10 Th'other, let it sleep with death:
Fitter, where it died, to tell,
Than that it lived at all. Farewell.

(BEN JONSON)

Not only does this memorial poem not have a controlling metaphor, it might be argued that it has nothing metaphorical about it at all. The thought comes straight at us. We are not presented with some striking comparison, some bold image, which first hits home and only then suggests the associative meaning it carries. In short, statement is the poetic tool Jonson uses, here as (for the most part) elsewhere. The poem is strong, as is its language; it is compelling, it is effective.

And yet, though not obviously metaphorical, neither is this poem a statement of that which is simply and literally true. "Underneath this stone doth lie," we are told, "as much beauty as could die." This is extravagant, but it is also more than that. Beauty is not some sort of indivisible thing, nor is it an imperishable abstraction, and neither is (nor was, nor could be) this dead lady, in life, the total embodiment of mortal beauty. Jonson (and his time) would have explained this as a fancy, a "conceit"—that is, an imaginative idea which allows a poet to say, "in a little" space, what otherwise would have to be belabored and elaborately spelled out. And what is a "conceit" but a different kind of metaphor, a metaphor which does not proclaim its metaphoricality (if there is such a word), but for all that ends by comparing, for purposes of illumination and explication, one thing to another? We *know* that "as much beauty as could die" does not lie interred "underneath this stone." But we also know, and approve of, and respond to, what Jonson wants us to understand, wants us to feel, by the use of this conceit. The methodology employed by a poet tends to be as much a matter of his or her particular sensibility as the material out of which his images are woven, or the subjects which he chooses to write about (or not to write about). Again, for the reader of poems it is a matter of learning to accept what the poet is and is not, what he tells us and what he does not.

To underline, finally, that wholly basic truth, consider as if juxtaposed against the Jonson poem just examined this intensely metaphorical poem by Emily Dickinson (like most of her poems, it has no title):

> The Spider holds a Silver Ball
> In unperceived Hands—
> And dancing softly to Himself
> His Yarn of Pearl—unwinds—
>
> 5   He plies from Nought to Nought—
> In unsubstantial Trade—
> Supplants our Tapestries with His—
> In half the period—
>
> An Hour to rear supreme
> 10 His Continents of Light—
> Then dangle from the Housewife's Broom—
> His Boundaries—forgot—

It is easy to see that spiders are at the heart of each of these twelve lines. But to what are they being compared? What is the true source of the metaphorical comparison being made? Dickinson makes it plain at the very start: she is talking about splendidly isolated creatures, oriented not toward actual accomplishment but toward the almost mystical achievement of "unsubstantial trade." And these creatures, in the end, are regularly swept away by "the Housewife's Broom," all their giant fabric of insubstantial but glorious "Tapestries" destroyed unthinkingly, uncaringly, by the inexorable forces of ordinary life. Line 1, accordingly, tells us that the spider holds a "Silver Ball." This is poetry, not biology; Dickinson is not giving us a naturalist's sound observations but an immediate poetic clue. "Silver Ball" is unmistakeably close to "crystal ball," an instrument of prophesy and prediction, though not necessarily useful prophesy and prediction. This magical instrument is being grasped, furthermore, not by spider legs but by the "Hands" of line 2. It is humans, not spiders, who work with hands. And these hands are "unperceived," unnoticed. This is sufficiently true of spiders so that the basis for comparison is established. But can we miss the linkage being made between spiders and human weavers of splendid and useless webs, human weavers who like spiders work in isolation, unseen, unknown? And can we miss the linkage between Dickinson's own life and career and these metaphorically brilliant and neglected human weavers? The connection is insisted upon throughout the poem, from the "Yarn of Pearl" (preciousness not lightly cast before swine) to the "Continents of Light," erected in the poet's mind as beautifully as they are created by the spider's webs.

Not only Emily Dickinson's poems but also her letters are extraordinarily metaphorical—they scarcely seem to be prose, and are at times not quite intelligible. "I did not deem that planetary forces annulled," she once wrote to a friend just become a soldier in the Civil War, "but suffered an exchange of territory, or world. I should have liked to see you before you became improbable. War feels to me like an oblique place." We can perhaps still better judge this typical mode of expression if we realize that the letter and the poem just quoted are almost exactly contemporaneous (the dating of her poems is largely conjectural). The year before, in response to some bewildered, uncomprehending (and not very positive) criticism of her poems, she had written to the same correspondent: "I thanked you for your justice, but could not drop the bells whose jingling cooled my tramp. Perhaps the balm seemed better, because you bled me first." Her frame of mind, clearly, is much the same no matter what literary form she chose to use for its expression. And to a very considerable extent metaphor is exactly that: a frame of mind, a way of looking out from within an inner world of essentially personal thoughts and feelings. In the very act of expressing such inner worlds, the poet shares them with us.

Poems Supplementary to Chapter 2

— 1 —

In this extended metaphor Dugan walks a difficult and delicate line, that between overidentification with the animal-victim and oversymbolization of it. The poem is just serious enough—its theology distinctly Catholic—and just mocking enough to preserve its balance.

Funeral Oration for a Mouse

This, Lord, was an anxious brother and
a living diagram of fear: full of health himself,
        he brought diseases like a gift
to give his hosts. Masked in a cat's moustache
5   but sounding like a bird, he was a ghost
        of lesser noises and a kitchen pest
for whom ladies stand on chairs. So,
Lord, accept our felt though minor guilt
for an ignoble foe and ancient sin:
10   the murder of a guest
who shared our board: just once he ate
        too slowly, dying in our trap
from necessary hunger and a broken back.

Humors of love aside, the mousetrap was our own
15   opinion of the mouse, but for the mouse
        it was the tree of knowledge with
        its consequential fruit, the true cross
        and the gate of hell. Even to approach
        it makes him like or better than
20   its maker: his courage as a spoiler never once
impressed us, but to go out cautiously at night,
        into the dining room—what bravery, what
        hunger! Younger by far, in dying he
was older than us all: his mobile tail and nose

25   spasmed in the pinch of our annoyance. Why,
then, at that snapping sound, did we, victorious,
begin to laugh without delight?

Our stomachs, deep in an analysis
of their own stolen baits
30   (and asking, "Lord, Host, to whom are we the pests?),
contracted and demanded a retreat
from our machine and its effect of death,
as if the mouse's fingers, skinnier
than hairpins and as breakable as cheese,
35   could grasp our grasping lives, and in
their drowning movement pull us under too,
into the common death beyond the mousetrap.

(ALAN DUGAN)

— 2 —

The key to this poem is perception of the governing metaphor, explained in lines 9–13. Once we know who (or rather what) the hero is—"halo," in line 7, anticipates the later explanation—the rest falls into place easily. Similarly, line 3 is baffling only until we think in terms of the physical comparison being made by the metaphor.

There He Was

on horseback, and
the saber's drawn,
lunar acuity
cut out a slice
5   of sunlight in mid-air.
He whirled it once
around his head, a halo, and
discharged it at a foe.
Charge forever, hero! Rear,
10   horse! The saber points
toward death, by means
of which he changed

into a statue in the square.
To you the glory, brother,
15 and to us the girls.

(ALAN DUGAN)

— 3 —

These four poems form a unit and must be considered as an integrated progression. The first presents us with unpopulated urban landscape: only the animal (line 12) actually moves. The second introduces inner consciousness. The third deepens that inner awareness, extending it out into the urban scene already fully described. The fourth places inner awareness and conscience squarely into the urban scene; in lines 48–51 the persona for the first time permits himself a reaction, and lines 52–54 conclude with helpless, bitter empathy.

Preludes

1.

The winter evening settles down
With smell of steaks in passageways.
Six o'clock.
The burnt-out ends of smoky days.
5   And now a gusty shower wraps
The grimy scraps
Of withered leaves about your feet
And newspapers from vacant lots;
The showers beat
10   On broken blinds and chimney-pots,°
And at the corner of the street
A lonely cab-horse steams and stamps.

And then the lighting of the lamps.

2.

The morning comes to consciousness
15   Of faint stale smells of beer

---

10 **chimney-pots** pipes at top of chimneys

From the sawdust-trampled street
With all its muddy feet that press
To early coffee-stands.
With the other masquerades
20 That time resumes,
One thinks of all the hands
That are raising dingy shades
In a thousand furnished rooms.

3.

You tossed a blanket from the bed,
25 You lay upon your back, and waited;
You dozed, and watched the night revealing
The thousand sordid images
Of which your soul was constituted;
They flickered against the ceiling.
30 And when all the world came back
And the light crept up between the shutters
And you heard the sparrows in the gutters,
You had such a vision of the street
As the street hardly understands;
35 Sitting along the bed's edge, where
You curled the papers from your hair,
Or clasped the yellow soles of feet
In the palms of both soiled hands.

4.

His soul stretched tight across the skies
40 That fade behind a city block,
Or trampled by insistent feet
At four and five and six o'clock;
And short square fingers stuffing pipes,
And evening newspapers, and eyes
45 Assured of certain certainties,
The conscience of a blackened street
Impatient to assume the world.

I am moved by fancies that are curled
Around these images, and cling:
50 The notion of some infinitely gentle
Infinitely suffering thing.

Wipe your hand across your mouth, and laugh;
The worlds revolve like ancient women
Gathering fuel in vacant lots.

(T. S. ELIOT)

— 4 —

Donne's metaphors in this poem are cumulatively progressive. The "strange sights" of the first stanza are recapitulated at the start of stanza two, which then proceeds to build toward a pilgrimage to the strangest sight of all, explained in line 18. Stanza three, though less extensively metaphorical than what has come before, nevertheless embodies an extended restatement and formulation of the point already made in line 18; in that sense, stanza three is a fanciful capping of all the metaphors in the poem.

Song

Go and catch a falling star,
    Get with child a mandrake root,°
Tell me where all past years are
    Or who cleft the Devil's foot,
5 Teach me to hear mermaids singing,
  Or to keep off envy's stinging,
          And find
          What wind
Serves to advance an honest mind.

10 If thou beest born to strange sights,
    Things invisible to see,
Ride ten thousand days and night,
    Till age snow white hairs on thee.
Thou, when thou return'st, wilt tell me
15 All strange wonders that befell thee,
          And swear
          No where
Lives a woman true,° and fair.°

---

2 **mandrake root** herb root in roughly human shape (often used as a fertility drug)   18 **true** faithful; **fair** beautiful

If thou find'st one, let me know;
20   Such a pilgrimage were sweet.
Yet do not, I would not go,
        Though at next door we might meet;
Though she were true when you met her,
And last till you write your letter,
25   Yet she
            Will be
False, ere I come, to two, or three.

(JOHN DONNE)

— 5 —

This entire short poem is founded on a clear metaphor: the thinning out of milk "spilt on a stone" is compared to the eventual end of those who "have done and thought." The first part of line 3, which is not metaphorical, provides the essential context by means of which the central metaphor is fully apprehended.

Spilt Milk

We that have done and thought,
That have thought and done,
Must ramble, and thin out
Like milk spilt on a stone.

(WILLIAM BUTLER YEATS)

— 6 —

Lines 13 and 14 provide the key to this poem: fed back into the three metaphors (lines 1–4, lines 5–9, and lines 10–12), they explain both the bitterness and the determined anti-intellectualism being expressed. Queen Emain had won her right to measure "a town" (in the legend, a palace) by defeating her own uncle in battle; Babylonian indifference is itself semilegendary; and lines 10–12 probably refer to the death of the sun god's own son, killed by Zeus when he attempted, with dangerous ineptitude, to drive the chariot of the sun.

The Dawn

I would be ignorant as the dawn
That has looked down
On that old queen° measuring a town
With the pin of a brooch,
5   Or on the withered men that saw
From their pedantic Babylon
The careless planets in their courses,°
The stars fade out where the moon comes,
And took their tablets° and did sums;
10 I would be ignorant as the dawn
That merely stood, rocking the glittering coach
Above the cloudy shoulders of the horses;
I would be—for no knowledge is worth a straw—
Ignorant and wanton as the dawn.

(WILLIAM BUTLER YEATS)

— 7 —

The ingenious simplicity of the two basic metaphors in this poem is heightened by the exceedingly deft rhymes and by the careful variations in line length. The quick unexpectedness of metaphor is joined to unexpectedness of rhyme and meter, each reinforcing the other.

Fire and Ice

Some say the world will end in fire,
Some say in ice.
From what I've tasted of desire
I hold with those who favor fire.

---

3 **that old queen** Emain, in an Irish legend   7 **courses** paths   9 **tablets** writing pads

5   But if it had to perish twice,
I think I know enough of hate
To say that for destruction ice
Is also great
And would suffice.

(ROBERT FROST)

— 8 —

Two basic stances underly the rich metaphors in this poem: (1) Wordsworth perceives good in Nature, and harm in "the world" of modern man, the commercial, industrial world that was already very much evident in England; and (2) though himself a firm Christian believer, *any* purity of belief seems to him to be preferable to corruption and impurity of belief. Lines 1–4 contain the basic information for comprehension of the first of these stances, and line 8 and the first part of line 9 the basic information for the second.

The World Is Too Much with Us

The world is too much with us; late and soon,
Getting and spending, we lay waste our powers;
Little we see in Nature that is ours;
We have given our hearts away, a sordid boon!°
5   This Sea that bares her bosom to the moon,
The winds that will be howling at all hours,
And are up-gathered now like sleeping flowers,
For this, for everything, we are out of tune;
It moves us not. —Great God! I'd rather be
10 A Pagan suckled in a creed outworn;
So might I, standing on this pleasant lea,°
Have glimpses that would make me less forlorn;
Have sight of Proteus° rising from the sea;
Or hear old Triton° blow his wreathèd horn.

(WILLIAM WORDSWORTH)

---

4 **boon** gift   11 **lea** open grassland, meadow   13 **Proteus** Old Man of the Sea   14 **Triton** son of the sea god Neptune

— 9 —

The mirror of the title is a literal mirror: the first line establishes that.
The rest of this poem is essentially a set of variations on the metaphori-
cal possibilities of mirrorness—culminating, in lines 67–70, in a sum-
mary statement of the powers of mirrorness, followed, in lines 71–73,
by a kind of creedal formulation of the poet-persona's own attitude
toward those powers.

A Mirror Driven Through Nature

It's six feet by six feet, the mirror
I help hoist into a pick up,
Delivering it because he's paid cash for it
Out of my house to his house.

5   Leering, he promises to hang it up over his bed.
I slip as we prop and angle the mirror
On furniture pads, tilting my house on its porch,
Upending the neighbors who sit watching
A cat claw for balance on solid ground.

10   He drives in the cab of his truck,
I sit on the deck in back, wind flicking
My hair in the great mirror now being driven
Out of the city, which seems to be shrinking
Into a tighter and tighter bundle of bricks,
15   Its skyline being replaced gradually by sky,
Blue sky, and so many parachutists hung up
In tree tops they seem to be clouds.

The world is more pleasing on its ear,
In motion, and reversed, as now the superhighway
20   Forks off like the thumb of a hitch-hiker
And the road turns to dirt;
                              now all nature is waltzed
On the shocks of the truck, and the hayfield cows
That have gathered in the mirror
25   Are rocked as they chew, or buck like horses

When a pothole bounces the truck.
                          Which is to say
The disposition of the mirror
Is a form of power over nature, while saying so
30   Is an ignoring of certain terrible
Natural certainties,
                          like the tow-head
Squinting now through the crotch of his slingshot
At a magpie—or is it at my mirror?
35   A moment will tell, for either the magpie
Will rise checkered out of its pecked cow carcase,
Or it will shatter and fall into a thousand
Magpies.
            But neither happens.
40   We are almost there,
And I begin to wonder, what kind of a man
Bolts a mirror over his head?
Will the mirror stay up? Will the ceiling?
What about that man's mistress? Imagine
45   Her scared blue eyes staring up
Into the heaven of his pumping ass—
And his eyes,
                  all pupil, staring back
Into hers from the oval of his hand mirror . . .
50   Seeing it for the first time from *that* angle,
How could she not regret it all,
Even the bastard children?

I'm sicker than he is, I think, imagining
Things like that, as already the pick up
55   Honks its horn, six children rush
Pell-mell out of a whitewashed farmhouse,
Scattering six chickens, and a soap-faced woman skips
From the slanting porch cradling twins
In her arms—
60   or are they magnolia blossoms
Gathered into pillowcases?

"These fell while you was away," she says

To her husband squinting at her as she snaps
Two fistfuls of cambric at the sky.
65   And instantly the air is awash with blossoms,
Chickens, children, kite tails, sunmotes—

And I believe whatever the mirror reflects
Is true, and whatever is not
May by the mirror be made lovely
70   Though never true,
                                being
Half in love with this world, half
With a vision of it.

(WILLIAM ZARANKA)

— 10 —

The simple act of sending small children to school is here viewed from the mothers' rather than from either the teachers' or the childrens' perspective. Although there is a supplementary metaphor in lines 5–7, the basic metaphor is that first established in lines 1–4, and then elaborated in lines 11–14. The old saw about "an apple for the teacher" is here transformed into a wry and powerful statement of maternal weariness and frustration.

The School Children

The children go forward with their little satchels.
And all morning the mothers have labored
to gather the late apples, red and gold,
like words of another language.

5   And on the other shore
are those who wait behind great desks
to receive these offerings.

How orderly they are—the nails
on which the children hang
10   their overcoats of blue or yellow wool.

And the teachers shall instruct them in silence
and the mothers shall scour the orchards for a way out,
drawing to themselves the gray limbs of the fruit trees
bearing so little ammunition.

(LOUISE GLÜCK)

— 11 —

The title of this poem establishes the true meaning; the first line establishes the metaphor. We humans are only "the moment's populace." Where we stand, or as line 2 puts it, "where we are," turns out to be surprisingly "inhabited," and just as surprisingly "what it always was." To savor the full meaning of the poem, read the information contained in line 12 back into lines 2 through 6—and especially into the pivotal meaning of "save" in line 7.

Population

Like a flat sea,
Here is where we are, the empty reaches
Empty of ourselves

Where dark, light, sound
5 Shatter the mind born
Alone to ocean

Save we are
A crowd, a population, those
Born, those not yet dead, the moment's

10 Populace, sea-borne and violent, finding
Incredibly under the sense the rough deck
Inhabited, and what it always was.

(GEORGE OPPEN)

— 12 —

Though the title is literal, this poem in fact containing two strophes, each spoken by a different voice, the central metaphor which gives the poem meaning is less obvious. The poem is plainly both wry and quasi-serious—which helps identify and locate the comparison being made, between the haunting presence of the literary greats (lines 8–11) and the writer/first voice's attempt to challenge, instead, a natural force, which at least defeats him easily and terminally. "I'll challenge myself," says line 1. But the metaphor tells us exactly what comes of such determination.

Two Voices

I'll challenge myself, I said.
I have read the classics;
my insides feel they'd like to be outside
catching air. It was cold
5   but sunny. I wore my coat,
no hat though. Adventure.
I would invite trouble at once.
Pneumonia. I'll escape Stendhal,
Baudelaire, Whitman, Eliot,
10 each pressing me in turn
to his heart. In the cold air
I hardened. Nearby stood a lake;
I jumped in.
        "We had to haul him
15 out, a block of ice, eyeballs
in a frozen stare. After melting him
down, we lost him. He had forgotten
how to breathe. 'Challenge the weather,'
he murmured. 'Challenge the weather.'
20 And he closed his eyes."

(DAVID IGNATOW)

— 13 —

This poem is not an obscure metaphor but a very fully extended one. The key word, employed in line 2 and again in line 20, is "waiting": line 3 tells us what the lapse of time, this "waiting," is all about, "for us to grow old too."

Calmly While the Roof Swells

Somewhere in a back room we're not even sure
exists in our house, the old people waiting
for us to grow old too and wear them hang
like wallpaper, peeling, our dry-cleaned suits,
5   and although we never
open the door
to look in, and although
we're not quite sure
there is a door, they murmur like the ceilings
10   in old houses do when it rains and the wood
swells to keep us dry; we listen

and hear the hairs inside that can't
find pores to push through
push and curl
15   back, a nest of hair inside.
And we hear the birds that circle within
and without for the choice nest-stuff to lay in,
and we sit talking calmly while the roof
swells and our grandparents murmur, we hardly
20   remember them now, their waiting through the walls.

(MICHAEL HETTICH)

— 14 —

The basic metaphor here is domestic, not to say culinary. The kitchen
comparisons of lines 1–4 culminate, however, in a theological affirma-
tion, and theological concerns dominate until, finally, in lines 13 and
14 of this sonnet, the domestic/culinary again takes over, completing
the metaphor started almost ten lines earlier.

my dreams, my works, must wait till after hell

I hold my honey and I store my bread
In little jars and cabinets of my will.
I label clearly, and each latch and lid

I bid, Be firm till I return from hell.
5   I am very hungry. I am incomplete.
And none can tell me when I may dine again.
No man can give me any word but Wait,
The puny light. I keep eyes pointed in;
Hoping that, when the devil days of my hurt
10 Drag out to their last dregs and I resume
On such legs as are left me, in such heart
As I can manage, remember to go home,
My taste will not have turned insensitive
To honey and bread old purity could love.

(GWENDOLYN BROOKS)

— 15 —

The single controlling metaphor—fungal blossom and desert flower in bloom—is doubly appropriate, since a fungus is in fact a growing "plant." The metaphor is very fully exploited; the poet rings multiple changes and modulations on it, ending in a kind of hymnal that is also deeply appropriate, for hymns are sung both in celebration and in mourning.

Coccidioidmycosis

probing tar for the hard edges of stone
flowers, he picks one, smells it, finds
a spore between petals: from here
to the doctor he wonders at the beauty
5 of the desert rose, coughs long and deep
trying to bring up what the x-ray
confirms

is a dark bud opening on his heart,
a fungal bloom for which there is no medicine
10 but thought from which there is no escape

---

coccidioidmycosis infectious lung disease of fungus origin

but faith in fictions or the desert sun
which may, if anything will, blunt
the blades of the flower,
his blossoming hollow of black.

(DOUGLAS ASPER)

~∽3∽~
HOW POETRY WORKS: APPROACHES AND TECHNIQUES

ONE OF THE hardest things for readers, as well as for young poets, to learn is that poetry must say something. Mere beauty of phrase, mere intensity of musicality, mere ingeniousness of technique, become irrelevant in the absence of solid substance. Meaning and metaphor, the subject matters of the first two chapters, are basically concerned with poetry's substance, and substance is without a doubt the most important aspect of poetry.

But like all the arts, poetry is a complex meshing of substance and manner, of thought and form, of argument and technique. We admire a particular singer, in matters musical, because we like the way he or she sounds, the quality of the voice, the way a song or an aria is delivered. *What* is being sung is important, but *how* it is being sung seems of almost equal importance. In painting, similarly, we respond to a certain painter's use of color, or to his use of line. At the ballet we gasp at a dancer's leaps, or turns. At a concert we applaud a pianist's unusually rippling arpeggios, or a trumpet player's brilliant upper notes, or a flutist's long-held breath. In fiction, a novelist's style, or his characterization, or his descriptions, sometimes thrill us quite as deeply as do the plots of his books, or even as deeply as do his books' ultimate significance. In short, an artist's craft can be and usually is a deeply important part of how we react to his art.

At the beginning of Chapter One, I defined poetry as follows:

Poetry is a (1) disciplined, compact verbal utterance, (2) in some more or less musical mode, (3) dealing with aspects of internal or external reality in some meaningful way.

Item 3 deals with substance; the first two elements, however, are matters of craft. The approaches, and also the techniques, by means of which a poet makes use of the craft aspects of his art range as widely up and down the scale as the ways that a dancer prepares for and then executes a particular maneuver. Craftsmen in any field, and not only the arts, can sit and discuss these details for hours: there seems to be no end to the variations, to the possibilities, to the things that even a master can still learn. The discussion in this chapter, accordingly, must be understood as no more than an outline of some of the high points of a virtually inexhaustible subject.

(1) Poetic Music

Verbal music (musicality) is poetry's bottom line. A poet who cannot hear or handle the music of his language is no more a poet than a violinist with defective pitch is truly a violinist, or than a color-blind painter can be considered a real painter. John Dryden, a fine poet and an even finer critic, once said, that "'Tis much like dancing on ropes with fettered legs: a man may shun a fall by using caution; but the gracefulness of motion is not to be expected. . . ." Musicality is, of course, a relative matter: some poets have better ears, some have worse, but none are totally tone-deaf to verbal music. Gregory Corso, however, comes pretty close:

From Another Room

Dumb genius blows
feeble breath into my windowless room
He—the sagacious mute
rap-tapping a code or doom
5   —the drunkard punched the wall to have his storm!
Through the crack! Through the crack!
My feast was in the easy blood that flowed.

The lack of musicality here—and throughout virtually all of Corso's work, which is often high-spirited, ingenious, even delightful, but which never sings—may not be immediately obvious, especially to the relative beginner in poetic matters. The poem should be read aloud, first of all (as indeed should all poetry). If "From Another Room" is read with attention to its natural stresses, it will sound something like a four-hundred-pound man in very flat sandals stomping across a marble floor. There is almost no rhythmic variety: bang, bang, bang, comes the poem, line after dull line. Even in a poem only seven lines long, so remarkable a lack of grace becomes oppressive.

Contrast this ponderous verbal music with the intensely graceful flow of a poem with more lines but of essentially the same length, written by Denise Levertov:

to the reader

As you read, a white bear leisurely
pees, dyeing the snow
saffron,

and as you read, many gods
5   lie among lianas:° eyes of obsidian°
are watching the generations of leaves,

and as you read
the sea is turning its dark pages,
turning
10   its dark pages.

It is easier to point to than it is to analyze the superb musicality of this poem, its delicacy of rhythm. Again, the real test is to read the poem aloud: criticism does not in truth have the tools to explain what ears can plainly hear. Levertov's major success, especially in contrast to the Corso poem, is clearly the achieving of rhythmic variety. Sounding the poem aloud, one never knows exactly what the next line will turn into, how it will move, whether it will resolve and end or whether it will coil on into the line after, and perhaps the line after that. There is a rhetorical structure—the repeated introductory statement, "As you read . . . and as you read . . . and as you read"—which both neatly divides the poem into its three sections, or strophes, and at the same time equally

---

5 **lianas** vines (usually tropical); **obsidian** dark, volcanic glass

neatly holds the poem together through its unity of statement. Corso's poem does not have a uniform line length, but there is no line much longer or much shorter than any other. Levertov has lines of one word and also lines of six or seven words. By itself this does not necessarily mean much. But given the plainly superior musical quality of Levertov's poem, even so crude a measurement is significant—as is, also, the fact that Corso's poem makes significant use of alliteration (words beginning with the same consonant, or beginning with any vowel) at most only twice, with the /b/ sounds in lines 1 and 2 and the /f/ sounds in line 7, while Levertov plays with alliteration in the /b/ /p/ usage in lines 1 and 2, uses /s/ alliteration in lines 2 and 3, /l/ alliteration in the first part of line 5 and vowel alliteration in the second part of that same line, with a return to partial /s/ alliteration in lines 6–10, four words ending with /s/ (I am not counting the particle "as," though one might count it), one key word, "sea," beginning with /s/. Counting instances of alliteration and partial alliteration, let me repeat, makes no great sense if it is used to *establish* some sort of qualitative judgment. But it does help *explain* the musical superiority of Levertov's poem in contrast to Corso's.

Poetic music, of course, implies a contrast with the music of prose. Prose does in fact have music, but it is a very different sort of music. Consider the following passages, the first from a prose history of England, the second from the *Anglo-Saxon Chronicle*, a historical account much of which is written in poetry rather than in prose. The events described are essentially the same, namely the death of the English king Edgar in A.D. 975.

But the peace which only a king could keep was destroyed when Edgar died, leaving two young boys, sons of different mothers. Though the elder, Edward the Martyr, was crowned by the archbishops, his step-mother would not submit. . . .

(KEITH FEILING, *A History of England*)

In this year ended the earthly pleasures
Of Edgar, King of England, who sought
A different and lovelier light and left
This worthless life for one more lasting.
5   And all men everywhere on earth, and in England,

> Properly schooled in the science of numbers,
> Know that the King, the young ring-giver,
> Left the world and his life in the month
> Named after Julius, and on its eighth day.
> 10 And after him his half-grown son
> Received the kingdom, and Edward became
> The chief of England's earls, and her King.

(translated from the Old English by BURTON RAFFEL)

The poetry of the *Anglo-Saxon Chronicle* is not precisely the sort of poetry we write or read today, but it is clearly poetry, and clearly musical in a very different way from the sturdy plain prose of Professor Feiling. Nor does it make the latter any more like poetry to arrange it down the page as if it were in fact poetry:

> But the peace which only
> a king could keep
> was destroyed when Edgar died,
> leaving two young boys,
> 5 sons of diffrent mothers.
> Though the elder, Edward the Martyr,
> was crowned by the archbishops,
> his step-mother would not submit. . . .

The eye alone might tell you that this latter version is indeed poetry: why else would it have the broken lineation of poetry? But read it aloud and, though it has a rhythm and a music, it is distinctly not the music of poetry, but still the music of good, straightforward prose. Apart from differences in perspective, and also in the sort of information conveyed, the chief distinction between the old chronicler and the contemporary historian is plainly that the former writes poetry and the latter prose. There is some literary rhetoric in the *Chronicle* poem—"a different and lovelier light," "the King, the young ring-giver"—but of course we expect that of poetry, and there is not a great deal of that sort of adornment here. This is, as poetry, pretty plain stuff—but that is its purpose, the *Chronicle* being as much history for its time as Professor Feiling's book, written in 1949, is history for us.

What then makes the *Chronicle* poem a poem? It is poetry because it has a form of musical organization (a musical mode), basically a four-beat line, with a good deal of linking alliteration. That is, both normal, natural speech rhythm and also usual prose rhythm are subordinated, in the *Chronicle* poem, to an overriding musical pattern. The mold into which the poet casts his ideas is neither the mold of ordinary speech nor the mold of usual prose.

There are musical differences between and among different speakers, and different writers of prose, just as there are musical differences between and among different poets. Anyone who has once heard former President Carter and former President Ford knows that their vocal patterns are as different from each other as each is from the vocal patterns of former President Nixon. There are differences in vocabulary, too, and differences in voice quality, but Carter employs a kind of crooning half-chant, Ford a choppy, recurringly unfinished matrix of exclamations, and Nixon a long-breathed whine of sermonic intensity. Nor does one need even to consider strictly literary prose in order to appreciate the difference in verbal music as between a federal income tax statute, a corporation's annual report, and an advertisement for the latest dishwasher soap.

There have always been writers of eloquent, musical prose; there have always been writers of what are called prose poems—that is, poems which employ the different music of prose within a framework of poetic structure and organization. The prose poem is an odd bird, very much a hybrid form. One example should suffice:

In the old days either the plaintiff or the defendant won or lost justly or unjustly according to the mood of the court; the innocent and the guilty were acquitted or condemned according to their luck or pull with justice. Nowadays they are all condemned to death by hard labor, together with the lawyers, juries, and arresting police. Then the boards of review condemn the presiding judges, too, for having wasted time. In this way, all those who are in any way connected with justice are impartially disconnected, and the clerk closes the court house to join the last judgment. This is not to say that there is no more justice: as an only natural human invention to begin with, it has turned into the needs of the state, which needs labor. The whole apparatus can be forgotten in the absence of individuals to whom to apply it, and the sensible man will have nothing to do with anything outside his inner, passional life except his position.

(ALAN DUGAN)

This has much of the compression of poetry; it plays with words, and with verbal surprises, as poetry does; and even the clearly prose rhythms employed by Alan Dugan have strong echoes of the poetic rhythms (or music) he employs. But if this is to be considered poetry, it is a different sort of poetry from anything we have examined thus far. There is almost nothing metaphorical (at least, not overtly metaphorical: one could argue that the whole thing is itself a metaphor, or small allegory). The sequence of ideas, as we proceed from sentence to sentence, is logical in the fashion that, in Chapter One, I called literal or linear. (Poetry tends to proceed nonliterally, nonlinearally.) There are no interrupted or broken ideas; everything is rounded off, completed.

And that is in fact what constitutes the basic difference between prose and poetry. Prose, and thus the musical organization of prose, is closely founded on what linguists call the syntax of a language, and what more traditionally minded folk like to call the grammar of a language. That is, prose written in the English language must pretty strictly adhere to the formal syntax (or grammar) of English. Poetry can and frequently must stray from that formal syntax. Look back at the two poems by Alan Dugan in the supplement to Chapter 2. "Funeral Oration for a Mouse," the longer and more fully elaborated of the two, is very close to the formal syntax of English; its rhythms are also noticeably more proselike, less lyrical. "There He Was," on the other hand, is shorter and plainly more lyrical—and also much less close to formal English syntax. This is all highly proper (not to say logical), for the chief purpose of prose is and always has been the conveying of information, and lyrical poetry would not do well at that goal: try to imagine governmental directives written in lyrical poetic effusions. Worse, try to imagine military directives written as lyrical poems. What we call literary prose has never been anything but a tiny percentage of the prose produced at any given time.

And syntax is more concerned with ideas than with emotions. That is, since prose is primarily designed to convey information, its structure is designed to maximize such idea-carrying attributes as clarity, balance, order, and linear organization in general. This necessarily has large implications for the rhythmical (or musical) qualities of prose, as opposed to poetry. Professor Feiling, for example, put his information about the death of King Edgar and the succession to his throne as follows: "But the peace which only a king could keep was destroyed when Edgar died, leaving two young boys, sons of different mothers." A contemporary poet, wanting to deal with this material, might have written, instead:

> Kings can keep peace
> If kings can keep the breath
> In their faces.
> But kings can die.
> 5   And Edgar died,
> And instead of a king
> There were two boys—
> And two mothers.

The significant thing about these freshly concocted lines is how very differently their music moves, in contrast to Professor Feiling's prose. It is not formal syntactic patterns which have determined word order here, or emphasis, or vocabulary, but other and more emotional considerations. Again, Professor Feiling's prose better conveys the information. The poem is nevertheless the better of the two as a carrier of certain emotional states and stances. And that is what poetry is all about, and why it has endured, though prose has long since displaced it—and properly displaced it, on the whole—as a carrier of information.

Poetic music is both personal and also timebound. If Alexander Pope, writing in the first half of the eighteenth century, had dealt with the material in Professor Feiling's prose sentence, he might have written something like this:

> A king who's firm on a throne holds peace in hand,
> A king who dies lets anarchy loose in a land.

Since Pope, of course, neither wrote the couplet just cited nor ever wrote on the death of King Edgar, consider for a moment one of his minor productions, "On a Lady Who Pisst at the Tragedy of Cato":

While maudlin Whigs deplored their Cato's fate,
Still with dry eyes the Tory Celia sate,
But while her pride forbids her tears to flow,
The gushing waters find a vent below:
5   Though secret, yet with copious grief she mourns,
Like twenty river-gods with all their urns.
Let others screw their hypocritic face,
She shows her grief in a sincerer place;
There Nature reigns, and passion void of art,
10   For that road leads directly to the heart.

A century or so earlier, had John Donne or one of his poetic followers written on poor King Edgar (surely never so mourned as in these pages), we might have seen a poem like this:

Give a king two flowers
To plant in his land
And see how mourning showers
Shake both petal and strand.

Again, Donne never having written these lines or on this theme, consider what he in fact did write: note especially how very differently the poetry sings, to what different melodies and phrasings:

Break of Day

'Tis true, 'tis day: what though it be?
O wilt thou therefore rise from me?
Why should we rise, because 'tis light?
Did we lie down, because 'twas night?
5   Love which in spite of darkness brought us hither
Should in despite of light keep us together.

Light hath no tongue, but is all eye;
If it could speak as well as spy
This were the worst that it could say,
10   That being well, I fain would stay,
And that I loved my heart and honor so
That I would not from him that had them go.

Must business thee from hence remove?
Oh, that's the worst disease of love;
15 The poor, the foul, the false, love can
Admit, but not the busied man.
He which hath business, and makes love, doth do
Such wrong, as when a martyred man doth woo.

The twisting, long-breathed complexity of Donne's music perfectly matches the twisting, long-breathed complexity of his thought. And yet the poem is not insistently complex: the music and the thought of the opening line are both simple and speechlike. The blunt wit of line four is neatly carried by a blunt, direct musicality—for musicality, like metaphor, is both a technique, a tool, and at the same time an intrinsic part of the indivisible substance of a poem.

Like metaphor, musicality is both a technique—a tool—and at the same time an intrinsic part of the indivisible substance of a poem. This is perfectly illustrated by two poems of the contemporary poet Philip Levine. The first, "A Late Answer," was published in a book that appeared eight years later than the book in which the second poem appeared. They are on different themes; they employ different structures; but most important of all, they are totally unlike in their music.

A Late Answer

Beyond that stand of firs
was a small clearing
where the woods ran out
of breath or the winds
5 beat them back. No one
was born there and no one
would be, but you could
bury a lonely man there
or an animal you didn't
10 want out for flies to eat.
As we passed under the trees
you were cold and took
my hand and felt a shiver
pass through me, but you
15 didn't let go. When you

spoke at last it was to ask
after my thoughts, but
just then we broke into light
so unexpected I had to close
20 my eyes and saw the fire
swimming there and had
such a vision of the end
of my life, the trees
turning to great flowers
25 of flame and the field ringed
with sword bearing angels.
I could say nothing,
but held on to your hand
and you to mine
30 both in the dream and in
that bare place where
the North Sea winds lashed
our faces with sudden spurts
of rain. Now, on the other side
35 of the world, years later,
I know the ant came here
believing he would rule
and he waits for the wren
to fall, the grass waits
40 blowing its breath
into this morning that rises
darkly on wet winds. Somewhere
the sea saves its tears
for the rising tide, somewhere
45 we'll leave the world weighing
no more than when we came,
and the answer will be
the same, your hand in mine,
mine in yours, in that clearing
50 where the angels come toward us
without laughter, without tears.

Starting with a shared memory, a sudden stumbling out of physical darkness and into physical light, followed by "a vision of the end of my life," Levine proceeds in line 34 to distance himself both in time and in geography. But neither time nor distance make a great deal of difference: here too the laws of the natural universe prevail, "the ant came here/ believing he would rule/ and he waits for the wren/to fall." Just so the grass waits: the ant and the earth take all, when death comes. It was cold and windy, there "where/ the North Sea winds lashed/ our faces." Here too is a "morning that rises/ darkly on wet winds." And though the persona has no great vision, this time, the old vision still holds. "The answer will be/ the same," and he and his beloved will be as they were before, and it will be neither joy nor sadness but just what it has always been, death. (I think there may be some comfort for the beginning reader of poetry in the confession, which I freely make, that I neither understand nor like the lines about the sea saving "its tears/ for the rising tide." I can understand the carefully balanced neutrality of the metaphor which is paired with this one, about leaving "the world weighing/ no more than when we came." This latter image fits neatly into the idea of the unchanging answer: we come and we go weighing the same, which is nothing at all. But why the sea weeps here I cannot fathom.)

"A Late Answer" moves swiftly, in long-breathed sweeps that run across many lines almost without pause. Lines 15–26, for example, are both a single sentence, syntactically, and also should, I think, be spoken at a single, sustained pitch level, though there are clear pauses (short pauses) at the two commas in the sentence. How utterly unlike this verse movement is that of the second poem:

Animals Are Passing from Our Lives

It's wonderful how I jog
on four honed-down ivory toes
my massive buttocks slipping
like oiled parts with each light step.

5   I'm to market. I can smell
the sour, grooved block, I can smell
the blade that opens the hole
and the pudgy white fingers

that shake out the intestines
10   like a hankie. In my dreams

the snouts drool on the marble,
suffering children, suffering flies,

suffering the consumers
who won't meet their steady eyes
15   for fear they could see. The boy
who drives me along believes

that any moment I'll fall
on my side and drum my toes
like a typewriter or squeal
20   and shit like a new housewife

discovering television,
or that I'll turn like a beast
cleverly to hook his teeth
with my teeth. No. Not this pig.

The persona is (and is not) a pig being driven to market. This particular animal is part machine, however, with "oiled parts," a pig who can think of himself as "like a typewriter," a pig who is given to unanimal-like dreams of his and his fellows' future. The swineherd boy may think him merely an animal, capable of turning "like a beast," but "this pig" knows reality from a dream and will not attempt to evade his inevitable fate. Consumers of meat may shun reality, so afraid of the dead animals being sold to them that they "won't meet their [the animals'] steady eyes," steady because fixed long since in death. But it is a consumer's fate to eat, a pig's fate to be eaten, and the bitter declaration of the last three words of the poem proclaim an ironical, hopeless bravery: "Not this pig." It is humans who "squeal/ and shit," not this pig. In the poem it is *pigs* who suffer children—"Suffer the little children to come unto me," says the Bible—and *pigs* who suffer flies. In this poem human beings are nothing more than consumers, passive, oppressive. For the poem to effect that sour reversal of roles, what better persona for the poet to assume than that of a market-bound porker? And how better to hammer this reversal at his readers than by the contained, the relatively short-breathed word packages into which the poem is arranged? There are similarities between these two Levine poems, similarities of verbal music as well as of other sorts. But it is the differences between these two poems which mark out a fundamental truth: the "magic" of a poem does not come from some extraordinary, some suprahuman power, but from all men's indefinable and undeniable uniqueness, the force of an individual personality. To the extent that a poet truthfully and uniquely expresses who and what he happens to be, his poems too will express that unique self, in music as in their other component parts. To the extent that he either lacks or is unable to get into his poetry a distinctive self, a distinctive set of ideas and emotions, so too will his poems lack a distinctive voice. If it is no harder to be a great poet than it is to be a great physicist, or a great architect, or a great anything else, surely it is no easier.

(2) Contrast; Balance

Metaphor is a process of comparison, which means a process of association. By linking A to B or to C we discover or illuminate aspects of A which we want to emphasize. But as nineteenth-century philosophers, and especially Hegel, have informed us, there is a great power in negative as well as in positive thinking. We can learn as much about A by comparing it to X, which it does *not* resemble, as we can by comparing it to B, which it does. Dissociation is indeed powerful, though it is neither every poet's cup of tea nor, all in all, quite so apparent to the reader. Perhaps the greatest master of dissociative contrast in all of English poetry is John Donne:

Woman's Constancy

Now thou hast loved me one whole day,
Tomorrow when thou leav'st what wilt thou say?
Wilt thou then antedate some new-made vow?
    Or say that now
5 We are not just those persons which we were?
Or that oaths made in reverential fear
Of Love, and his wrath, any may forswear?
Or as true deaths true marriages untie,
So lovers' contracts, images of those,
10 Bind but till sleep, death's image, them unloose?
    Or your own end to justify

For having purposed° change and falsehood, you
Can have no way but falsehood to be true?
Vain lunatic, against these scapes° I could
15   Dispute, and conquer, if I would,
        Which I abstain to do,
For by tomorrow I may think so too.

    The long list of contrasts out of which this fundamentally dissocia-
tive poem is made begins, indeed, in the very first line. The woman has
loved him "one whole day": love is supposed to be eternal, but as the
title proclaims, this poet knows better. The adjective "whole" slyly
informs us that an unbroken twenty-four hours of love is frequently
more than one has a right to expect—from a woman. There is, of
course, another implicit dissociative comparison being made, as
between unconstant women and (the poet implies) stalwart, faithful,
unchanging men. At least, that implicit contrast *seems* to be present
here; the end of the poem turns that too on its head.
    She leaves him "tomorrow," of course. That is all the future she can
possibly contain in her fickle heart. What does she say as she departs?
Perhaps that she is in love with someone else ("some new-made vow"),
which declaration to be sure she will fabricate, making it seem to have
existed long before she met the persona. Perhaps, a "whole day" being
so huge a span of time, "now/ we are not just those persons which we
were?" The adjective "just" expresses exactly the small-minded nit-
picking the poet is aiming for. Perhaps, he goes on, you (woman) will
argue that a love oath is invalid precisely because it is a love oath. That
is, anything sworn to merely out of fear is invalid—and are not all
lovers afraid of the god of love? In lines 8–10 Donne heightens all of
these dissociative metaphors with an elaborately negative contrast,
beautifully typical of the sort of writing that gave his poetry the name
of "metaphysical"—i.e., the forcible linking of unlike things. A real
marriage inevitably ends, as all things human end, in death. A lover's
"contract" is only an image of a marriage—a mere anticipatory reflec-
tion, as it were. So when the lovers sleep—sleep being itself only an
image, a pale reflection, of a much greater "sleep," death—that too
ought to end such transitory things as lovers' agreements to love. And
Donne piles it on: lines 11–13, equally dissociative, wonder if a woman,

---

12 **purposed** intended   14 **scapes** thoughtless errors

who after all *intended* to be false, can be true to her falsehood only by being false. Well, the poem concludes, this is all "vain," and the persona could "dispute, and conquer, if I would"—but he does not, and he will not. A man is capable of better things, but why bother, considering that it is women with whom love associations are to be established? Why not join what you cannot hope to overcome, except in "dispute" and debate?—the title of the poem, remember, is "Woman's Constancy," which is intended itself to be a dissociative notion, a contradiction in terms.

No century has ever made more effective use of dissociation than that time of the so-called heroic couplet (see the next chapter for explication of the term). Alexander Pope is, of course, the ultimate master of the rhymed couplet, but there are other poets who rang exquisite variations on Pope's approach or who, like Matthew Prior, themselves helped teach Pope the sort of song he might want to sing:

An Epitaph

Interred° beneath this marble stone
Lie sauntering Jack, and idle Joan.
While rolling threescore years and one
Did round this globe their courses° run;
5   If human things went ill or well;
If changing empires rose or fell;
The morning passed, the evening came,
And found this couple still the same.
They walked and ate, good folks: what then?
10 Why then they walked and ate again:
They soundly slept the night away:
They did just nothing all the day:
And having buried children four,
Would not take pains to try for more.
15 Nor sister either had, nor brother:
They seemed just tallied° for each other.

Their moral and economy
Most perfectly they made agree:
Each virtue kept its proper bound,

---

1 **interred** buried   4 **courses** usual ways, paths   16 **tallied** matched, fitted

20 Nor trespassed on the other's ground.
    Nor fame, nor censure they regarded;
    They neither punished, nor rewarded.
    He cared not what the footmen did:
    Her maids she neither praised, nor chid:°
25 So every servant took his course;
    And bad at first, they all grew worse.
    Slothful disorder filled his stable;
    And sluttish plenty decked° her table.
    Their beer was strong; their wine was port;
30 Their meal was large; their grace was short.
    They gave the poor the remnant-meat,
    Just when it grew not fit to eat.

    They paid the church- and parish-rate;°
    And took, but read not the receipt:
35 For which they claimed their Sunday's due
    Of slumbering in an upper pew.

    No man's defects sought they to know;
    So never made themselves a foe.
    No man's good deeds did they commend;
40 So never raised themselves a friend.
    Nor cherished they relations poor:
    That might decrease their present store:
    Nor barn nor house did they repair:
    That might oblige their future heir.

45 They neither added, nor confounded;°
    They neither wanted,° nor abounded.
    Each Christmas they accounts did clear;
    And wound their bottom° round the year.
    Nor tear, nor smile did they employ
50 At news of public grief, or joy.
    When bells were rung, and bonfires made,
    If asked, they ne'er denied their aid:

---

24 **chid** chided, scolded   28 **decked** covered   33 **parish-rate** parish tax   45 **confounded**
wasted   46 **wanted** lacked   48 **bottom** spool of thread

Their jug° was to the ringers carried,
Whoever either died, or married.
55 Their billet at the fire was found,
Whoever was deposed, or crowned.

Nor good, nor bad, nor fools, nor wise;
They would not learn, nor could advise:
Without love, hatred, joy, or fear,
60 They led—a kind of—as it were:
Nor wished, nor cared, nor laughed, nor cried:
And so they lived; and so they died.

I count over thirty grammatical negatives, which comes to about one for every two lines in the entire poem. But the dissociative negations make the percentage considerably higher. "Their beer was strong; their wine was port;/ Their meal was large"—and having set us up with three hearty positives, Prior follows with the negative, dissociative "their grace was short." Time to eat, and to excess, they had. Time to say their thanks to God for that food they did not have. It would be hard to find a clearer dissociative line than "slothful *disorder* filled his stable," but Prior matches the man's negative capabilities with the woman's: "*sluttish* plenty decked her table" (italics added). The summation is biting: "Without love, hatred, joy, or fear"—could anything be more dissociated from life and its positive features?—"they led—a kind of—as it were." Delicately, Prior indicates that what these dissociated folk lived could not be called "life." "And so they lived; and so they died"—and so what? They were nothing, and they went back to nothing, and it made no difference—perhaps not even to them.

"An Epitaph" is the title, and epitaphs are usually positive, remembering some aspect or aspects of a departed person's life. In that sense, therefore, the entire poem is a negative metaphor, a dissociative comparison—for what could there be to remember, or to eulogize, of people like these two? "They did just nothing all the day."

Contemporary poets use dissociative, contrasting metaphors differently, but to no less powerful an effect. T. S. Eliot's "Preludes," quoted in the supplement to Chapter 2, makes extensive use of the technique.

---

53 **jug** jug of ale or beer

"The winter evening settles down/ With smell of steaks in passage-ways." The personification of the evening leads us to expect a positive comparison; we are given, instead, the "smell of steaks" in rooming-house corridors. "Smoky days" could arguably be attached to a stun-ningly positive comparison; here it is linked to the discarded cigarette butt tossed into the street, for these are "the burnt-out ends of smoky days." Section two opens, similarly, with the morning coming to consciousness—and that too is usually positive, a return to vitality, to life. Not here: "consciousness *of faint stale smells of beer* . . ." (italics added).

Balance is not a substantive issue, but a technical one. The only sort of balance one can find, in matters substantive, would be even-handedness of treatment, equal time to differing points of view. Such an approach makes sense in legislation; it makes no sense in art, which is not inherently symmetrical. Technical balance, indeed, is not a ques-tion of even-handedness at all, but a question of final harmony. Rather than touching all bases, representing all possible points of view, artistic balance seeks the functional integration of working parts. It can be divided into three major components: continuity, consistency, and appropriateness. But it remains a matter of functional integration, what those trained in the classical languages often prefer to call *mensura*—things in their proper places, in the proper order. And func-tional integration is best demonstrated, rather than simply talked about:

The City

You said, "I will go to another land, I will go to another sea.
Another city will be found, a better one than this.
Every effort of mine is a condemnation of fate;
and my heart is—like a corpse—buried.
5   How long will my mind remain in this wasteland.
Wherever I turn my eyes, wherever I may look
I see black ruins of my life here,
where I spent so many years destroying and wasting."

You will find no new lands, you will find no other seas.
10 The city will follow you. You will roam the same
streets. And you will age in the same neighborhoods;
and you will grow gray in these same houses.
Always you will arrive in this city. Do not hope for any other—
There is no ship for you, there is no road.
15 As you have destroyed your life here
in this little corner, you have ruined it in the entire world.

(C. P. Cavafy, translated from the Greek by RAE DALVEN)

Deceptively simple, because perfectly organized, Cavafy's poem is virtually a model of balance. The complainant's case is stated plausibly, clearly; the language, even in the stripped-down mode which to some degree translation must inevitably be, is totally appropriate, keyed to exactly what is being said. And then, after a crucial spatial break, the complainant is answered, once again in exactly the same register. He has said, "I will go to another land, I will go to another sea." The answer is, "You will find no new lands, you will find no other seas." He has said, "Another city will be found, a better one than this." The answer assures him, "The city will follow you." It may seem simple, it may even seem easy, but it is not: to develop so seamless an organization, without falling into monotony, is the very farthest thing from easy. Note, for example, how Cavafy does not answer in the same terms, although the tonal register is the same. That there will be no new lands, no new seas, comes as a straight negation of the complaint, but that the city will follow after the complainant is a subtle new development and one that is immediately pursued. Lines 10–13 expand and ramify the point: "Do not hope for any other." Everything is a "wasteland," the complainant moans; everything he sees is "black ruins." Line 14 of the answer returns to the response already given in line 9, but in different terms: "There is no ship for you, there is no road." And the final two lines of the response, and of the poem, pick up some of the language of lines 7 and 8 of the complaint, as well as encapsulating the poem's final message: your life is ruined, not just here, "in this little corner," but "in the entire world." It is the message of the despairingly realistic Devil, in Christopher Marlowe's play *Doctor Faustus*. Asked, "How comes it then that thou art out of hell?" the Devil replies, "Why this is hell, nor am I out of it." In short, a denizen of hell carries his endless dwelling place with him; he is his own punishment. Mere physical movement takes him, in truth, to noplace different.

Cherry-ripe

Cherry-ripe, ripe, ripe, I cry,
Full and fair ones; come and buy.
If so be, you ask me where
They do grow? I answer: There,
5   Where my Julia's lips do smile.
There's the land, or cherry-isle,
Whose plantations fully show
All the year, where cherries grow.

(ROBERT HERRICK)

Balance has no necessary connection with profundity. A perfectly balanced poem, like "Cherry-ripe," can have a subject matter so light, so frothy, that it almost blows away in the soft breeze of the words. His beloved's lips are so red that they seem to him "the land, or cherry-isle . . . where cherries grow." That is all there is to the poem, in substantive terms. But Herrick has not padded that elementary message. Rather, he has expanded it emotionally, nonliterally. He begins with a street vendor's cry, apparently a vendor seeking to sell cherries. But beginning with line 3 we see that this is not an actual vendor but an appropriation of street-vendor tactics by the persona of the poem. And this substitution of poetic voice for street-vendor voice shapes the basic nonliteralness of the entire poem, for the place where these nonliteral cherries grow is "where my Julia's lips do smile." The metaphor is straightforward, but by *seeming* to take it literally—what else can a street vendor sell but literal cherries?—the poet transforms it into a kind of magical never-never land. And this, in turn, is exactly what he sees in his Julia's smile: the magic "plantations" where, not in just one season, or two, but "all the year" the glowing magic cherries blossom. Absolutely nothing is out of place in this poem: everything is beautifully, supremely ordered.

Composed upon Westminister Bridge, September 3, 1802

Earth has not anything to show more fair:
Dull would he be of soul who could pass by
A sight so touching in its majesty;
This city now doth, like a garment, wear
5   The beauty of the morning; silent, bare,
Ships, towers, domes, theaters, and temples lie
Open unto the fields, and to the sky;
All bright and glittering in the smokeless air.
Never did sun more beautifully steep
10 In his first splendor, valley, rock, or hill;
Ne'er saw I, never felt, a calm so deep!
The river glideth at his own sweet will:
Dear God! the very houses seem asleep;
And all that mighty heart is lying still!

(WILLIAM WORDSWORTH)

The transcendent beauty of a giant city, when daylight has broken but the whole huge place is "silent, bare," with nothing of its regular bustle and noise, is richly and yet simply evoked. The basic stance, namely, that a city is natural too, and can "wear/ The beauty of the morning" as gorgeously as any "valley, rock, or hill," perfectly expresses the poet's own surprise at the discovery. He has never thought that "a calm so deep" could emanate from what he has always seen as an inhuman, unnatural construct. But seeing the city (London) "all bright and glittering in the smokeless air," he realizes that the city is in truth as human as he is. "The very houses seem asleep," he exclaims, and then goes still further. Not only can the component parts of the city act as other human creatures act, by sleeping, but the city has a heart—and not an ordinary one, but a "mighty heart." The change in approach is not total; Wordsworth does not suggest that he will now see London, awake, as beautifully steeped in anything. But a sleeping heart remains a heart, even when it wakes: to that extent the change in attitude is far-reaching, permanent. And the poem is so balanced, so tightly controlled, so carefully paced, that we understand in enormous detail, and in enormous depth, just how stunningly far-reaching the change in attitude truly is.

The Magi

Toward world's end, through the bare
beginnings of winter, they are traveling again.
How many winters have we seen it happen,
watched the same sign come forward as they pass
5 cities sprung around this route their gold
engraved on the desert, and yet
held our peace, these
being the Wise, come to see at the accustomed hour
nothing changed: roofs, the barn
10 blazing in darkness, all they wish to see.

(LOUISE GLÜCK)

How better to express the absence of change than to combine two age-old and unchanging phenomena, the coming of winter ("world's end": at one point the year was thought to begin with spring, not on the first of January) and the coming to the Christ child of the Magi? Timelessness is highlighted over and over, from the parallel phrases of lines 1 and 2 ("toward . . . through . . .") to the explicit reminders: "They are traveling again," "how many winters . . . ," "the same sign come forward," "at the accustomed hour." We are meant to feel, and we feel, that holding our peace in the face of such endless, inevitable reiteration is only appropriate, for these are "the Wise" and, in truth, there is "nothing changed." But the splendid evocation of the manger scene, "the barn blazing in darkness," is subtly modified by the poem's final words. What the Magi, "the Wise," see when as usual they come to look is also "all they wish to see." Theirs is a perfect, unchanging faith, and to that sort of faith is given unchanging sight. But for the rest of us, rather wearily holding our peace—that is, not having peace but keeping our mouths shut? It is quietly disquieting, and a deft end to a magnificently managed poem.

For poetic art *is* verbal management, and in exactly the same sense as we talk of managing the economy, or a corporation, or a difficult child. When a poet has the sort of balance I have here been talking of, he has the power to point his poem in any direction he desires. He must, to be sure, have something worth managing; he must not use his poetic skills merely to display his verbal facility. That, however, is not a question of poetic balance but of personal insight and integrity.

(3) Precision

Precision (exactness rather than mere correctness) may seem of lesser importance. It is indeed essentially a word-by-word matter: each choice of a word must do for the line, for the stanza, for the poem, precisely what is required, and on all the possible levels of both the word, the line, the stanza, and the poem. Put in such detailed terms, precision may begin to seem less insignificant—and a great deal less simple.

Elegy

I know but will not tell
you, Aunt Irene, why there
are soapsuds in the whiskey:
Uncle Robert had to have
5 a drink while shaving. May
there be no bloodshed in your house
this morning of my father's death
and no unkept appearance
in the living, since he has
10 to wear the rouge and lipstick
of your ceremony, mother,
for the first and last time:
father, hello and goodbye.

(ALAN DUGAN)

The language is so utterly subdued that in all fourteen lines there are only two words—"appearance" and "ceremony"—with more than two syllables, and they have but three. This is an elegy, seemingly (these things are, again, not always as literal as they may seem) written on the "morning of my father's death." The persona-son wants no quarreling ("no bloodshed"—though this also refers to the drink that

Uncle Robert had to have "while shaving," presumably to steady his hand and thus eliminate bloodshed in a more literal sense). The house must be suitably hushed, to honor the dead. Nor must shaving or other proper rituals be disrupted, so that the dead man's memory can be properly reverenced—for the corpse, though masculine in life, in death "has to wear the rouge and lipstick of your ceremony, mother, for the first and last time." That is, the undertakers will have "primped" the corpse, with makeup and the like, to try to blot out the signs of death and to make the dead man look at least something like what he looked in life. *Frater, ave atque vale*, wrote the Latin poet Catullus, "Brother, hail and farewell," and Dugan echoes that two-thousand-year-old poem, also a funeral poem, with his own "hello and goodbye."

The precision is dazzling. Try, for example, to substitute even a closely equivalent word for any word in "Elegy." "I understand but will not say, Aunt Irene . . ." "Uncle Robert needed a drink while shaving," "no disorder among the living," "for the only time in his whole long life." Every word in the poem is doing double and sometimes triple duty. "No unkept appearance" means nothing untidy, disorderly, but it also suggests the keeping of appearances, and further suggests, though less explicitly, the keeping of other things, responsibilities, promises, commitments. "Had to have" a drink means was required to have a drink as well as needed a drink; it also quietly hammers its point, with a quick burst of /h/ alliteration. "Bloodshed" means quarreling, and the shedding of blood while shaving, and further evokes the blood which is necessarily "shed" in death: there is already a necessary shedding of blood, "this morning of my father's death," so let us have no more than is necessary. "Rouge and lipstick" precisely evokes both the cosmetic art of women and that of the undertaker; it also highlights the loss of living blood, with its emphasis on the two reddening aspects of those cosmetic arts. Women and undertakers do other things, in their cosmetic applications; the poet does not speak of them, though they would be equally truthful, because they would not heighten the substance of his poem as "rouge and lipstick" do. "Ceremony" refers to his mother's regular ritual of applying cosmetics, but it also evokes the solemn quality of this day's very special ritual, a funeral. "First and last" means for the only time, but "first and last" forcefully underlines the finality of it all—and what is more final than death? "First and last" also prepares the reader for the finality of the "hello and goodbye" farewell,

In greeting his father, this final day, the son knows he will never greet his father again.

This Window

I sit on the inside of this window
doing piece-work: woodcut, quilt square,
the shape of things to come.

Next door, you putter,
5   running water. Soon you will bring me
coffee, years before I need it.

Outside in the twilight,
a child playing some street game
calls: *come closer*

10   as the bark on the tree
darkens with evening and the last
light empties from a curve of sky.

I have been smelling coffee
all my life. Cold and so much
15   older when you bring me some,

I sit on the inside
of this window, close
as I can come.

(CANDICE WARD)

There are three kinds of people, and three individual people, in this poem: the woman who is the persona; the man, presumably her husband ("next door, you putter"); and "a child playing some street game." So too there are three physical locations: "inside . . . this window," where the woman sits; "outside in the twilight" or "next door," where the man and the child are; and that transitional place, neither in nor out, where the woman sits as "close as I can come" to the other two and to the life outside the window, where "the bark on the tree/ darkens with evening and the last/ light empties from a curve of sky." We are not told exactly why the woman is in a different location;

we do not need to be told, for we are informed that she is "doing piece-work," and this is still further spelled out for us as "woodcut, quilt square." That is, she is doing "women's work," and "women's work" physically as well as psychologically separates her from the "child playing" or the man puttering. That which links them, a simple domestic act carefully and very precisely selected, is the making of coffee, which act the husband is performing. He will bring her coffee, "soon"—but "years before I need it." Why is it thus premature, this domestic linking of the two? We are given three indirect but very precise answers: (1) what she is making, as she does her "women's work," is "the shape of things to come"; that is, she is preparing for a future state not yet arrived (because she is pregnant? We are not told); (2) "I have been smelling coffee/ all my life"; that is, not drinking it, but smelling it: coffee has always, like "the shape of things to come," been something in preparation, as life too is always in preparation but not yet lived; and (3) when the coffee does actually arrive, the persona will be "cold and so much/ older"—not, surely, in the literal sense, but psychologically older, and cold in both physical and psychological ways, because it grows dark and so cold, and because though life is outside the window, she is kept "on the inside." We do not need to know why her being a woman has so isolated her: we know some of the details, and we know that such things can and do happen, and not at all infrequently. We also know, in part because the whole poem is filled with regret, in part because the final lines tell us explicitly, that the persona not only wishes it were otherwise, but understands that it is as it has to be. All she can do, in addition to going on as she must go on, is to try to be as "close as I can come."

Individual words in "This Window" do perhaps even more multiple duty than in the Dugan poem. The thrust of the poem is deliberately less explicit, more emotional than rational. We are being shown a state of mind, a state of being, quite as much as the clear consequences of some particular though inevitable event. Individual words, accordingly, must be freighted with information and emotion, almost to the limit of their carrying power. "Next door, you putter" is a perfect illustration. We are here told (1) that the person addressed is not with the persona, but "next door"; (2) that the person addressed is specifically located in another dwelling, "next door," rather than in the same dwelling as the persona; (3) that in a poem so intensely preoccupied with the persona's femaleness, the "you" is very likely to be her husband, though this is not clearly asserted; and (4) that if the "you" is both masculine and her husband, as seems likely, then just as she does "piece-work," or "women's work," so he too does, in his puttering, "man's work." This is a heavy load for only four words to carry—and yet it is accomplished, and in good part because each of those four words is precisely slotted for the precise burden it needs to transmit. The "child playing some street game" does not speak to her, calling *"come closer,"* but in another sense, both because the child is outside and she is inside, and because the child *is* a child and she is a woman, the call is also addressed to her. And that hanging implication is picked up and strengthened, at the end of the poem, when she tells us that although she cannot come out she will sit "close as I can come." The words of the child's call must, for the art and for the effect of the poem, be harmonized absolutely with the woman's need to be (1) close to the outside, (2) close to the child, and (3) close to her husband, as well as to the life he and the others lead "outside in the twilight." Language cannot be obliged to do this much work: it must be worked with and not against the grain.

(4) Obscurity

Poetry is not always and invariably easy, but few things that are always easy are worth very much. Nor is difficulty, or comparative difficulty, in any way necessarily synonymous with obscurity—that dreaded and largely undeserved label, applied for the most part to what they do not understand by those who ought (and who could pretty readily) know better.

But poetry has acquired a special reputation for obscurity. William Blake's famous lines "Tiger! Tiger! burning bright/ In the forests of the night" seem to too many people Poetry with a large capital P. That is, no one needs to inquire what the lines mean, and really, no one could find out if they wanted to. Nor does it matter—for Poetry (with that capital P) is fancy language, highfalutin, "a tale . . . full of sound and fury,/ Signifying nothing," or at least next to nothing.

And in the case of bad or fake poets, of whom there are alas a great many (as of course we have bad plumbers and fake experts on anything and everything known to man), obscurity may be not much more than a smokescreen for flatulent mouthings and rantings. And even good and honest writers, of whom also there are a very great many, sometimes write less well, or less carefully, than perhaps they ought to if, like their father in heaven, they were perfect. William Blake is neither a bad nor a fake poet, and his famous poem is neither obscure nor in any way impenetrable.

The Tiger

Tiger! Tiger! burning bright
In the forests of the night,
What immortal hand or eye
Could frame thy fearful symmetry?

5   In what distant deeps or skies
Burned the fire of thine eyes?
On what wings dare he aspire?
What the hand, dare seize the fire?

And what shoulder, & what art,
10   Could twist the sinews of thy heart?
And when thy heart began to beat,
What dread hand? & what dread feet?

What the hammer? what the chain?
In what furnace was thy brain?
15   What the anvil? what dread grasp
Dare its deadly terrors clasp?

When the stars threw down their spears,
And watered heaven with their tears,
Did he smile his work to see?
20   Did he who made the lamb make thee?

Tiger! Tiger! burning bright
In the forests of the night,
What immortal hand or eye
Dare frame thy fearful symmetry?

First: why write about a tiger at all? There are several answers. Blake wrote about tigers more than once (as he also wrote about lambs more than once), as creatures both wild and free, creatures often ferocious but also capable of spontaneity and even generosity. In his poems "The Little Girl Lost" and "The Little Girl Found" tigers guard rather than consume the child: her parents "saw their sleeping child/ Among tigers wild." It was a time of immense social upheaval, and a time also of immense change. The Industrial Revolution had started, in Blake's lifetime, and science had begun to assume something like the stature it now enjoys. But there were social and psychological costs, as there must be in times of change, and Blake mourned what had been lost. The tiger "burning bright/ in the forests of the night" represented for him a state of primitive human power and freedom, now on the way to being lost. The God who could and did make the tiger could not be the same God of whom the priests of his day spoke.

Second: what use does Blake make of the tiger? He does not show the animal hunting, or indeed doing much of anything else. Most of the poem, indeed, is about the force which created the tiger—namely, God. Lines 3–20, the vast bulk of the poem, are on this subject. "Did he smile his work to see?" Was God pleased? The answer is quite obviously yes. "Did he who made the lamb make thee?" Again, surely he did, and meant to, and we must never forget that God is not made in the priestly image, Blake insists.

Third: why does Blake assume that the "fire of [the tiger's] eyes" came from some "distant deeps or skies?" Because, simply, he does not see the tiger as a literal beast, but as a symbolic force. Can he do this? Is it legitimate? Why not?

Fourth: why does he speak of the tiger's creation as a kind of mechanical process, involving hammers, furnaces, anvils, and the like? Precisely because his was a time of Industrial Revolution and he was disturbed to the very core by the enormous power of the increasingly omnipresent Machine. Again, this is a symbolic, nonliteral tiger, not one borrowed from the zoo.

Fifth: what has happened to the syntax in lines 11 and 12? "What dread hand? & what dread feet"—what? Well, Blake is not his father in heaven, and he is not perfect. In an earlier version of the poem this line continued, "Could fetch it from the furnace deep?" Blake revised the poem, the syntax was fractured, and he liked it fractured and left it that way.

Sixth: how do the stars get into the poem, and what are they supposed to be doing when they throw "down their spears" and water "heaven with their tears"? Surely that is obscure? It is, yes, and once more the fact must be admitted. Blake associated astronomy with rationalism, and disliked both; he saw the stars surrendering, here, in the face of a greater harmony, God's harmony, and being prepared for the reconciliation (only two lines farther on in the poem) of tiger and lamb. It is hard for the nonscholar to know this—but Blake was hardly the most concerned of workmen, in such matters. He was a visionary, and thought himself a prophet and much of his writing prophetic.

Let us, then, add up the scorecard. We find in a poem of twenty-four lines one plain obscurity, but hardly a crucial one to the poem as a whole, and one obviously careless solecism (grammatical error). Are these sufficient grounds to condemn a poem of such self-evident power and beauty? And is the relatively slight effort required to more fully understand the poem worthwhile? What is involved, after all, is some minimal knowledge of England in the Industrial Revolution, and some reading of Blake's other poems. We ought to know the former, and the latter is hardly prohibitively difficult. We do as much every time we try to find out who the lead singer in XYZ Band is, and what he recorded before he recorded something we happen to be fond of. We do rather more every time we have a math problem, or in making a report to our superior at work, and in a myriad contexts of all our daily lives.

Romance

Your father kneels on the roof, cleaning
gutters while your mother
types letters to magazines
thanking them, and you
5   walk around
your bedroom, doors closed, humming all
afternoon, identifying
birds in your head, in your shadows on the wall.

The woman you'll marry is talking politics,
10   silence, the war that is not quite
happening all
over the world
and the ones that are killing nobody

you've ever known, but you haven't met her yet.
15 She lives down the street. You won't touch her for years.

(MICHAEL HETTICH)

Let us repeat the questions just asked. Is "Romance" obscure? Is Michael Hettich worth the effort? The answers are, first, no, "Romance," though not perhaps the easiest poem in the world, is far from obscure (I will set out a truly obscure poem in a moment), and second, yes, it is definitely worth the effort. The key problem in the first of the poem's two strophes is likely to center in lines 7 and 8, where the persona, after "humming all afternoon," is said to be "identifying birds in [his] head, in [his] shadows on the wall." This is a male child; he has parents, in this poem, and the actions of parents and child are likely to be related, even if only negatively. The father is tending to his home, in the best suburban style; the mother is rather vacuously typing "letters to magazines/ thanking them," though we are not told why. Do we need to be told why? Isn't the suburban vacuity of the mother related to the practical suburbanness of the father? And is not the son's mental bird-watching related to what his parents do? The mother thanks magazines—for nothing, so far as we know. The son identifies birds that exist only in his head, or at best in "shadows [which he casts] on the wall," as he walks around in his bedroom. The mother is not fully in touch with the realities; the father is; the son cannot satisfactorily relate to or imitate either of his parents, and is this obscure—or only something that requires careful reading and thought?

The second strophe hurls us into the future, but ends by assuring us that that future is still far off. The future wife of the persona is herself unhappy in her context; she speaks of the "war that is not quite/ happening all/ over the world," the "small" wars that we all read of in our daily newspapers. But the romance is all in the future. And that is the important thrust of the poem: romance is not something born out of fairy tales, but out of human contexts, and human contexts are almost never as straightforward, as rational, as predictable as we often like to think (or pretend?) they are. Hettich challenges the straightforward and the rational. He asserts the power—and also the charm, for this is both a powerful and a beautiful poem—of the irrational, the nonlinear. And by asserting it, and by helping us to face and to deal with it, he seems to me to be doing something deeply significant, deeply worthwhile.

I have promised a truly obscure poem: here it is.

There Are Many Pathways to the Garden

If you are bound for the sun's empty plum
there is no need to mock the wine tongue
but if you are going to a rage of pennies
over a stevedore's wax ocean
5   then, remember: all long pajamas are frozen dust
unless an axe cuts my flaming grotto.

You are one for colonial lizards
and over bathhouses of your ear
skulls shall whisper
10   of a love for a crab's rude whip
and the rimless island of refusal shall seat itself
beside the corpse of a dog
that always beats a hurricane
in the mad run for Apollo's boxing glove.

15   As your fingers melt a desert
an attempt is made to marry the lily-and-fig-foot dragon
mermaids wander and play with a living cross
a child invents a sublime bucket of eyes
and I set free the dawn of your desires.

20   The crash of your heart
beating its way through a fever of fish
is heard in every crowd of that thirsty tomorrow
and your trip ends in the mask of my candle-lit hair.

(PHILIP LAMANTIA)

I have no idea what this is all about; I recognize surrealist techniques, but what they are meant to do I simply do not know. This is, in my judgment, impenetrable. There are respectable people who like this poem, and other works of this poet, and other poems by other poets like him. I do not, and this is the only place in this book where you will encounter Philip Lamantia or anyone who writes as he does. I believe in poetry as communication, but not in poetry as befuddlement.

This is not to say that poetry is always or even perfectly penetrable even by the most zealous and dedicated reader. Just as we all say or write things that are hard for others to understand, despite our best efforts to the contrary, so too poets sometimes strain language in their attempt to turn the partially ineffable into the fully comprehensible. Some poets are obscure more often than are other poets, as some politicians, teachers, and friends can be more difficult to understand than others. Different subjects, too, can elicit more or less obscure responses—and poems. Poets like other people change, also, sometimes growing more obscure as they age and develop (Ezra Pound is a perfect example), sometimes growing less obscure (the later poems of John Donne are a good deal less tangled, on the whole, as the later poems of William Butler Yeats are more direct and plain spoken). A reader separated from the time of a poem's composition by as little as a century can find things obscure that to the poet's contemporaries were quite obvious. Extend the time gap to several centuries, and all sorts of apparent obscurities can arise. Virtually all poets in Shakespeare's time, for example, knew something of ancient Roman culture in general and the ancient poet Ovid in particular; almost all poets in that time had read and knew well the Bible. Their references to such literary sources were not obscure in their own time, but have to many readers today become very obscure indeed. (See the section on "allusion" in the next chapter.)

To a large extent, accordingly, obscurity is a deeply relative matter rather than something fixed and definite. But it remains true, for all that, that poetry like Philip Lamantia's—which resolutely sets its face against communication—is obscure as a matter of operating principle. And that, at least, cannot be said of any of the other poets represented in this book: if they are obscure it is a failing, or the effect of differences in chronology or culture. They do not *try* to be obscure; they have a fundamental respect for and commitment to communicating with their readers. Obscurity is not something they desire, though sometimes they may feel themselves forced to risk it in the interest of communicating things that may not be entirely within their reach. It is the nature of language, as it is the nature of human beings who have invented and

Poems Supplementary to Chapter 3

— 1 —

This poem is about World War One, when people did essentially the same things that people do today—but did not talk about them. All sorts of verbal taboos prevailed (underwear, for example, is still referred to as "unmentionables"). Cummings here uses a most "unpoetic" word, "etcetera," as a way of mocking poetic and verbal taboos, and mocking too the social taboos that underlie them. The poem's dry, sparse music matches its mocking tone.

"My Sweet Old Etcetera"

my sweet old etcetera
aunt lucy during the recent

war could and what
is more did tell you just
5   what everybody was fighting

for,
my sister
isabel created hundreds
(and
10   hundreds) of socks not to
mention shirts fleaproof earwarmers

etcetera wristers etcetera, my
mother hoped that

i would die etcetera
15   bravely of course my father used
to become hoarse talking about how it was
a privilege and if only he
could meanwhile my

self etcetera lay quietly
20   in the deep mud et

cetera
(dreaming,
et
        cetera, of
25   Your smile
eyes knees and of your Etcetera)

                                    (e e cummings)

— 2 —

Though George Herbert is in fact one of the outstanding metrical and
formal innovators in the history of English poetry, he is even more
remarkable for the continual sweetness of his verse. There is a perpet-
ual brightness in Herbert's poems, closely matching the deeply felt
religious beliefs about which he writes; his life, too, closely matched the
sacred fervor of his poetry.

The Pulley

        When God at first made man,
Having a glass of blessings standing by,
"Let us," said he, "pour on him all we can;
Let the world's riches, which dispersèd lie,
5   Contract into a span."°

        So strength made first a way;
Then beauty flowed, then wisdom, honor, pleasure;
When almost all was out, God made a stay,°
Perceiving that alone of all his treasure
10   Rest in the bottom lay.

        "For if I should," said he,
"Bestow this jewel also on my creature,
He would adore my gifts instead of me,
And rest in Nature, not the God of Nature.
15   So both should losers be.

---

5 **span** small space   8 **stay** halt, stop

"Yet let him keep the rest,
But keep them with repining° restlessness:
Let him be rich and weary, that at least
If goodness lead him not, yet weariness
20   May toss him to my breast."

(GEORGE HERBERT)

— 3 —

Balance and contrast are the mainsprings of this wonderfully nasty little poem. The animal metaphor, for example, is employed only in lines 3 and 5—and only in muted fashion, in line 5. The last two words of line 6 frame a devastating contrast, and line 7, following immediately thereafter, concludes the poem with yet another contrast.

On Mauros the Rhetor°

Lo, I beheld Mauros,
Professor of Public Speaking,
Raise high his elephant-snout
And from between his lips
5   (12 oz. apiece) give vent
To a voice whose very sound is accomplished murder.

I was impressed.

(Palladas, translated from the Greek by DUDLEY FITTS)

— 4 —

Quietly yet vividly musical, Frost's poem also involves a fine asymmetrical balance, with three stanzas devoted to the woods and only one to the "promises [I have] to keep," and as delicate a contrast as a poet can muster, in the final stanza.

---

17 **repining** discontented   **rhetor** orator, teacher of oratory

Stopping by Woods on a Snowy Evening

Whose woods these are I think I know,
His house is in the village though;
He will not see me stopping here
To watch his wood fill up with snow.

5   My little horse must think it queer
To stop without a farmhouse near
Between the woods and frozen lake
The darkest evening of the year.

He gives his harness bells a shake
10 To ask if there is some mistake.
The only other sound's the sweep
Of easy wind and downy flake.

The woods are lovely, dark and deep.
But I have promises to keep,
15 And miles to go before I sleep,
And miles to go before I sleep.

(ROBERT FROST)

— 5 —

Yeats was always a superbly musical poet; at the beginning of his career he lacked the power and intensity his work came to enjoy. Contrasting forces and destinies meld into an early climax, in lines 10 and 11 of this mature sonnet; thereafter the poem moves almost tangentially, with a strangely detached diminuendo effect, to its muted conclusion. "Leda and the Swan" is as fine an example of perfect balance as exists.

Leda and the Swan°

A sudden blow: the great wings beating still
Above the staggering girl, her thighs caressed

Leda and the Swan Zeus seduced Leda by assuming the shape of a swan; Helen of Troy and Clytemnestra, wife and murderess of Agamemnon, were born to Leda of Zeus

By the dark webs, her nape° caught in his bill,
He holds her helpless breast upon his breast.

5   How can those terrified vague fingers push
The feathered glory from her loosening thighs?
And how can body, laid in that white rush,°
But feel the strange heart beating where it lies?

A shudder in the loins engenders there
10 The broken wall, the burning roof and tower
And Agamemnon dead.
             Being so caught up,
So mastered by the brute blood of the air,
Did she put on his knowledge with his power
Before the indifferent beak could let her drop?

                (WILLIAM BUTLER YEATS)

— 6 —

Yeats here juggles the sharply contrasting images of decrepit old schol-
ars and lusty young poets, bringing the two strands suddenly and
sharply together in lines 11 and 12. Lines 1 through 6 sweep forward,
all one syntactical unit, all one long breath. Lines 7 through 10, in
contrast, are short, abrupt. The final two lines open out the rhythm
once more, though not quite so sweepingly as at the start.

The Scholars

Bald heads forgetful of their sins,
Old, learned, respectable bald heads
Edit and annotate the lines
That young men, tossing on their beds,
5   Rhymed out in love's despair
To flatter beauty's ignorant ear.
All shuffle there; all cough in ink;
All wear the carpet with their shoes;
All think what other people think;

---

3 **nape** back of the neck   7 **rush** reeds

10   All know the man their neighbor knows.
       Lord, what would they say
       Did their Catullus° walk that way?

                   (WILLIAM BUTLER YEATS)

— 7 —

Wyatt's is an odd, distinctive, and as yet imperfectly understood musicality. The balance in this poem is straightforward and symmetrical. Stanza one contrasts past and present; stanza two gives us one past encounter in some detail; and stanza three draws, in bitter and ironical language, the logical moral of lines 20 and 21. It is in good part the intensity of Wyatt's characterization which gives the poem its power, and much of the characterization is based on remarkably precise use of adjectives—as, for example, in lines 10–12.

    They flee from me that sometime did me seek
       With naked foot stalking in my chamber.
    I have seen them gentle, tame, and meek
       That now are wild and do not remember
5   That sometime they put themselves in danger
    To take bread at my hand; and now they range°
    Busily seeking with a continual change.

    Thanked be fortune, it hath been otherwise
       Twenty times better; but once in special,
10 In thin array after° a pleasant guise,°
       When her loose gown from her shoulders did fall,
       And she me caught in her arms long and small;
    Therewithal sweetly did me kiss,
    And softly said, "Dear heart, how like you this?"

15 It was no dream; I lay broad waking.
       But all is turned through my gentleness°
    Into a strange° fashion of forsaking;

---

12 **Catullus** Roman poet, bawdy and sensual, dead at thirty 6 **range** roam, stray 10 **after** according to; **guise** style, way, manner 16 **gentleness** courtesy, good breeding 17 **strange** cold, impersonal

And I have leave to go of her goodness,
And she also to use new fangledness.
20 But since that I so kindly am served,
I would fain know what she hath deserved.

(SIR THOMAS WYATT)

— 8 —

Great poetry can be written about literally anything: Mandelstam, who was one of the very greatest of twentieth-century poets, here builds a powerful short poem out of the metrical aspects of classical Greek verse. Note how the metaphorical comparison between Greek meters and Nature, introduced in line 3, is brought to extensive fruition in stanza two—yet without detracting in any way from the basic metaphor.

Orioles sing in trees, and metrical
verse is measured in vowels.
Once a year Nature has quantity
too, like Homer's lines.

5 A day, that day, cavernous like a caesura:°
peaceful, sluggish; ox at the grass,
air too heavy to be blown through a reed
for as long as a single full note.

(Osip E. Mandelstam, translated from the Russian
by BURTON RAFFEL and ALLA BURAGO)

— 9 —

This poem is addressed, not to a woman, but to Byron's poet friend Thomas Moore. Both were famous carousers; both were renowned for their amorous exploits. After a night's wild festivities, Byron wrote this poem and sent it to Moore with a letter expressing weariness and hope in about equal measure.

---

5 **caesura** metrical pause, hiatus

So we'll go no more a-roving
    So late into the night,
Though the heart be still as loving,
    And the moon be still as bright.

5   For the sword outwears its sheath,
    And the soul wears out the breast,
And the heart must pause to breathe,
    And Love itself have rest.

Though the night was made for loving,
10   And the day returns too soon,
Yet we'll go no more a-roving
    By the light of the moon.

                (LORD BYRON)

— 10 —

This sonnet is at once deeply autobiographical and a perfect example of Romantic feeling. Keats did indeed die before his pen had "gleaned [his] teeming brain," and the woman who did not return his desperately passionate love, Fanny Brawne, was by his death taken from him. But the poem's final line *asserts* at the same time as it means to *deny* the powers of both love and fame.

When I have fears that I may cease to be
    Before my pen has gleaned° my teeming brain,
Before high-pilèd books, in charact'ry,°
    Hold like rich garners° the full-ripened grain;
5 When I behold, upon the night's starred face,
    Huge cloudy symbols of a high romance,
And think that I may never live to trace
    Their shadows, with the magic hand of chance;
And when I feel, fair creature of an hour,
10   That I shall never look upon thee more,
Never have relish in the faery power
    Of unreflecting love!—then on the shore

---

2 **gleaned** gathered   3 **charact'ry** writing   4 **garners** granaries

Of the wide world I stand alone, and think
Till Love and Fame to nothingness do sink.

(JOHN KEATS)

— 11 —

Taken from a cycle of fifty-four poems, written in Catalan, this is a
beautifully organized lyric, framed between two different voices saying
almost (but not quite) the same thing in two different contexts. The
wind's voice, in the final lines, echoes and reinforces, even as it subtly
alters, what the persona has begun the poem by saying. And between
these two echoing assertions the poem evokes the ancients of days, the
moon and the earth, the birds and the wind, and by reference all things
timeless and enduring, to emphasize the unchanging, unchangeable
truths here displayed.

> Men are different, and speech is different,
> And there are many many names for one unique love.
>
> The delicate old silver° decides to stay late
> And keeps its light in the fields.
> 5 With its thousand perfect ear-traps
> The earth has snared the birds singing in the air.
>
> Yes: understand, and take yours, too,
> From the olive trees,
> The simple, lofty truth of the wind's captive voice:
> 10 "Speech is different, and men are different,
> And there will be many many names for one unique love."

(Salvador Espriu, The Bull-Hide: XXX, translated from the
Catalan by BURTON RAFFEL)

— 12 —

Lines 16–18 are the key here: they are anticipated, in one way or
another, in line 2, in line 4, and in lines 8–10. That is, in this poem

---

3 **delicate old silver** the moon

about "hanging around in forms," there is in fact an unusually high formal consistency. The poem, once fully understood, is both tighter and a great deal less complex than it at first seems.

On Visiting Central Park Zoo

The animals, hanging around in forms,
are each resigned to be what each one is,
imprisoned twice, in flesh first, then in irons.
The Bactrian camel° is adjusted or is not
5   as, with his humps collapsed for lack of need
for water and with useless tufts of hair
like hummocks on the great plains of his flanks,
he stands around in shape and chews
a curd of solace, whether bitter, bland, or sweet,
10 who knows? Such is his formal pride,
his gargoyle's face remains a stone
assertion as he pisses in between his splayed,°
seemingly rachitic° legs and stays
that way, in place, for want of something else
15 to do, caught in his double prison all the time.
Whatever he is, he goes on being what he is,
although ridiculous in forced review,
perseverant in not doing what he need not do.

(ALAN DUGAN)

— 13 —

Both clever and poignant, this poem is squarely founded in its author's real experience. The clipped syntax, the choppy rhythm, and the incessant playing with words give an entirely deceptive appearance of obscurity and difficulty.

---

4 **Bactrian camel** Asian or two-humped camel   12 **splayed** spread out   13 **rachitic** bent by rickets

Water-Dole: A Prison Poem

Half a basin:
Have a bath, have tea.
Have tea but no bath.
Have a bath and no tea.

(Ho Chi Minh, translated from the Vietnamese by BURTON RAFFEL)

— 14 —

The stumbling, roundabout progression of this poem exactly matches
the stumbling, roundabout gait of the drunkard. The persona seems,
but only seems to seem, to also stumble into truthfulness: lines 1 and 2
clearly indicate that he knows exactly what he's doing.

Going on the Wagon

Whenever I'm drunk
I want to go on the wagon. Really
I want to, but I like it,
I like it, and I can't, really,
5   I mean I can but
I won't.

(Nguyen Khuyen, translated from the Vietnamese by BURTON RAFFEL)

~4~
WHAT POETRY USES: DEVICES

EVERY CRAFT HAS its tricks; most of them are either useful or interesting only to practitioners. None of the six devices to be discussed here is to be found in every poem or in every poet. But these are in general the most significant as well as the most widely used poetic devices, in the tradition of poetry written in English:

(1) Rhyme
(2) Alliteration
(3) Repetition; Refrain
(4) Allusion; Acrostics
(5) Imitation; Parody
(6) Onomatopoeia

(1) Rhyme

Rhyme (sometimes spelled rime) usually means end rhyme—that is, words at the end of one line having the same vowel sound as words at the end of one or more other lines; rhyming words that do not end with a vowel sound, further, customarily also end in the same consonant or combination of consonants.

> They say Argyll's a Wit, for what?
> For writing? no—for writing not.

> (ALEXANDER POPE)

In phonemic transcription—a system for recording the significant sounds of a language—the rhyme words in Pope's couplet would look like this: /wat/ and /nat/. This is called full rhyme, or complete rhyme, or whole rhyme, or in a coverall usage I myself prefer, *rime riche* or "rich rhyme," avoiding terminological confusion by using French. The *spellings* do not rhyme; the *sounds* do. English spelling is often a very poor guide to actual sound, and rhyme is built on actual sound—though there is a device called eye rhyme, in which spellings fit and sounds do not. John Milton uses eye rhyme twice in this eighteen-line poem:

On the University Carrier° who sickened in the time of his vacancy,° being forbid to go to London, by reason of the Plague

Here lies old Hobson, Death hath broke his girt,°
And here, alas, hath laid him in the dirt,
Or else the ways being foul, twenty to one
He's here stuck in a slough,° and overthrown.
5 'Twas such a shifter,° that if truth were known
Death was half glad when he had got him down;
For he had any time this ten years full
Dodged with him, betwixt Cambridge and the Bull.°
And surely Death could never have prevailed
10 Had not his weekly course of carriage failed.
But lately finding him so long at home,
And thinking how his journey's end was come,
And that he had tane° up his latest° inn,
In the kind office of a chamberlin
15 Showed him his room where he must lodge that night,
Pulled off his boots, and took away the light.
If any ask for him it shall be said
Hobson has supped, and's newly gone to bed.

---

carrier porter, coachman; **vacancy** leisure, unemployment   1 **girt** belt on a packhorse, such as Hobson drove 4 **slough** impassable muddy place 5 **shifter** trickster, cunning fellow 8 **Bull** name of an inn 13 **tane** taken; **latest** last

In phonemic transcription, again, the rhymes of lines 5 and 6 read /nown/ and /dawn/, and the rhymes of lines 11 and 12 read /howm/ and /kəm/. The sounds do not match, the spellings do. And in this poem there is yet another imperfect rhyme, that in lines 3 and 4, where neither the spellings nor the sounds match. "One" and "overthrown" is not an eye rhyme; in transcription it is clear that it is not *rime riche* either: /wn/, /ovirƟrown/. This particular weakened form of rhyme can be called part or imperfect rhyme or, once more in French, *rime faible*, "feeble rhyme." It can also, depending on who is naming things, be called assonance, which ought to mean simply vowel rhyme in which the consonants do not match, but which is frequently extended to cover all manner of part or imperfect or *faible* rhyme.

Rhymes can occur at other points in a poem than at the ends of lines. If these inner rhymes follow a pattern, occurring in the same place in two or more lines, they are called internal rhyme. If they occur randomly, they are usually called slant rhyme, but—the confusion in terminology being an extensive one—random inner rhyme is also sometimes called internal rhyme. Here are some examples, first an example of internal rhyme from Tennyson's *The Princess* and then a delicate blend of almost throbbing internal rhymes and neat slant rhymes in a Christina Rossetti poem well titled "Echo":

The Splendor Falls

The splendor falls on castle walls
    And snowy summits old in story;
The long light shakes across the lakes,
    And the wild cataract leaps in glory.
5 Blow, bugle, blow, set the wild echoes flying,
Blow, bugle; answer, echoes, dying, dying, dying.

O, hark, O, hear! how thin and clear,
    And thinner, clearer, farther going!
O, sweet and far from cliff and scar°
10 The horns of Elfland faintly blowing!
Blow, let us hear the purple glens° replying,
Blow, bugle; answer, echoes, dying, dying, dying.

---

9 **scar** precipice, crag   11 **glens** small, narrow, secluded valleys

O love, they die in yon rich sky,
  They faint on hill or field or river;
15 Our echoes roll from soul to soul,
  And grow for ever and for ever.
Blow, bugle, blow, set the wild echoes flying,
And answer, echoes, answer, dying, dying, dying.

    (ALFRED, LORD TENNYSON)

Echo

Come to me in the silence of the night;
  Come in the sleeping silence of a dream;
Come with soft rounded cheeks and eyes as bright
  As sunlight on a stream;
5   Come back in tears,
O memory, hope, love of finished years.

O dream how sweet, too sweet, too bitter sweet,
  Whose wakening should have been in Paradise,
Where souls brimful of love abide and meet;
10   Where thirsting longful eyes
   Watch the slow door
That opening, letting in, lets out no more.

Yet come to me in dreams, that I may live
  My very life again though cold in death:
15 Come back to me in dreams, that I may give
  Pulse for pulse, breath for breath:
   Speak low, lean low,
As long ago, my love, how long ago.

I have been defining rhyme, and to some extent illustrating those definitions. But a full explanation of rhyme's use, and even more its significance, would be a very much longer discussion, and plainly beyond the scope of this book. Historically, rhyme did not really come into use at all, in English poetry, until after the Norman Conquest of 1066. The earliest English poetry—*Beowulf* and its contemporaries— made virtually no use of rhyme. There is a single example of a rhyming poem in the entire surviving corpus of Old English poetry (Old English poetry extends from roughly the eighth century to the time of the Conquest). And when rhyme does begin to show itself in English poetry, in the twelfth and thirteenth centuries, its practice is at best uncertain. Here for example is a little four-line poem from about 1150:

> Myrie songen the monkes binne Ely
> Whan Cnut Kyng rewe therby:
> Roweth, knightes, neer the lond
> And here we thise monkes song.

> Merry sang the monks within [inside] Ely [a monastery]
> When King Cnut rowed thereby:
> Row, knights, near the land
> And let us hear these monks' song.

The rhyme of lines 3 and 4 is, to say the least, defective, nor is there much sense that even the rather mechanical rhyme of lines 1 and 2 is fully understood by whatever poet produced this little poem. A hundred years later, in about 1250, awkwardness can still be seen:

> Sey me, wight in the broom,
> Teche me how I shal don
> That myn housebonde
> Me loven wolde.

5 > "Hold thy tonge stille
> And have al thy wille."

> Tell me [say to me], creature in the brush [wood],
> Teach me how I ought to do [behave]
> So that my husband
> Ought to love me.

> "Hold your tongue still
> And have all your will."

Only the third of the three rhyming pairs seems fully sounded; the rhyme of lines 3 and 4, "housebonde" and "wolde," seems unusually defective.

But by the time of Geoffrey Chaucer, who died in 1400, rhyme had become an integral and totally integrated part of English poetry. Indeed, it had by that point almost entirely replaced the earlier alliterative verse (see Chapter 6 for a brief discussion).

Chaucers Wordes unto Adam, His Owne Scriveyn

Adam scriveyn, if ever it thee bifalle
Boece or Troylus for to wryten newe,
Under thy long lokkes thou most have the scalle,
But after my makyng thou wryte more trewe;
5 So ofte a-daye I mot thy werk renewe,
It to correcte and eek to rubbe and scrape;
And al is thorugh thy negligence and rape.

Chaucer's Words to Adam, His Scribe [Secretary]

Scribe Adam, if ever it happens to you
To write out once again [my poems] *Boethius* and *Troilus*,
May you have scabies under your long locks
Unless you write more accurately as I have composed [these
    poems];
So often day after day I'm obliged to renew [repair] your work,
Correcting it and also rubbing and scraping [at it, erasing];
And it's all because of your negligence and haste.

The language is somewhat unfamiliar, but even without understanding what Chaucer is saying it is evident that he handles rhyme with ease and grace. Furthermore, Chaucer has abandoned the simple rhyming couplets of earlier Middle English poetry for a very much more intricate rhyme scheme. This stanza rhymes A B A B B C C—which is in fact more than just intricate. Indeed, the rhyme patterning is to some degree substantive here, as the poet leads us through the first part of the poem with alternating rhymes, leans on the second of those rhymes in line 5, then sums up his message in the rhyming couplet of lines 6 and 7. The rhyme is truly part of the poem, truly organic and supportive to the poem's meaning, no longer a kind of fumbling decoration. Rhyme *is* decorative, to be sure, but just as the first poets to use it knew how much easier poetry could be remembered if it rhymed, so too subsequent poets have known that rhyme is in its way as functional as form, or meter, or metaphor, or any other component part of the larger whole which constitutes a poem.

Consider the exhilarating use made of rhyme in George Herbert's magnificent "The Collar":

I struck the board° and cried, "No more;
   I will abroad!°
What? shall I ever sigh and pine?
My lines and life are free, free as the road,
5 Loose as the wind, as large as store.°
    Shall I be still in suit?
Have I no harvest but a thorn
 To let° me blood, and not restore
What I have lost with cordial° fruit?
10   Sure there was wine
Before my sighs did dry it; there was corn
   Before my tears did drown it.
Is the year only lost to me?
   Have I no bays° to crown it,
15 No flowers, no garlands gay? All blasted?
    All wasted?
No so, my heart; but there is fruit,
   And thou hast hands.
Recover all thy sigh-blown age
20 On double pleasures: leave thy cold dispute
Of what is fit and not. Forsake thy cage,
   Thy rope of sands,
Which petty thoughts have made, and made to thee
 Good cable, to enforce and draw,
25   And be thy law,
While thou didst wink and wouldst not see.
   Away! take heed;
   I will abroad.
Call in thy death's-head there; tie up thy fears.
30   He that forbears

---

1 **board** table; **abroad** out, away   5 **store** abundance   8 **let** shed   9 **cordial** reinvigorating, cheering   14 **bays** laurel wreaths

> To suit and serve his need
> Deserves his load."
> But as I raved and grew more fierce and wild
> At every word,
> 35 Methought I heard one calling, *Child!*
> And I replied, *My Lord*.

Some changes in the pronunciation of English make this poem perhaps seem less closely rhymed than in fact it is. In George Herbert's time (the poem was printed in 1633), "abroad" made a perfect rhyme with "road" and "load"; "blasted" and "wasted" formed a perfect rhyme; "fears" and "forbears" probably made a perfect rhyme, and so too did "word" and "lord." The passionate frenzy of the rebellious Christian (Herbert was an Anglican priest), struggling more and more desperately to shake off his spiritual "collar," and demonstrating in the process considerable "choler" or "hot anger," is exhibited in full flight, mounting ever more excited and ever less rational. By the repetition of "I will abroad," in line 28—and "will" then meant something much closer to "wish" or "desire" than it does today—the persona is so out of control that, in the very next line, he can declare himself totally free of any fear of death. (Good Christians frequently kept skulls about them, to remind them of the inevitable, and to help keep them obedient to what they understood to be God's laws.) In line 33 the poem assures us, in the most explicit terms, that the persona is raving, "more fierce and wild/ at every word." But all it takes to calm and control him is the single word, spoken (note the italics, as if to indicate something utterly different from the speech marked by quotation marks in lines 1 and 32) presumably by God. The collar is immediately restored, the choler is ended, and the persona is back in a state of grace and proper obedience: *My Lord*, he concedes.

The supporting role played by the poem's rhyme can at best be outlined, given the subtlety of the effects involved and the formal freedom (that is, the nonprescriptive structure) of "The Collar." All sorts of rhyme schemes are employed. Lines 1–5 run A B C B A —and the C rhyme is not picked up until line 10. (The rhyme for line 13 is not picked up, if indeed it can be considered to be picked up at all, until line 23!) There is feminine rhyme—that is, two-syllable rhyme, with the second syllable unstressed or weak (and therefore "feminine")—in lines 12 and 14. No line rhymes with the line that follows it until lines 15 and

16, and not again until lines 24 and 25, but then this rhyming pattern is quickly repeated in lines 29 and 30—and never repeated again. In short, just as the persona is out of balance, so too are the rhyme patterns and the freely constructed form of the poem, which is in the usual sense no form at all, since the poet varies line length, and spatial position of the beginning of a line, according to no known pattern whatever. We cannot predict where the rebellious Christian is going to go next, or what he is likely to say next. But neither can we predict the form, the meter, or the rhyme of anything he is going to say—until, perhaps, the final two rhymes, when "child" chimes beautifully against "wild," and that having taken place, so too does "lord" chime against "word." (Perhaps yet another pun, since the Bible, God's Word, was often known simply as "the Word.")

Another master of rhyme, Lord Byron, used it in his greatest poem, the unfinished comic masterpiece *Don Juan* (deliberately mispronounced, throughout, to rhyme with "ruin"), to effect some of the wittiest, subtlest, and most outrageous jokes and puns and comic juxtapositions in all of English poetry. Here are three stanzas, numbers 5, 8, and 9 of Canto the First:

Brave men were living before Agamemnon
    And since, exceeding valorous and sage,
A good deal like him too, though quite the same none;
    But then they shone not on the poet's page,
5 And so have been forgotten:—I condemn none,
    But can't find any in the present age
Fit for my poem (that is, for my new one);
So, as I said, I'll take my friend Don Juan.
 . . . .

In Seville was he born, a pleasant city,
10   Famous for oranges and women—he
Who has not seen it will be much to pity,
    So says the proverb—and I quite agree:
Of all the Spanish towns is none more pretty,
    Cadiz perhaps—but that you soon may see;
15 Don Juan's parents lived beside the river,
    A noble stream, and called the Guadalquivir.

His father's name was José—*Don*, of course—
    A true Hidalgo, free from every stain
Of Moor or Hebrew blood, he traced his source
20   Through the most Gothic gentlemen of Spain;
A better cavalier ne'er mounted horse,
    Or, being mounted, e'er got down again,
Than José, who begot our hero, who
Begot—but that's to come—Well, to renew:

—And on he rattles, dashing this way and that, mocking, tender, martial, all tumbled on top of each other. The rhymes are a high point of every stanza: the pattern is A B A B A B C C, and Byron's way of filling in the pattern is delightfully slapdash. Agamemnon was a great Greek hero, one who met a tragic death at his own wife's hands. Byron mocks all this ancient heroism by rhyming Agamemnon first with "same none" and then with "condemn none." Note that this is a feminine rhyme, which is hard to manage in the first place, and in addition the English is required to push and pull to match with what is, after all, a Greek name, Agamemnon. "New one" and "Don Juan" is mocking in a different way: this is not the Don Juan of old lecherous fame, seducing women here, there, and everywhere, but indeed a "new one," a very different hero. The poem starts in Spain and Byron—who was in fact a magnificent linguist—mocks the Spanish names he chooses to use. Seville, normally acented on the second syllable, is here required to be accented on the first, because of the metrical pattern employed. And /gwàdâlkwiyvír/—that is, the Spanish sounding of the city's name, with a secondary accent on the second syllable and the primary accent on the final syllable—is obliged by the rhyme to be pronounced with the accent on the third syllable, which is further required to be shortened from /iy/ to /i/, to match the sound of "river." Byron puts the acute accent on the father's name, José, but then so manages the meter that the word must be pronounced with the first syllable stressed. And the rhyme of lines 23 and 24 helps underline the sideways motion the poet is using, digressing at will, but always returning, sooner or later, to his main narrative thread.

A later, lesser, but still very funny descendant of this side of Lord Byron is Ogden Nash. Like Byron, Nash turns forms and procedures on their heads: anything goes, from misspellings that point up a

rhyme to absurd line lengths that either hold back or accelerate
a rhyme.

Suppose He Threw It in Your Face

Please don't anybody ask me to decide anything, I do not know
    a nut from a meg,
Or which came first, the lady or the tiger, or which came next,
    the chicken or the egg.
It takes a man of vision
To make a decision,
5 And my every memory
Is far too dilemmary.
I am, alas, to be reckoned
With the shortstop who can't decide whether to throw to first or to
    second,
Nor can I decide whether to put, except after c,
10 E before i, or i before e.
But where this twilight mind really goes into eclipse
Is in the matter of tips.
I stand stricken before the triple doom,
Whether, and How Much, and Whom.
15 Tell me, which is more unpleasant,
The look from him who is superior to a tip and gets it, or from
    him who isn't and doesn't?
I had rather be discovered playing with my toes in the Boston
    Aquarium
Than decide wrongly about an honorarium.
Oh, to dwell forever amid Utopian scenery
20 Where hotels and restaurants and service stations are operated
    by untippable unoffendable machinery.

In the hands of a skilled poet, rhyme can be used in a wide variety
of ways, as an integrated, supportive device that adds to both point
and pleasure. Not all poets use it, especially today, but its potential
remains and it is hard to imagine an English-language poetry which
does not continue, when and as it chooses, to employ rhyme for poems
both serious and funny.

(2) Alliteration

Like many apparently simple poetic devices, alliteration—the use of words beginning with the same consonant, or with no consonant—has deeper roots, and vastly more complex possibilities, than the uninitiated might assume. Old English verse, in which alliteration played a strong and structural role, will be briefly discussed in Chapter 6. Here I want to outline the basic purposes and patterns of alliteration in poems written in what linguists call Modern English (i.e., from about 1500 to date).

> When all my five and country senses see,
> The fingers will forget green thumbs and mark
> How, through the halfmoon's vegetable eye,
> Husk of young stars and handfull zodiac,
> 5 Love in the frost is pared and wintered by,
> The whispering ears will watch love drummed away
> Down breeze and shell to a discordant beach,
> And, lashed to syllables, the lynx tongue cry
> That her fond wounds are mended bitterly.
> 10 My nostrils see her breath burn like a bush.
>
> My one and noble heart has witnesses
> In all love's countries, that will grope awake;
> And when blind sleep drops on the spying senses,
> The heart is sensual, though five eyes break.
>
> (DYLAN THOMAS)

There is in fact more alliteration, and more consistent alliteration, in this adaptation of the sonnet form than there is rhyme. Some of the rhyme is perfect; much is very imperfect, including such pairings as mark/zodiac, beach/bush, and witnesses/senses. But the alliteration is almost insistent, and for the most part follows a tighter pattern than does the rhyme: Thomas tends to pick up a line's alliteration from something in the line just before it. The two /f/ words that alliterate in line 2 follow on the single /f/ word of line 1. Line 3 has two slightly separated alliterative /h/ pairings, whch are then reinforced in line 4. The single /w/ word of line 5 is underlined by the two /w/ alliterations of line 6, which line in turn has a single /d/ word that becomes the two /d/ alliterations of line 7. Whether or not the /l/ alliteration of line 8 (two alliterative pairings and the imperfect but pronounced /l/ sounds of the word "syllables") is anticipated by the /l/ sound in "shell," in line 7, the pattern is again resumed in the /b/ word of line 9, which leads us into the three /b/ sounds of line 10. The pattern is inverted in lines 11 and 12, with two /w/ alliterations in the first of these lines ("one" does not look like a /w/ alliterative pairing, but in sound it is) and something less than two in the second line ("awake" is a clear alliteration; "will," being an auxiliary, receives less linguistic stress and so less aural prominence). The same reversal is employed in lines 13 and 14, with three /s/ alliterations (and the terminal /s/ in "drops") in the first of the lines and "sensual" in the second line (with, also, the terminal /z/ of "eyes").

It is a sensual poem, and the alliteration helps emphasize the earthiness which the poet wants to stress. Lines 1–10 deal with "country senses"; what the "senses *see*" (italics added) is expressed by a powerful parade of sensual images, for which the alliteration forms a kind of aural background. In line 11 this parading of sensual images is linked to the heart within; the senses are the heart's "witnesses," that is, its sense-perceiving agents. In the final two lines we are told that when "blind sleep" closes down these outer agents of perception, the heart still remains sensual: the "five eyes," or five senses, may be suspended, but the heart is palpable and pumping and as sensual as when its outer agents are awake and actively at work.

Indeed, the poem is so distinctly oriented toward its sensual stresses that, plainly, its semantic stress suffers somewhat. It is difficult to know, in the usual sense of verbal communication, what Thomas is "saying" in this poem, beyond what I have already indicated can be perceived through its form and manner. There is some clear loss of meaning but not, I think, a crippling loss.

Lewis Carroll too, in "Jabberwocky," uses alliteration (as well as other poetic devices, of course) as a kind of compensation for partially lost meaning. The "toves," we are told, "gyre and gimble." The "Jabberwock" has "claws that catch"; the victorious hero is a "beamish boy." There is much partial alliteration as well, with the alliterating consonants in medial positions rather than in initial ones: "'Twas bri*ll*ig, and the *sl*ithy toves," "the mome *r*aths outg*r*abe." The poet employs different degrees of linguistic stress for alliteration, as in "*B*eware the Jujub *b*ird," and straightforward repetitions, as in "*th*rough and *th*rough" or "*sn*icker-*sn*ack." And in the end, as in the Dylan Thomas poem, meaning emerges out of and in part transcends the mere sounds of words and their arrangement into assorted patterns. "Jabberwocky" is not perhaps as "serious" as "When all my five and country senses see," but in addition to delightful nonsense, and to serious parody, Carroll's poem evokes primal images that we may not fully "understand" but to which we cannot help but respond. That is surely meaning enough for any poem.

Just as deliberate, but a great deal more delicate, is David Young's use of alliteration (spiced with doses of rhyme, in several varieties) in "A Country Postcard":

September here, a haze on things,
diamond mornings, dying corn.
We have green fields here, white-flecked,
we have blue fields here, chicory,
5   yellow fields, four kinds of goldenrod,
and a man in a white shirt
and a red face
a man made out of words
stands by the B&O tracks
10   listening for the express
that disappeared west
before the tracks
began to rust.

There's a stillness
15   this morning, that the man
made out of words must walk through
listening
as he wades
in chicory, alfalfa,
20   wild carrot, goldenrod,
the nodding, growing
dew-decked, soon-to-die
words.

The poem is a closely woven fabric, its principal metaphors being involved with the fragility of things—plants, the seasons, poems. (The "man made out of words" is yet another metaphorical way of saying "poet"; the "soon-to-die words" at the end of the poem are of course the poems produced by this poet.) The old train tracks, too, now rusted out and both useless and unused, underline the same basic theme—and the heaviest rhyme of all further underlines the point: express/west. More subtle, because more imperfect, are the rhymes of things/mornings, made/wades, goldenrod/nodding. But again, as in the Thomas poem, alliteration is still more common than rhyme, and a good deal more consistent, though never as insistent as in the Thomas poem. Line 1 has /h/ alliteration, line 2 has /d/ alliteration, line 3 has both /h/ and /f/ alliteration, line 4 has /h/ alliteration (used so much, I suspect, because it is inevitably more subtle, more delicate: the /h/ sound is an odd one, in English, being articulated partly like a consonant, partly like a vowel), line 5 has both /f/ alliteration and the partial alliteration of /k/ and /g/. Except for line 8, which has /m/ alliteration, regular alliterative occurrence drops out of the poem until line 15, which again has /m/ alliteration, and line 16, which has both /m/ and /w/ alliteration; the poem does not alliterate thereafter until line 22, the penultimate line, and here the delicate pattern—no more than one alliterative pair to any line—is for the first and last time broken, with three instances of /d/ alliteration, not accidentally one of the heaviest sorts of alliteration available in modern English. The emphasis is subtly evident: it is the metaphorical comparison of all the other elements in the poem to the fragile impermanence of poetry that really matters to the poet, and around which he has therefore built both the meaning and the sound structure of his poem. The sound structure serves to underline, though not to carry, the poem's meaning: supportive roles, not lead roles, are what rhyme and alliteration and other such devices are used for.

Alliteration can be used in a wide variety of patterns; as the following poem shows, it can be used to great effect with insistent rhyme, as well as without it:

Dying Speech of an Old Philosopher

I strove with none, for none was worth my strife:
    Nature I loved, and, next to Nature, Art:

I warmed both hands before the fire of Life;
 It sinks; and I am ready to depart.

(WALTER SAVAGE LANDOR)

Line 1 has both /s/ and /n/ alliteration, line 2 has three instances of /n/ alliteration and also the vowel alliteration of and/art, line 3 has /b/ alliteration and a complex of /f/ alliterations—and other than the partial /r/ alliteration of the last line, the only alliteration employed, suddenly, is the soft vowel alliteration of and/I/am. Again, sound devices support meaning: it is of course the last line alone that deals directly with the speaker's imminent death, the earlier lines being a rapid recapitulation of the life he has lived. (If your ear is sharply tuned, you will have heard the alliteration in the last sentence, for prose too employs, though very differently, the same sound devices used in poetry.)

Cor Cordium [Heart of Hearts]

O heart of hearts, the chalice of love's fire,
 Hid round with flowers and all the bounty of bloom;
 O wonderful and perfect heart, for whom
The lyrist° liberty made life a lyre;
5 O heavenly heart, at whose most dear desire
 Dead love, living and singing, cleft his tomb,
And with him risen and regent in death's room
All day thy choral pulses rang full choir;
O heart whose beating blood was running song,
10 O sole thing sweeter than thine own songs were,
  Help us for thy free love's sake to be free,
True for thy truth's sake, for thy strength's sake strong,
 Till very liberty make clean and fair
The nursing earth as the sepulchral sea.

(ALGERNON CHARLES SWINBURNE)

Devices in poetry can run away with a poet, especially a poet too in love with devices and possessing little balance. Some of the lines in

---

4 **lyrist** lyric poet, singer

Swinburne's sonnet, written in memory of the poet Shelley, plainly use alliteration excessively: line 4, for example, with its four /l/ alliterations, or line 10, with three /s/ alliterations as well as three "th" alliterations, or line 12, with initial /t/ alliteration, ending in a violent display of /s/ alliteration. Swinburne was well aware that he was overly fond of alliteration, and once mocked himself in a poem which began, "From the depth of the dreamy decline of the dawn through a notable nimbus of nebulous moonshine,/ Pallid and pink as the palm of the flag-flower that flickers with fear of the flies as they float . . ." But recognition of one's faults is not quite so useful as curing them: Swinburne, and others like him, stand as a warning that manner cannot race ahead of matter, but must forever stand behind and to some degree in the shadows—a helper, important and useful, but not the star of the show.

(3) Repetition; Refrain

Repetition can be of a single word, or of a phrase or a line; when it becomes a regularly repeated feature of a poem, it turns into refrain, which simply means a line (or even a stanza) which recurs again and again, usually at regular intervals. Repetition is a form of emphasis: in perhaps the most famous use of it in all English poetry, John Milton has the blinded hero Samson bemoan his extinguished sight, saying (*Samson Agonistes*, lines 80–82), "O dark, dark, dark, amid the blaze of noon,/ Irrecoverably dark, total Eclipse/ Without all hope of day!" Emphasis need not be quite so overwhelming as Milton's use of it, which is effective because of the enormity of Samson's loss.

> Fly, fly, my friends, I have my death wound: fly!
> See there that boy,° that murdering boy I say,
> Who like a thief, hid in dark bush doth lie,
> Till bloody bullet get him wrongful prey.
> 5 So tyrant he no fitter place could spy,
> Nor so fair level° in so secret stay,°
> As that sweet black which veils the heavenly eye:
> There himself with his shot he close° doth lay.

---

2 **boy** the God of Love, Cupid   6 **level** vantage point; **stay** waiting place   8 **close** secretly

Poor passenger,° pass now thereby I did,
10   And stayed,° pleased with the prospect° of the place,
      While that black hue from me the bad guest hid;
But straight° I saw notions of lightning grace,
      And then descried the glist'ring° of his dart:
      But ere I could fly hence, it pierced my heart.

(SIR PHILIP SIDNEY, *Astrophil and Stella*, #20)

The poet uses no less than four kinds of repetition, some of them deeply ingenious, to underline the highly wrought, consciously artificial tone of his sonnet. The three uses of "fly" in line 1 might be taken seriously, if line 1 was not immediately followed by line 2, which is plainly light and distinctly not serious—an effect created, in part, by phrasal repetition, "that boy, that murdering boy." There is syntactic repetition in line 6: "so fair level . . . so secret stay." In line 9 the repetition is punlike abstraction of a verb from out of a noun: "poor passenger, pass now . . ." Finally, in line 14 we have an echoic use of the triple repetition of line 1, "fly." None of these repetitions themselves determines the poem's meaning, but each of them helps support and emphasize that meaning.

Caelius
it's Lesbia, my Lesbia, that Lesbia
the Lesbia whom Catullus loved
more than self and all he calls his own
5   now at the corners
and down the back alleys
ashes she hauls ashes
for Father Remus' every bastard son.

(Catullus #58, translated from the Latin by FRANK O. COPLEY)

Much of the poignancy of this bitter love lament comes from the carefully orchestrated repetition of his beloved's name, each time slightly differently: "*it's* Lesbia, *my* Lesbia, *that* Lesbia, *the* Lesbia . . ."

---

9 **passenger** passerby 10 **stayed** stopped, delayed; **prospect** view 12 **straight** immediately, at once 13 **glist'ring** glittering

(italics added). The specifically sexual image of line 7, too, uses variant repetition: "ashes, she hauls ashes . . ." There is even a suggestion of syntactic repetition—not fully articulated, but sufficiently hinted at to be noteworthy—in lines 5 and 6. Had "now" been repeated, a phrasal repetition would be explicit.

> I read the *Christabel*;
>   Very well:
> I read the *Missionary*;
>   Pretty—very:
> 5   I tried at *Ilderim*;
>   Ahem!
> I read a sheet of *Marg'ret of Anjou*;
>   *Can you?*
> I turned a page of Webster's *Waterloo*;
> 10   Pooh! pooh!
> I looked at Wordsworth's milk-white *Rylstone Doe*;
>   Hillo!
> I read *Glenvaron*, too, by Caro. Lamb—
>   God damn!

                              (LORD BYRON)

The syntactic repetition—"I read . . . tried . . . turned a page of . . . looked at . . . ."—is a basic pattern, suggesting not only the bored, endlessly repetitive nature of the reading, but also the boring, endlessly repetitive nature of the writing. The rhyme plainly is deployed to exactly the same end, though even Byron is defeated by *Glenvaron*— or, perhaps, allows himself cheerfully to seem defeated, in order to lighten his poem with a bit of variation. There is a minor example of visual repetition, too, when in line 8 the critical comment, like the titles of the various literary works being commented upon, is put in italics. It may look easy to do this sort of thing; it is not. The craft requirement is large, and there are not many professional poets, much less amateurs, who can handle it as Byron does.

Visual repetition becomes quasi-structural in poems like the following:

A Valentine for a Lady

Darling, at the Beautician's you buy
Your [a] hair
      [b] complexion
      [c] lips
5   [d] dimples, &
      [e] teeth.
For a like amount you could just as well buy a face.

(Lucilius, translated from the Greek by DUDLEY FITTS)

There is basic repetition in the poem, in its Greek original, but as can be seen from comparing this translation to others, less successful in English, it is this translator who has seen and exploited the structural possibilities of repetition.

You bought hair, rouge, cream, teeth and paste.
It'd cost the same to buy a face.

(translated by ANDREW SINCLAIR)

Shopping Tip

Lady, you went to the market
and picked up hair, rouge, honey, wax and teeth.

For a like amount
      you might have bought a face.

(translated by WILLIS BARNSTONE)

Sinclair sharply subordinates repetition to rhyme, which is indeed the chief device of his poem, and I suspect the chief reason why his is the least effective of the three versions. Barnstone combines the word repetition of line 2 with a kind of syntactic repetition, as between lines 1 and 2 and lines 3 and 4, for emphasis here separated by a space. It works quite well—and better than Sinclair's version, precisely because Barnstone's translation does not have to put all its eggs in the one rhyming basket.

To even more sharply illustrate the dangers as well as the advantages of repetition, consider the following poem:

A Ballad of Trees and the Master

Into the woods my Master went,
    Clean forspent, forspent.
Into the woods my Master came,
    Forspent with love and shame.
5 But the olives they were not blind to Him,
The little gray leaves were kind to Him:
The thorn-tree had a mind to Him
    When into the woods He came.

Out of the woods my Master went,
10   And He was well content
Out of the woods my Master came,
    Content with death and shame.
When Death and Shame would woo Him last,
From under the trees they drew Him last:
15 'Twas on a tree they slew Him—last
    When out of the woods He came.

(SIDNEY LANIER)

This is, as the British say, a much of a muchness—in a word, too much of a good thing. Repetition is used and overused. There is straight word repetition in line 2; phrasal repetition as between lines 1 and 3; more word repetition in line 4; syntactic repetition, heavily (and unnecessarily) reinforced by rhyme, in lines 5–7; and then more phrasal repetition in line 8. Without detailing the repetitions of the second stanza, let me at least note that that entire stanza is in a sense a syntactic/structural repetition on the first stanza, "into the woods" being transformed into "out of the woods." There are other reasons for this poem's inferior quality; it is sentimentalized, its diction is cloying, it has a rather mechanical shift in meter between the first and second half of each stanza. But the sheer pounding overuse of repetition surely plays a large role, too.

To underline the cardinal point in the use of this as other poetic devices, namely, that balance and moderation are usually essential, consider the following poem, in which phrasal and syntactic repetition are used in delicately shifting combinations, each and all perfectly integrated with the poem's meaning:

Door

I open and close
my favorite door
to hear the whine
of hinges; it doesn't
5   lead anywhere
but dark, and I never
go out. I have
binoculars, good eyes.
Door seems to have
10   grey eyes; I'm not sure.

He never smiles
but is always friendly
in his way.
I catch the scent
15   of forest, pine needles,
mushrooms when I open him,
sometimes when I stand close
and knock.

I think he's a bear
20   sometimes when I wake late—
I wish he were.
He could protect me.
And I could walk with him
in the daylight, ask him questions
25   about how it feels.
He never growls.

And when I wake
he's just my door

through which, someday,
I'll leave.

(MICHAEL HETTICH)

There is straight word repetition—"sometimes," in lines 17 and 20—but mostly there is phrasal and syntactic repetition, never entirely repetitive, always slightly varied, surprising. "I never go out . . . He never smiles . . . He never growls . . ." Or, more closely juxtaposed, "I have binoculars, good eyes" and "Door seems to have grey eyes . . ." The very folktale-like tone of the poem fits with this constant repetition; so too does the heavy, insistent use of simple declarative sentences, each beginning with "I." And, of course, that is part of the poem's meaning: the persona "never go[es] out," he is like a character in a fairy story, locked into his room, seeing and imagining all sorts of things. To personify a door, in that sort of context, is hardly surprising—and the poet nicely prepares us with "the whine of its hinges," in lines 3 and 4, and then the half-impersonal, half-personified "Door seems to have grey eyes" of lines 9 and 10. So too the wistful "I think he's a bear" of line 19 is built toward, expertly, by the forest imagery of the second strophe. The most perfect use of repetition, because technically imperfect, is in my judgment the extension of the present tense "sometimes," repeated in lines 17 and 20, into the future tense "someday" of the penultimate line. It seems to me to suggest, though I cannot be completely sure, that "someday" too is wistful, and that the persona himself knows it to be a day that may well never come. Technical devices alone, however, can almost never effect so decisive a substantive point—and perhaps that is the poet's reason for using a technical device, at this point, rather than something blunter and more emphatic. That is, perhaps it is the poet's conscious, deliberate intention to leave us as uncertain as the persona himself: will he? won't he? Who knows, who can tell?

Refrain needs less comment; it is both more familiar and less complex, associated as it is with such musical-derived poetic forms as the ballad. Many refrains are indeed simple sound repetitions, essentially without verbal significance. Take, for example, the refrain of the old ballad "The Three Ravens." One stanza is sufficient to make the point:

There were three ravens sat on a tree,
Down a down, hay down, hay down,
There were three ravens sat on a tree,
With a down,
5   There were three ravens sat on a tree,
They were as black as they might be,
With a down derry, derry, derry, down, down.

So familiar and predictable is this usage that texts are customarily printed, as this one usually is too, with the refrain in the first (and occasionally but not invariably in the last) stanza, but not in the many other stanzas. Everyone knows about refrains; everyone can understand from the fact that the poem is a ballad, and that the first stanza exhibits a refrain, that the refrain by its nature runs throughout.

Poets use a variety of approaches to make the refrain less purely musical and more substantive. One approach is to keep using a refrain, but not the same refrain:

Why so pale and wan, fond lover?
    Prithee, why so pale?
Will, when looking well can't move her,
    Looking ill prevail?
5   Prithee, why so pale?

Why so dull and mute, young sinner?
    Prithee, why so mute?
Will, when speaking well can't win her.
    Saying nothing do't?
10   Prithee, why so mute?

Quit, quit, for shame; this will not move,
    This cannot take her.
If of herself she will not love,
    Nothing can make her:
15   The devil take her!

(SIR JOHN SUCKLING)

There are a number of forms of repetition used, as well as the shifting refrain. The rhyme word of lines 2 and 7 is repeated from lines 1 and 6 (where, however, it is not used in rhyming position). "Will" and "well" are used in the same syntactic sense in both lines 3 and 8; indeed, lines 3 and 4 and then lines 8 and 9 are repetitive interrogatives. Note how Suckling carefully sets up and then just as carefully breaks these particular repetitive patterns: the third and final stanza does not pick up the rhyme of its second line from a word in its first line, and the third and fourth lines of that final stanza are not only not interrogative but, continued into the fifth line by a lead-in colon, they end as the poem does in an exclamation point.

The next poem does something similar, though not identical. Here the refrain is indeed repeated verbatim, but it is used each time as the second line in a rhymed couplet, and the first line of that couplet is different each time. The refrain is thus in a sense renewed, each time we hear it, and it becomes thereby more substantive than it would had it been simply repeated.

>Queen and huntress, chaste and fair,
>Now the sun is laid to sleep,
>Seated in thy silver chair,
>State in wonted° manner keep;
>5 Hesperus° entreats thy light,
>Goddess excellently bright.
>
>Earth, let not thy envious shade
>Dare itself to interpose;
>Cynthia's° shining orb was made
>10 Heaven to clear, when day did close.
>Bless us then with wishèd sight,
>Goddess excellently bright.
>
>Lay thy bow of pearl apart,
>And thy crystal-shining quiver;
>15 Give unto the flying hart°
>Space to breathe, how short soever.
>Thou that mak'st a day of night,
>Goddess excellently bright.

(BEN JONSON)

---

4 **wonted** usual   5 **Hesperus** evening star   9 **Cynthia** the moon (as emblem of Artemis, the virgin huntress)   15 **hart** deer

William Blake, finally, so employs the refrain device that it is not only varied, it is not only substantive, but so like the repetitive tone of the poem is it that it scarcely seems a refrain at all.

The Lamb

  Little Lamb, who made thee?
  Dost thou know who made thee?
Gave thee life & bid thee feed,
By the stream & o'er the mead;°
5 Gave thee clothing of delight,
Softest clothing wooly bright;
Gave thee such a tender voice,
Making all the vales rejoice!
  Little Lamb who made thee?
10 Dost thou know who made thee?
  Little Lamb I'll tell thee,
  Little Lamb I'll tell thee!
He is callèd by thy name,
For he calls himself a Lamb:
15 He is meek & he is mild,
He became a little child:
I a child & thou a lamb,
We are callèd by his name.
  Little Lamb God bless thee.
  Little Lamb God bless thee.

(4) Allusion; Acrostics

Like everyone else, poets have always made allusions. There is nothing intrinsically esoteric about the process. People living in a particular place have geographical and cultural phenomena in common, and refer to them, often in shorthand style: "Let's go to the Tower, let's go down to Philly, let's go see your old man." People who share a common history, sometimes a very long common history, similarly refer to events long past: "What did you do in the War? Did your grandfather come from the Old Country? Did your family land on the

---

4 **mead** meadow

Rock?" People who have a common religion, and a common scriptural book, can refer to the contents of that book, assuming—as in the following poem—that in the year 1655 every Englishman would know enough of the Bible to understand the reference without difficulty:

> When I consider how my light is spent,°
>   E're half my days in this dark world and wide,
>   And that one Talent which is death to hide
>   Lodg'd with me useless, though my soul more bent
> 5 To serve therewith my Maker, and present
>   My true account, lest he returning chide;
>   Doth God exact° day labor, light denied,
>   I fondly° ask; but patience to prevent
> That murmur, soon replies, God doth not need
> 10   Either man's work or His own gifts, who best
>   Bear His mild yoke, they serve Him best, His state
> Is kingly. Thousands at His bidding speed
>   And post o'er land and ocean without rest:
>   They also serve who only stand and wait.

(JOHN MILTON)

Knowing that Milton had gone blind, and not knowing the Bible, we might assume that "Talent" in line 3 referred to his poetic gift. It does, surely, but there is a good deal more to it than that, for the basic reference is to Matthew 25:14–30, the so-called parable of the talents. The parable tells of three servants, each entrusted with talents, then the name of a coin, by a master about to go off on a journey. One servant got five talents, and "traded with the same" and so could give back to his returning master five plus five talents. A second servant got two, made two additional, and so could give back to his master two plus two talents. But the third servant, who got just one talent, was afraid and hid it, and so could give back to his master only that which he had been given to start with. The third servant is sharply scolded and the single talent is taken from him and given to the first servant.

This not only makes the reference to a "Talent" more wide-ranging

---

1 **spent** used up (Milton had gone blind)   7 **exact** require   8 **fondly** foolishly

and profound, but it also makes lines 4–7 take on a whole new light, and indeed makes the entire poem communicate in a different and richer way. That sort of additional richness is precisely what allusions are meant to do. The problem is, of course, that this is not 1655, and there is no reason to assume that everyone who can read the poem has also read the Bible. What was the very farthest thing from esoteric, in John Milton's day, has become distinctly a matter of specialized learning. The poem has thus become, through no fault of its own, or of its author, distinctly unapproachable except through specialized and perhaps even esoteric knowledge, no longer communally shared.

So too with the Latin classics, and many of the Greek ones, too; once similarly the common property of every educated man in Europe or the United States, they are now basically esoterica and known to very few.

> Swell me a bowl with lusty wine,
> Till I may see the plump Lyaeus swim
> >   Above the brim:
> I drink as I would write,
> 5   In flowing measure, filled with flame, and spright.°

> (BEN JONSON)

Much of the poem can be understood without understanding the allusion in line 2, "plump Lyaeus," but lacking the classical learning to decipher it is plainly a severe handicap. Lyaeus is another name for Dionysus, as is also Bacchus—and with that information in hand the poem all fits together.

A Thought from Propertius

> She might, so noble from head
> To great shapely knees
> The long flowing line,
> Have walked to the altar
> 5   Through the holy images

---

5 **spright** spirit

At Pallas Athene's side,
Or been fit spoil for a centaur
Drunk with the unmixed wine.

(WILLIAM BUTLER YEATS)

Full understanding of this eight-line lyric requires knowledge of both Greek and Latin material. Propertius, first of all, is a Roman poet, most of whose poems have to do with love. The altar, known to most Christians, is however not the Christian altar at all, but that of the "pagan" Greeks, for Pallas Athene is the daughter of Zeus, ruler of the gods in the Greek pantheon. The centaurs were legendary creatures, half man and half horse—and all lust. It was, finally, the Greek custom not to drink wine undiluted, but with the addition of water: to drink "unmixed wine" was to court certain and rapid drunkenness. Again, something of the poem's meaning is apparent, without knowing the things I have just outlined, but the poem is incomparably richer once they are known.

The Crimes of Bernard

They were always arguing that we
were either the Devil's puppets or
God's marionettes, so when I said,
"What's the difference?, the latter
5 has us by the long hairs, the former
by the short, the best thing
about Commedia dell'Arte is
improvisation," they said, "There
are only two sides to a question: to
10 propose a third is treason if true.
Traitors we snatch bald, we
cut off their balls, we set them out
naked on the road to nowheres
as two-bit Abélards, two-bit whores,
15 and go on arguing as before."

(ALAN DUGAN)

Rather than Greek and Latin learning, this poem takes us into medieval matters. The kind of furious but essentially empty arguing, here described, is what has been called the "how-many-angels-can-dance-on-the-head-of-a-pin" approach—better known as Scholasticism. Abélard was a learned and talented monk, tutor to a beautiful young girl, Eloise. He seduced her, and her relatives castrated him. The once common reference to long hairs, those which grow on our heads, and short hairs, those which grow on our groins, is no longer in common usage. And Commedia dell'Arte (an allusion, I must admit, that I have never been unable to understand, in the context of this poem) is an Italian form of street theater. Published in 1963, Dugan's poem depends for full comprehension on a degree of learning that most people do not have—but this is not, as in the poems discussed a moment ago, knowledge that most people did have at one time but have no longer. Knowledge of medieval philosophy and history has never been common. Dugan's poem thus illustrates a relatively new phenomenon, namely, a poet consciously writing for an audience which represents only a very small part of the literate population of his time. Dugan's audience is a distinctly learned one, and surely poets like John Milton and Ben Jonson wrote for other men as learned, or nearly as learned, as themselves. But there is a crucial difference, for in that earlier time all the readers of poetry, and indeed all the readers of anything in any literary form, were learned: indeed, in their time you could avoid punishment, even for murder, if you could demonstrate your ability to read aloud from a Latin text, any Latin text shoved under your nose.

The world has become a different place; the world's poetry too has changed; and the relationship between poets and their readers has changed quite as much. Ezra Pound, along with his friend and onetime disciple, T. S. Eliot, are more than any other individuals responsible for excessive use of allusion in modern poetry. But they like most of us are also part of a larger historical tide—as much swept up by forces more powerful than any single man as they are innovators and initiators. Marianne Moore wrote the following poem in 1932:

No Swan So Fine

"No water so still as the
   dead fountains of Versailles." No swan

with swart° blind look askance
and gondoliering legs, so fine
5   as the chintz china one with fawn-
brown eyes and toothed gold
collar on to show whose bird it was.

Lodged in the Louis Fifteenth
        candelabrum-tree of cockscomb-
10   tinted buttons, dahlias,
sea-urchins, and everlastings,°
        it perches on the branching foam
of polished sculptured
flowers—at ease and tall. The king is dead.

We can understand the quotation with which the poem begins: it is someone visiting the onetime pleasure palace of the kings of France. It would be nice to know why the statement is in quotation marks, whether it is taken from the poet's diary or notebook, or from some other source. We are not told (though Miss Moore is fond of appending footnotes to her poems, to give us exactly such information as this), and there is something inherently pedantic in using quotation marks but not explaining them. There is something even more pedantic in assuming that all readers will know that Italian gondoliers paddle from the stern rather than from the bow of their crafts. There is something pedantic beyond description in Miss Moore's footnote to line 9's "candelabrum-tree": "A pair of Louis XV candelabra with Dresden figures of swans belonging to Lord Balfour." Is this an auction-sale catalogue or a poem?

Like Marianne Moore, H.D. (Hilda Doolittle) is very much a member of the poetic generation which includes Pound and Eliot. This is the first of two poems entitled "Acon":

Bear me to Dictaeus,
and to the steep slopes;
to the river Erymanthus.

I choose spray of dittany,
5   cyperum, frail of flower,

---

3 **swart** dark, black   11 **everlasting** flowers that can be dried without loss of color

> buds of myrrh,
> all-healing herbs,
> close pressed in calathes.
>
> For she lies panting,
> 10   drawing sharp breath,
> broken with harsh sobs,
> she, Hyella,
> whom no god pities.

There are two sorts of allusions here, one Greek sites and names, the other plants. The problem is that the first sort is basically indecipherable, and the second is both difficult to decipher and in one case confusing. What (and where) is Dictaeus? What is its significance in this poem? I have tried to track the allusion down; I cannot. Is it real? legendary? imaginary? I do not know. The same with the river Erymanthus: if it exists, I have not been able to locate it, and certainly I do not know what it is doing in the poem. Hyella too may be intended as a specific reference, or it may not: I cannot discover, no matter where I hunt. I can learn that dittany is a labiate, herbal plant, and that cyperum is a sedgelike plant; the former has had medicinal usages, the latter (so far as I can learn) has not. Since myrrh too is known for its perfume, rather than for any medicinal properties, the reference to "all-healing herbs" in line 7 is more or less baffling. Nor does it help to find that calathes is *either* a flower-shaped basket *or* a genus of tropical American herbs. In short, whether there is true historical and botanical allusion in the poem, or whether some (or all) of the allusions are concocted, there is almost no way of knowing—and without understanding so many of the important words, how can one hope to understand the poem? (I do not myself understand even the title: what "Acon" means I do not know.)

Over-allusiveness is not, to be sure, the mark of all modern poetry; it is definitely the mark of some modern poetry. To some extent, what is and what is not too much allusion must be a relative matter: some people are more learned in some areas than in others, just as some people are more learned than other people. There are no hard-and-fast rules, no absolute standards. It becomes, in the end, a matter of taste.

Acrostics are even more playful than allusions, and much less frequently used. A poet writing an acrostic uses (almost invariably) the first letter of the first word in each line as a steppingstone. Put all the first letters of all the first words in all the lines together, and what do you get?

> Give me your patience, sister, while I frame
> Exact in capitals your golden name;
> Or sue the fair Apollo and he will
> Rouse from his heavy slumber and instill
> 5   Great love in me for thee and Poesy.
> Imagine not that greatest mastery
> And kingdom over all the Realms of verse,
> Nears more to heaven in aught, than when we nurse
> And surety give to love and Brotherhood.
>
> 10   Anthropophagi° in Othello's mood;
> Ulysses storm'd and his enchanted belt
> Glow with the Muse, but they are never felt
> Unbosom'd so and so eternal made,
> Such tender incense in their laurel shade
> 15   To all the regent sisters of the Nine°
> As this poor offering to you, sister mine.
>
> Kind sister! ay, this third name says you are;
> Enchanted has it been the Lord knows where;
> And may it taste to you like good old wine,
> Take you to real happiness and give
> Sons, daughters and a home like honied hive.

(JOHN KEATS)

What you get, plainly, is GEORGIANA AUGUSTA KEATS, the poet's sister-in-law. What you do not get, equally plainly, is particularly memorable poetry: acrostics are the trickiest of the tricks, and rarely distinguished as much for the quality of their verse as they are for its ingenuity.

One Esdras Barnivelt honored Pope by writing an admiring commentary on *The Rape of the Lock*. Pope then honored Barnivelt with the following acrostic poem:

---

10 **anthropophagi** man-eaters, cannibals   15 **the Nine** the nine Muses (female)

B arrels conceal the liquor they contain,
A nd sculls° are but the barrels of the brain.
R ipe politics the nation's barrel fill,
N one can like thee its fermentation still,
5 I ngenious writer, lest thy barrel split,
V nbarrel thy just sense, and broach thy wit.
E xtract from Tory barrels all French juice,
L et not the Whig's Geneva's stumm° infuse,°
T hen shall thy barrel be of gen'ral use.

But if neither John Keats nor Alexander Pope can do better than this, why need we linger any longer over the acrostic form?

(5) Imitation; Parody

The difference between imitation and parody, by and large, is the difference between high praise and low praise (or gentle criticism). A poet imitates in order to acknowledge a debt, or to free himself from an influence. A poet parodies in order to humorously (and sometimes nastily) highlight negative aspects of another poet's work (or at times, his own work).

Bright is the Ring of Words

Bright is the ring of words
  When the right man rings them,
Fair the fall songs
  When the singer sings them.
5 Still they are carolled and said—
  On wings they are carried—
After the singer is dead
  And the maker buried.

Low as the singer lies
10 In the field of heather,
Songs of his fashion bring
  The swains together.

---

2 **sculls** sculleries (?)   8 **stumm** unfermented or partly unfermented grape juice; **infuse** be poured

And when the west is red
With the sunset embers,
15 The lover lingers and sings
And the maid remembers.

(ROBERT LOUIS STEVENSON)

The great days of Swinburne's fame have long since faded away, but anyone who knows his work even casually can easily recognize how closely this imitates him—in subject, in form, in tone, in technique, even in meter and music. Swinburne's obsessive alliteration is not parodied here, but it is distinctly echoed. Swinburne's emphasis on music rather than on substance, his determined vagueness, his insistent enthusiasms—though for exactly what it is sometimes hard to tell—and even some of Swinburne's favorite words ("bright, ring, fair, fall, songs, singer, wings, maker, field, fashion, swains," and more): it is all here. This is Stevenson's poem, but it is a tribute to Swinburne's once massive, overwhelming influence on other poets, and a loving tribute, as poetic imitation always is.

Do the Dead Know What Time It Is?

The old guy put down his beer.
Son, he said,
       (and a girl came over to the table where we were:
       asked us by Jack Christ to buy her a drink.)
5 Son, I am going to tell you something
The like of which nobody ever was told.
       (and the girl said, I've got nothing on tonight;
       how about you and me going to your place?)
I am going to tell you the story of my mother's
10 Meeting with God.
       (and I whispered to the girl: I don't have a room,
       but maybe . . .)
She walked up to where the top of the world is
And He came right up to her and said
15 So at last you've come home.
       (but maybe what?

      I thought I'd like to stay here and talk to you.)
   My mother started to cry and God
   Put His arms around her.
20   (about what?
      Oh, just talk . . . we'll find something.)
   She said it was like a fog coming over her face
   And light was everywhere and a soft voice saying
   You can stop crying now.
25   (what can we talk about that will take all night?
      and I said that I didn't know.)
   You can stop crying now.

                    (KENNETH PATCHEN)

Patchen's poem clearly can stand on its own. But for those familiar
with Cummings' use of slang, and his abrupt transitions, and his insis-
tent juxtapositioning of the trivial and the serious, and the way he turns
conversation into high drama, there can be no question of the influence
of Cummings on this poem (and this poet). But as the following tribute
indicates, Cummings' style is one that contemporary poets love to play
with:

one

   lit a cigarette with it
   and the crowd went wild
   another did
   the famous disappearing egg trick
5   and popped off
   in a customer's face and everyone's
   knees began banging
   so we were ready
   for the last
10 who took three minutes
   to get it warmed up and then
   blew out 240 matches
   with a single twitch, my god
   240 matches, if I
15 could knock out poems like that
   with e.e.'s

onetwothree
punch I'd
say hello Sid King°, let me
20 show you a trick that
will have them cumming
in the aisles

(DOUGLAS ASPER)

Asper has caught not only the tone and the technique, in this affection-
ate spoof, but much of the substance as well, for Cummings is both a
magnificent love poet and equally adept at bawdy verse, frequently of a
satiric sort. The outrageous pun in line 21 almost seems to *be* the
original, rather than an echoing of it. And much the same must be said
of the next poem, a deeply fond and yet nicely mocking send-up of
Emily Dickinson:

Because I Could Not Dump

Because I could not Dump the Trash—
Jow kindly stopped for Me—
The Garbage Truck held but Ourselves—
And Bacterial Colonies—

5 We slowly drove—Joe smelled of Skunk—
Yet risking no delay
My hairdo and composure too,
Were quickly Fumed away—

We passed a School, where Dumpsters stood
10 Recycling—in the Rain—
We picked up Yields of Industry—
Dead Cats and Window Panes—

Or rather—Joe picked up—
Seeing maggot-lined cans—I recoiled—
15 When heir to smelly Legacies,
What sort of Woman—Spoils?

---

19 **Sid King** burlesque theater operator

We paused before a Dump that seemed
A Swelling of the Ground—
The Soil was scarcely visible—
20 Joe dropped—his Booty—down.

Since then—'tis a fortnight—yet
Seems shorter than the Day
I first set out the Old Fish Heads
And hoped Joe'd come my Way—

(ANDREA PATERSON)

That only another poet could so delicately echo another poet's manner
is plain. But that affection need not be the only motivation is also clear.
It would be hard to decide whether the pseudo-Dickinson poem is
more imitation or more parody, since there is so significant a lowering
of substance as well as a deft echoing of style. But the malice in this
next poem is obvious: here we have plainly crossed the line that sepa-
rates imitation from out-and-out parody:

Mr. Housman's Message

O woe, woe,
People are born and die,
We also shall be dead pretty soon
Therefore let us act as if we were dead already.

5 The bird sits on the hawthorn tree
But he dies also, presently.
Some lads get hung, and some get shot.
Woeful is this human lot.
        Woe! woe, etcetera . . . .

10 London is a woeful place,
Shropshire is much pleasanter.
Then let us smile a little space
Upon fond nature's morbid grace.
        Oh, Woe, woe, woe, etcetera. . . .

(EZRA POUND)

A. E. Housman is not a difficult poet to make fun of, but no one has ever done it better than, in this poem, Pound has done it. T. S. Eliot has been perhaps better parodied than, in the following poem, he himself parodied himself, but the self-analytical and good-humored criticism is sufficiently remarkable so that we can end this section with it:

Lines for Cuscuscaraway and Mirza Murad Ali Beg

How unpleasant to meet Mr. Eliot!
With his features of clerical cut,
And his brow so grim
And his mouth so prim
5 And his conversation, so nicely
Restricted to What Precisely
And If and Perhaps and But.
How unpleasant to meet Mr. Eliot!
With a bobtail cur
10 In a coat of fur
And a porpentine cat
And a wopsical hat:
How unpleasant to meet Mr. Eliot!
        (Whether his mouth be open or shut).

(T. S. ELIOT)

(6) Onomatopoeia

Words are not the things they describe, but (relatively speaking) abstractions of those things, verbal symbols which we can use in communicating to other human beings. But words are also sounds, and can be made to communicate both as meaning and, additionally, as sounds evocative of meaning. (Possibly such words as "cuckoo" and "whip-poorwill" originated in some such fashion.) Onomatopoeia is the poetic device by which sound is used to communicate sense. It is, however, not nearly so common in poetic practice as many theoreticians seem to believe. When poets do use it, they use it fleetingly, in passing: I cannot recall a single poem, anywhere in English or American literature, which makes use throughout its length of onomatopoeia. The closest thing to such a poem that I know of is "Silent Poem," by Robert Francis:

> backroad leafmold stonewall chipmunk
> underbrush grapevine woodchuck shadblow
>
> woodsmoke cowbarn honeysuckle woodpile
> sawhorse bucksaw outhouse wellsweep
>
> 5 backdoor flagstone bulkhead buttermilk
> candlestick ragrug firedog brownbread
>
> hilltop outcrop cowbell buttercup
> whetstone thunderstorm pitchfork steeplebush
>
> gristmill millstone cornmeal waterwheel
> 10 watercress buckwheat firefly jewelweed
>
> gravestone groundpine windbreak bedrock
> weathercock snowfall starlight cockcrow

But even "Silent Poem" is only partially onomatopoetic. The poem plainly experiments with syntactical effects (omitting all connectives, and especially verbs), visual effects, internal rhymes, and so on, as well as with sheer sound effects. More usually, if a longish passage rather than a single line is involved, the poet is consciously trying to make a point about this craft device—as for example in the famous lines of Alexander Pope:

> 'Tis not enough no harshness gives offence,
> The sound must seem an echo to the sense.
> Soft is the strain when Zephyr gently blows,
> And the smooth stream in smoother numbers° flows;
> 5 But when loud surges lash the sounding shore,
> The hoarse, rough verse should like the torrent roar.
> When Ajax strives, some rocks' vast weight to throw,
> The line too labors, and the words move slow;
> Not so, when swift Camilla scours the plain,
> 10 Flies o'er th'unbending corn, and skims along the main.

---

4 **numbers** poetic music, prosody

This is fearfully ingenious: Pope was one of the master craftsmen of all time. This passage is from his poem *An Essay on Criticism*, whose subject is the proper evaluation of poetry. At the same time that Pope is discussing the effects of onomatopoeia he is demonstrating its effects. But onomatopoeia is not a device which needs much consideration. I mention it here, indeed, in good part because too much has been made of it elsewhere.

SHAPES AND STRUCTURES

THE DIVIDING LINE between the outer and the inner, between form and content, is essentially impossible to draw. Even which came first, outer or inner, form or content, is frequently impossible to establish. The artist himself often feels, as did the Russian poet Osip Mandelstam, that poems preexist, and that the poet's job is only to discover them—both form and content not so much created as found.

And in every art the forms influence what is put into them, as what is put into a form also influences that form. In music, for example, the kind of melodies and harmonies and orchestration that go into a symphony are different from the kind that go into an overture or a concerto, just as Haydn's use of the minuet form becomes something altogether different in Beethoven's hands—and something almost unrecognizable in Mahler's. I want to discuss shapes and structures in poetry in order to help outline what various forms offer to the poet, and what various poets have done with various forms. I neither can nor want to separate form and content, and most emphatically I do not propose to establish neat (and totally false) guidelines for judging which is more (or less) important.

My discussion of poetic shapes and structures will be divided into eight sections. The division is not watertight, but neither is it totally arbitrary:

(1) Couplets; Quatrains
(2) Ballads and Hymns

(3) Sonnets (Italian, Shakespearian, Spenserian)
(4) Songs (Lyrics)
(5) Dialogues; Monologues
(6) Other Traditional Forms (ballade, limerick, rhyme royal, rondeau, sestina, spenserian, terza rima, triolet, villanelle)
(7) Free Forms
(8) Concrete Poetry

(1) Couplets; Quatrains

A couplet is a two-line form, usually rhyming A A. The length of the line is variable; the heroic couplet, however, requires both that the line be a uniform length (pentameter, or five metrical feet) and that the sense of the couplet usually be contained within the two lines themselves, not spilling over into the lines which follow. Generally, each line of a couplet must have the same length (number of metrical feet). Couplets have been written with lines of unequal length; couplets have been written without rhyme.

The couplet is almost but not quite the smallest form possible. Poems have been written which are only one line in length; the formal aspects of one-line poems are both elementary and obvious. The addition of the second line, however, and of the rhyme gives the poet much much more than twice the formal opportunity offered by the one-line form.

> Nature, and Nature's laws lay hid in Night.
> God said, *Let Newton be!* and all was Light.
>
> (ALEXANDER POPE)

The couplet's two parts, its first line and its second, are something like such natural forms as question and answer, push and pull, advance and retreat. Pivoting the form on the rhyme, the poet can play the first part against the second, using the first to announce and dramatize a subject and the second to resolve and still further heighten what has already been dramatized. Indeed, so basic is this opposition of the two parts to the couplet's poetic nature that it emerges whether or not the poet chooses also to employ rhyme:

I never dared be radical when young
For fear it would make me conservative when old.

(ROBERT FROST)

And wit—what is more naturally witty than the balancing of *this* against *that?*—fairly flows into couplet form, not only in Pope's couplets but in the couplets of poets of every time and every disposition:

Reflection on a Wicked World

Purity
Is obscurity.

(OGDEN NASH)

Salvationists: I

Come, my songs, let us speak of perfection—
We shall get ourselves rather disliked.

(EZRA POUND)

I am unable, yonder beggar cries,
To stand, or move; if he say true, he *lies*.

(JOHN DONNE)

On an Innkeeper, Nicknamed "The Marquis"

Here lies a mock Marquis, whose titles were shammed,
If ever he rise, it will be to be *damned*.

(ROBERT BURNS)

To Alchemists

If all you boast of your great art be true,
Sure, willing poverty lives most in you.

(BEN JONSON)

Not that wit is the only logical beneficiary of the couplet's antithetical balancing of *this* against *that*:

> Be not dismayed, though crosses cast thee down;
> Thy fall is but the rising to a crown.
>
> (ROBERT HERRICK)

On a Very Old Glass°

> We both are mortal; but thou, frailer creature,
> May'st die like me by chance, but not by nature.
>
> (JONATHAN SWIFT)

In a Station of the Metro°

> The apparition of these faces in the crowd;
> Petals on a wet, black bough.
>
> (EZRA POUND)

ana-MARY/ARMY-gram

> How well her name an *Army* doth present,
> In whom the *Lord of Hosts* did pitch his tent!
>
> (GEORGE HERBERT)

The couplets I have been discussing, to this point, have all been independent poems—small, but more than self-sufficient. But the couplet is much more than the fine but small form we have so far seen: it is also a major building block, with which poets of all varieties and of most times have erected larger forms.

Glass mirror   **Metro** Paris subway

Lines on the Mermaid Tavern°

Souls of poets dead and gone,
What Elysium° have ye known,
Happy field or mossy cavern,
Choicer than the Mermaid Tavern?
5   Have ye tippled° drink more fine
Than mine host's Canary wine?
Or are fruits of Paradise
Sweeter than those dainty pies
Of venison? O generous food!
10 Drest as though bold Robin Hood
Would, with his maid Marian,
Sup and bowse° from horn and can.

I have heard that on a day
Mine host's sign-board flew away,
15 Nobody knew whither, till
An astrologer's old quill
To a sheepskin gave the story,
Said he saw you in your glory,
Underneath a new-old sign
20 Sipping beverage divine,
And pledging with contented smack
The Mermaid in the Zodiac.

Souls of poets dead and gone,
What Elysium have ye known,
25 Happy field or mossy cavern,
Choicer than the Mermaid Tavern?

(JOHN KEATS)

Keats does not maintain a strict couplet form throughout this celebratory poem. The rhymes are consistent; the couplets begin to run over,

---

Mermaid Tavern London site of an Elizabethan literary club   2 Elysium heaven, paradise   5 tippled drunk (especially alcoholic beverages)   12 bowse drink, especially to excess in line 9, and from that point to about line 19 the couplets are at best loose. But the basic underlying shape of the verse, even when it strays from perfect realization of that shape, remains the couplet.

Again, the form survives without rhyme as well as with it, in these larger structures:

> The great Eliot° has come the great Eliot
> has gone and where precisely are we now?
>
> He moved from the Mississippi to the Thames°
> and we moved with him a few miles or inches.
>
> 5   He taught us what to read what not to read
> and when he changed his mind he let us know.
>
> He coughed discreetly and we likewise coughed;
> we waited and we heard him clear his throat.
>
> How to be perfect prisoners of the past
> 10 this was the thing but now he too is past.
>
> Shall we go sit beside the Mississippi
> and watch the riftraft driftwood floating by?
>
> (ROBERT FRANCIS)

Francis has Americanized the couplet here, as few modern poets have been able to do. The laconic, terse New England voice is deftly matched to the tight form: the dry pauses of Maine or Massachusetts speech are bent to the metrical pauses out of which metrical variety must, in the couplet, be built. The master of those pauses was, of course, Alexander Pope:

On Lord John Caryll

> A manly form; a bold, yet modest mind;
> Sincere, though prudent; constant, yet resigned;
> Honor unchanged; a principle professed;
> Fixed to one side, but mod'rate to the rest;

---

1 **Eliot** the poet T. S. Eliot   3 **Mississipi to the Thames** born in St. Louis, Missouri, Eliot emigrated to England, becoming a British citizen

5   An honest courtier, and a patriot too;
   Just to his Prince, and to his country true:
   All these were joined in one, yet failed to save
   The wise, the learn'd, the virtuous, and the brave;
   Lost, like the common plunder of the grave!
10   Ye few, whom better genius does inspire,
   Exalted souls, informed with purer fire!
   Go now, learn all vast Science can impart;
   Go fathom Nature, take the heights of Art!
   Rise higher yet: learn ev'n yourselves to know;
15   Nay, to yourselves alone that knowledge owe.
   Then, when you seem above mankind to soar,
   Look on this marble, and be vain no more!

If it is hard to do justice to Pope's marching couplets, in small space, nevertheless even this minor example of his use of the form shows how the metrical pauses are varied, balanced and unbalanced with infinite skill. Note that lines 7–9 are a once common variant on the couplet, called a triplet—that is, three lines rather than two, rhyming A A A. The triplet flourished in the seventeenth and especially in the eighteenth century; it is now almost totally unused. (One common form of the triplet has the third line contain an extra metrical foot; Pope keeps the three lines to the same length.)

The couplet extended—to whatever length the poet may choose—is still a couplet. The quatrain, or basic four-line form, is usually something more than two couplets joined. The normal rhyme scheme for the quatrain is A B A B; there are variants which drop one of the rhymes, usually the first, and follow the pattern A B C B; there are variants that cluster one rhyme and separate the other, following the pattern A B B A; there are variants that do not rhyme at all. Generally speaking the quatrain, properly so called, has a length of either four or five metrical feet, and keeps the same length throughout: this is, in fact, one of the chief distinguishing features separating the true quatrain from the ballad stanza, to be discussed shortly.

Edward Fitzgerald used quatrains of great deftness in his superb Englishing of "The Rubaiyat of Omar Khayam." The poem as a whole is too long to reproduce here, but the first twelve quatrains—the last of

which is among the most famous and most often quoted stanzas of any
sort in our language—illustrate the form nicely:

> Wake! For the Sun who scatter'd into flight
> The Stars before him from the Field of Night,
>   Drives Night along with them from Heav'n and strikes
> The Sultan's Turret with a Shaft of Light.
>
> 5 Before the phantom of False morning died,
> Methought a Voice within the Tavern cried,
>   "When all the Temple is prepared within,
> Why nods the drowsy Worshipper outside?"
>
> And, as the cock crew, those who stood before
> 10 The Tavern shouted— "open then the Door!
>   You know how little while we have to stay,
> And, once departed, may return no more."
>
> Now the New Year reviving old Desires,
> The thoughtful Soul to Solitude retires,
> 15   Where the WHITE HAND OF MOSES on the Bough
> Puts out, and Jesus from the Ground suspires.°
>
> Iram indeed is gone with all his Rose,
> And Jamshyd's Sev'n-ring'd Cup where no one knows;
>   But still a Ruby kindles in the Vine,
> 20 And many a Garden by the Water blows.
>
> And David's lips are locked; but in divine
> High-piping Pehlevi°, with "Wine! Wine! Wine!
>   Red Wine!"—the Nightingale cries to the Rose
> That sallow cheek of hers to incarnadine.°
>
> 25 Come, fill the Cup, and in the fire of Spring
> Your Winter-garment of Repentance sling:
>   The Bird of Time has but a little way
> To flutter—and the Bird is on the Wing.
>
> Whether at Naishapur or Babylon,
> 30 Whether the Cup with sweet or bitter run,

---

16 **suspires** sighs, breathes   22 **Pehlevi** Pahlavi, a language   24 **incarnadine** turn red

The Wine of Life keeps oozing drop by drop,
The Leaves of Life keep falling one by one.

Each morn a thousand Roses brings, you say;
Yes, but where leaves the Rose of Yesterday?
35   And this first Summer month that brings the Rose
Shall take Jamshyd and Kaikobad away.

Well, let it take them! What have we to do
With Kaikobad the Great, or Kaikhosru?
      Let Zal and Rustum bluster as they will,
40 Or Hátim call to supper—heed not you.

With me along the strip of Herbage strown
That just divides the desert from the sown,
      Where name of Slave and Sultan is forgot—
And Peace to Mahmud on his golden Throne!

45 A Book of Verses underneath the Bough,
A Jug of Wine, a Loaf of Bread—and Thou
      Beside me singing in the Wilderness—
Oh, Wilderness were Paradise enow°!

Early in his career, William Blake made similarly heavy use of
quatrains:

Holy Thursday

Is this a holy thing to see,
In a rich and fruitful land,
Babes reduced to misery,
Fed with cold and usurous hand?

5 Is that trembling cry a song?
Can it be a song of joy?
And so many children poor?
It is a land of poverty!

And their sun does never shine,
10 And their fields are bleak & bare,

---

48 **enow** enough, sufficient

And their ways are filled with thorns;
It is eternal winter there.

For where-e'er the sun does shine,
And where-e'er the rain does fall,
15 Babe can never hunger there,
Nor poverty the mind appall.

George Herbert, one of the most innovative of all poets in the matter of form, rang a number of variations on the quatrain, including the following poem, written in lines of three rather than of four feet:

Bitter-Sweet

Ah, my dear angry Lord,
Since thou dost love, yet strike;
Cast down, yet help afford;
Sure I will do the like.

5 I will complain, yet praise;
I will bewail, approve;
And all my sour-sweet days
I will lament and love.

Finally, to show the almost endless possibilities of variation, starting with the two-line couplet and building larger blocks of that, here is what might be called a sestet, or six-line stanza, clearly itself framed in an underlying couplet form.

Ode Written in the Beginning of the Year 1746

How sleep the brave who sink to rest
By all their country's wishes blest!
When Spring, with dewy fingers cold,
Returns to deck their hallowed mold,
5 She there shall dress a sweeter sod
Than Fancy's feet have ever trod.

By fairy hands their knell is rung,
By forms unseen their dirge is sung;

There Honor comes, a pilgrim gray,
10   To bless the turf that wraps their clay,
And Freedom shall awhile repair,°
To dwell a weeping hermit there!

(WILLIAM COLLINS)

(2) Ballads and Hymns

Ballads and hymns are probably the poetic forms most familiar to most people. Both are, in a sense, folk forms; their subject matters are usually different, but since they are technically similar, and since this is a chapter primarily focused on form, I have here linked them together.

from a familiar hymn

A mighty fortress is our God,
   A bulwark never failing;
Our helper He amid the flood
   Of mortal ills prevailing.

from a traditional ballad

And it's fare you well, my dearest dear,
   And it's fare you well for ever,
And if you don't go with me now,
Don't let me see you never.

Hymns and ballads are oral forms, meant to be sung rather than read, which probably accounts for their regular rhythm (four metrical feet in one line, three in the next) and also for the perfect rhymes of the even-numbered lines. Both forms are almost invariably in quatrains, with a pause at the end of the second line; the quatrain is thus in a way divided into two couplets, though the rhyme extends across from one couplet to the other. Nor is this simply an enumeration of dry technical characteristics: the internal division is basic to the form. In general, hymns and ballads advance a bit like children playing king of the hill:

---

11 **repair** go

one step forward, one step back. Whatever is said in the first line of a quatrain is essentially repeated in the second line; similarly, whatever is said in the third line is essentially repeated in the fourth line. All of which means that the real unit of expression is the couplet, and not the line. For example, in the hymn quatrain quoted above, line 1 says, "A mighty fortress is our God." All line 2 says, however, is that the "fortress" is a "bulwark," and instead of "mighty" that it is "never failing." God is "our helper," says line 3, "amid the flood," and line 4 explains that the flood is "of mortal ills" and that it is in fact a flood because it is "prevailing." So too with the ballad stanza, quoted above. Line 1 says goodbye and line 2 says goodbye for ever; line 3 says come with me, please, and line 4 says it's *really* goodbye if you don't come.

Here are two more brief examples, as before first of a hymn stanza and then of a ballad stanza:

hymn

O holy Child of Bethlehem!
   Descend to us, we pray;
Cast out our sin, and enter in,
   Be born in us today.

ballad

Will ye go to the Highlands, Leezie Lindsay?
   Will ye go to the Highlands wi me?
Will ye go to the Highlands, Leezie Lindsay,
   My pride and my darling to be?

The first couplet of the hymn quatrain (that is, lines 1 and 2) invokes the "holy Child." The second couplet explains why. The invocation of that "holy Child of Bethlehem" is not significantly added to by line 2, "Descend to us we pray," since the notion of Christ descending is inherent in the attempt to call out to him. There is some minor increment of sense; the two lines are not absolutely identical; but it is at best a very minor increment. So too, in line 3, to "cast out our sin" clearly implies the incarnation spelled out in line 4, namely, "Be born in us today." Lines 3 and 4, then, also function essentially as a couplet.

The patterning in the ballad stanza is too clear, I think, to need much comment. It is reminiscent of the old joke about the world-famous, universally successful preacher. Asked his secret, he replies: "First I tell them what I'm going to tell them. Then I tell them. Then I tell them what I've told them." Oral forms tend to require exactly that sort of patient forward movement: a little forward, a little back. Otherwise the listener, who does not have a printed text in front of him, from which he can verify what his ears are telling him, may well be left behind, uncomprehending. Every link in an oral chain must be clearly established—but the written form, once literate folk take over the oral forms and make them their own property, is a very different matter. Structural, formal variation and, especially, greater complexity are likely to emerge in the written form; after a time, too, the divergence is likely to become so great that the onetime oral form is almost unrecognizable in its later, literary descendant. Here is an early literary ballad, already significantly changed:

Hark, hark! the lark at heaven's gate sings,
    And Phoebus° 'gins arise,
His steeds to water at those springs
    On chaliced° flowers that lies;
5 And winking Mary-buds begin
    To ope their golden eyes:
With every thing that pretty is,
    My lady sweet, arise:
    Arise, arise!

(WILLIAM SHAKESPEARE, *Cymbeline*)

In the small collection of literary ballads and hymns that follows, note in particular how the shape of the original ballad form is changed in line length. The permutations and combinations are almost too numerous to try to exhibit; those that follow are illustrative only.

Ode on Solitude

Happy the man whose wish and care
    A few paternal acres bound,

---

2 **Phoebus** another name for Apollo, god of the sun   4 **chaliced** having a cuplike blossom

Content to breathe his native air,
    In his own ground.

5   Whose herds with milk, whose fields with bread,
    Whose flocks supply him with attire,
Whose trees in summer yield him shade,
    In winter fire.

Blest, who can unconcernedly find
10   Hours, days, and years slide soft away,
In health of body, peace of mind,
    Quiet by day,

Sound sleep by night; study and ease,
    Together mixed; sweet recreation;
15 And innocence, which most dost please
    With meditation.

Thus let me live, unseen, unknown;
    Thus unlamented let me die;
Steal from the world, and not a stone
20   Tell where I lie.

              (ALEXANDER POPE)

Death of the Day

My pictures blacken in their frames
    As night comes on,
And youthful maids and wrinkled dames
    Are now all one.

5   Death of the day! a sterner Death
    Did worse before;
The fairest form, the sweetest breath,
    Away he bore.

        (WALTER SAVAGE LANDOR)

The Foil

       If we could see below
The sphere of virtue, and each shining grace

As plainly'as that above doth show;
This were the better sky, the brighter place.

5   God hath made stars the foil
To set off virtues; griefs to set off sinning:
    Yet in this wretched world we toil,
As if grief were not foul, nor virtue winning.

                (GEORGE HERBERT)

We flash across the level.
    We thunder thro' the bridges.
We bicker° down the cuttings.°
    We sway along the ridges.

5 A rush of streaming hedges,
    Of jostling lights and shadows,
Of hurtling, hurrying stations,
    Of racing woods and meadows.

We charge the tunnels headlong—
10   The blackness roars and shatters.
We crash between embankments—
    The open spins and scatters.

We shake off the miles like water,
    We might carry a royal ransom;
15 And I think of her waiting, waiting,
    And long for a common hansom.°

          (WILLIAM ERNEST HENLEY)

North Labrador

A land of leaning ice
Hugged by plaster-grey arches of sky,
Flings itself silently
Into eternity.

---

3 **bicker** hurry; **cuttings** excavations   16 **hansom** cab

5   "Has no one come here to win you,
     Or left you with the faintest blush
     Upon your glittering breasts?
     Have you no memories, O Darkly Bright?"

     Cold-hushed, there is only the shifting of moments
     That journey toward no Spring—
     No birth, no death, no time nor sun
     In answer.

                                        (HART CRANE)

     What I can do—I will—
     Though it be little as a daffodil—
     That I cannot—must be
     Unknown to possibility—

                (EMILY DICKINSON)

     We play at Paste—
     Till qualified, for Pearl—
     Then, drop the Paste—
     And deem ourself a fool—

5   The Shapes—though—were similar—
     And our new Hands
     Learned *Gem*-Tactics—
     Practicing *Sands*—

                (EMILY DICKINSON)

     I send Two Sunsets—
     Day and I—in competition ran—
     I finished Two—and several Stars—
     While He—was making One—

5   His own was ampler—but as I
     Was saying to a friend—
     Mine—is the more convenient
     To carry in the hand.

                (EMILY DICKINSON)

It knew no lapse, nor Diminution—
But large—serene—
Burned on—until through Dissolution
It failed from Men—

5   I could not deem these Planetary forces
Annulled—
But suffered an Exchange of Territory—
Or World—

(EMILY DICKINSON)

(3) Sonnets

Sonnet comes from the Italian *sonetto*, meaning "a little sound, a little song." The form too comes from Italian practice, and the version which closely follows the Italian model is known, appropriately, as the Italian sonnet. The two chief versions in English, other than the Italian, are the Shakespearean and the Spenserian, each named for the poet who developed and popularized them early in the sonnet's English history. Virtually all sonnets have fourteen lines, are closely rhymed, are written in lines of five metrical feet, and have internal divisions which I will specify in a moment. Gerard Manley Hopkins developed a "curtal" or shortened sonnet; there is a variant of eighteen lines, sometimes called the "heroic" sonnet; there are free verse sonnets, blank verse sonnets (that is, unrhymed, but having still the traditional five metrical feet in each line), and some poems that are called sonnets but bear no particular relation to the form most poets know and almost all poets, still, have worked with.

(a)— Italian sonnet

Structurally, the Italian sonnet has two parts, the first of eight lines (known as the octave), the second of six lines (known as the sestet). Since Italian is (as English most definitely is not) a rhyme-rich language, the rhyme patterns are very tightly woven. The octave rhymes A B B A A B B A; the sestet rhymes C D E C D E or, at times, C D C D C D. It is a stately form, as well as lyrical; not accidentally, one of the principal proponents of the Italian sonnet is John Milton, arguably the stateliest of all the poets who have ever written in English. Not that Milton invariably wrote in the Italian sonnet form: his sonnet "On

Shakespeare" is in fact written in rhymed couplets rather than in any of the accepted sonnet versions. But it was overwhelmingly his favorite version of the sonnet.

      Cyriack,° this three years day these eyes, though clear
         To outward view of blemish or of spot,
         Bereft of light their seeing have forgot,
         Nor to their idle orbs doth sight appear
5   Of sun or moon or star throughout the year,
         Or man, or woman. Yet I argue not
         Against heav'ns hand or will, nor bate° a jot°
         Of heart or hope; but still bear up and steer
  Right onward. What supports me, dost thou ask?
10   The conscience, Friend, t'have lost them overplied°
         In liberty's defence, my noble task,
  Of which all Europe talks from side to side.
         This thought might lead me through the world's vain masque°
         Content though blind, had I no better guide.

Milton's rhyme scheme is Italian; his structuring of the octave and the sestet is slightly variant, since the octave runs over into the first part of line 9. The internal structuring of the octave and sestet are also slightly variant: in the octave the poet is supposed to develop a main statement, which is answered or resolved in the sestet. Milton develops two statements in the octave, one as to the nature of his blindness, the other his assertion that he does not quarrel with God because of his affliction. The sestet, too, is structurally almost more of a quatrain followed by a couplet: the resolution is complete by the end of line 12, and the final two lines are, though not rhymed as a couplet, more of a moral gloss (of the sort that the Shakespearean sonnet regularly employs).

    Christina Rossetti, not as powerful a poet, manages the Italian sonnet form more gracefully as well as more traditionally:

---

1 **Cyriack** Cyriack Skinner, once a pupil, later a friend of Milton's   7 **bate** abate, reduce; **jot** a little bit   10 **overplied** overused   13 **masque** dramatic performance, with pantomime, music, and sometimes dialogue

In an Artist's Studio

One face looks out from all his canvases,
    One selfsame figure sits or walks or leans:
    We found her hidden just behind those screens,
That mirror gave back all her loveliness.
5 A queen in opal or in ruby dress,
    A nameless girl in freshest summer-greens,
    A saint, an angel—every canvas means
The same one meaning, neither more nor less.
He feeds upon her face by day and night,
10 And she with true kind eyes looks back on him,
Fair as the moon and joyful as the light:
    Not wan with waiting, not with sorrow dim;
Not as she is, but was when hope shone bright;
    Not as she is, but as she fills his dreams.

Gerard Manley Hopkins, like Milton, tended to prefer the Italian form of the sonnet:

God's Grandeur

The world is charged with the grandeur of God,
    It will flame out, like shining from shook foil;
    It gathers to a greatness, like the ooze of oil
Crushed. Why do men then now not reck° his rod?
5 Generations have trod, have trod, have trod;
    And all is seared with trade; bleared, smeared with toil;
    And wears man's smudge and shares man's smell: the soil
Is bare now, nor can foot feel, being shod.

And for all this, nature is never spent;
10 There lives the dearest freshness deep down things;
And though the last lights off the black West went
    Oh, morning, at the brown brink eastward, springs—
Because the Holy Ghost over the bent
    World broods with warm breast and with ah! bright wings.

---

4 **reck** heed

Most poets who use the Italian form do not so clearly separate it from the other sonnet versions, marking the octave and the sestet, as Hopkins has done, with a space between the two. Cummings, who experimented with form in a great many of his poems, almost—but not quite—uses the Italian sonnet in its traditional pattern:

> when thou hast taken thy last applause, and when
> the final curtain strikes the world away,
> leaving to shadowy silence and dismay
> that stage which shall not know thy smile again,
> 5   lingering a little while i see thee then
> ponder the tinsel part they let thee play;
> i see the large lips vivid, the face grey,
> and silent smileless eyes of Magdalen.
> The lights have laughed their last; without, the street
> 10 darkling awaiteth her whose feet have trod
> the silly souls of men to golden dust:
> she pauses on the lintel of defeat,
> her heart breaks in a smile—and she is Lust . . .
>
> mine also, little painted poem of god

(b) Shakespearean sonnet

Both rhyme patterns are different in this version of the sonnet. It has four basic sections, instead of two: three quatrains, each separately rhymed, and a concluding couplet, rhymed separately as well. In short, this version of the sonnet recognizes and exploits the less sweeping, less freely rhyming, but more pithy nature of English as compared to Italian. Shakespeare did not invent the form (probably the Earl of Surrey did), but he certainly perfected it.

> That time of year thou mayst in me behold
> When yellow leaves, or none, or few, do hang
> Upon those boughs which shake against the cold,
> Bare ruined choirs° where late° the sweet birds sang.
> 5 In me thou see'st the twilight of such day
> As after sunset fadeth in the West,

---

4 **choir** part of a church used by singers   **late** lately

Which by-and-by black night doth take away,
Death's second self, that seals up all in rest.
In me thou see'st the glowing of such fire
10 That on the ashes of his youth doth lie,
As the deathbed whereon it must expire,
Consumed with that which it was nourished by.
　　This thou perceivest, which makes thy love more strong,
　　To love that well which thou must leave ere long.

The rhyme pattern here is A B A B C D C D E F E F G G—and as I noted, it is related to more substantive and structural matters than mere sound. In the Shakespearean sonnet the poet is obliged to frame not one statement, as in the octave of the Italian form, but three statements, capping them with a concise, often epigrammatic couplet. The three statements are usually (though not necessarily) clearly separate; in practice, accordingly, they tend to become more of a sequence than, as in the Italian form, simply an extended description. The poet is thus obliged to think more in developmental than in descriptive terms, which is more natural to the quatrain form than it is to the eight-line octave. The separate rhyming pattern of each quatrain, therefore, further aids the poet in thinking developmentally. Further: in order to build the poem toward the final, capping couplet (which structuring is yet another inducement to developmental rather than descriptive thinking), the three quatrains tend to become more dramatic, even challenging. Inevitably, and in good part in response to their different structural natures, the Shakespearean sonnet tends to be bolder, brighter, while the Italian sonnet tends more toward the discursive and meditative.

Bright star, would I were steadfast as thou art—
　　Not in lone splendor hung aloft the night
And watching, with eternal lids apart,
　　Like nature's patient, sleepless Eremite,°
5 The moving waters at their priestlike task
　　Of pure ablution° round earth's human shores,
Or gazing on the new soft fallen mask
　　Of snow upon the mountains and the moors—

---

4 **Eremite** hermit   6 **ablution** a cleansing with water, a ceremonial purification

No—yet still steadfast, still unchangeable,
10 Pillowed upon my fair love's ripening breast,
To feel forever its soft fall and swell,
  Awake forever in a sweet unrest,
Still, still to hear her tender-taken breath,
And so live ever—or else swoon to death.

           (JOHN KEATS)

Keats tended to prefer the Italian sonnet, but he did at times use the Shakespearean form. Here there is some blurring of the inner struc-ture: the first two quatrains, though rhymed in the Shakespearean form, tend more toward the octave's descriptive approach. But begin-ning with line 9, the Shakespearean form reasserts itself—and the con-cluding couplet would be impossible in anything but this form, or the Spenserian modification of it.

 For perfect Shakespearean sonnets, we need to return to the source itself:

Let me not to the marriage of true minds
Admit impediments. Love is not love
Which alters when it alteration finds,
Or bends with the remover to remove.
5 Oh, no! it is an ever-fixèd mark,
That looks on tempests and is never shaken;
It is the star to every wandering bark,°
Whose worth's unknown, although his height be taken.
Love's not Time's fool, though rosy lips and cheeks
10 Within his bending sickle's compass come;
Love alters not with his brief hours and weeks,
But bears it out even to the edge of doom.
If this be error and upon me proved,
I never writ, nor no man ever loved.

         (WILLIAM SHAKESPEARE)

---

7 **bark** small sailing vessel

My mistress' eyes are nothing like the sun;
Coral is far more red than her lips' red;
If snow be white, why then her breasts are dun;°
If hairs be wires, black wires grow on her head.
5   I have seen roses damasked,° red and white,
But no such roses see I in her cheeks;
And in some perfumes is there more delight
Than in the breath that from my mistress reeks.
I love to hear her speak, yet well I know
10   That music hath a far more pleasing sound;
I grant I never saw a goddess go;
My mistress, when she walks, treads on the ground.
And yet, by heaven, I think my love as rare
As any she belied° with false compare.

(WILLIAM SHAKESPEARE)

When to the sessions of sweet silent thought
I summon up remembrance of things past,
I sigh the lack of many a thing I sought,
And with old woes new wail my dear time's waste:
5   Then can I drown an eye, unused to flow,
For precious friends hid in death's dateless night,
And weep afresh love's long since cancelled woe,
And moan the expense° of many a vanished sight:
Then can I grieve at grievances foregone,
10   And heavily from woe to woe tell o'er
The sad account of fore-bemoanèd moan,
Which I new pay as if not paid before.
But if the while I think on thee, dear friend,
All losses are restored and sorrows end.

(WILLIAM SHAKESPEARE)

---

3 **dun** dull grayish-brown   5 **damasked** woven or adorned in elaborate designs   14
belied misrepresented   8 **expense** loss, sacrifice

(c) Spenserian sonnet

Least popular of the three major sonnet forms, the Spenserian sonnet is in effect a compromise between the other two, the Italian and the Shakespearean. It has three quatrains and a concluding couplet, like the Shakespearean form, but instead of being separated, from quatrain to quatrain, the rhymes are interlinked, more as are the rhymes in the Italian form. The rhyme pattern is A B A B B C B C C D C D E E. Strictly speaking, it is not so much a form in its own right as it is an Italian-oriented variation on the Shakespearean form. It needs no more comment than that, and requires no more than a single illustration, drawn of course from Spenser's sonnet sequence *Amoretti*:

My love is like to ice, and I to fire:
    How comes it then that this her cold so great
    Is not dissolved through my so hot desire,
    But harder grows the more I her entreat?
5 Or how comes it that my exceeding heat
    Is not delayed by her heart, frozen cold—
    But that I burn much more in boiling sweat,
    And feel my flames augmented manifold?
What more miraculous thing may be told
10   That fire which all things melts, should harden ice.
    And ice, which is congealed with senseless cold,
    Should kindle fire by wonderful device?
Such is the power of love in gentle° mind,
    That it can alter all the course of kind.°

(4) Songs (Lyrics)

"Song" originally referred to a poem intended to be sung, often by the poet himself and often with musical accompaniment. By a gradual process of change it has come to mean no more than a poem which is particularly lyric, or songlike. Structurally, it has very nearly infinite variants: it can be identified, more often than not, by the comparatively short length of its lines, and by the overriding musicality of its expression.

---

13 **gentle** noble, courteous, polite   14 **kind** nature

Under the greenwood tree
Who loves to lie with me,
And turn° his merry note
Unto the sweet bird's throat,
5   Come hither, come hither, come hither!
Here shall he see
No enemy
But winter and rough weather.

(WILLIAM SHAKESPEARE, *As You Like It*)

This was, of course, a song meant to be sung: it comes by its musicality honestly. We can notice, also, close and sometimes intricate rhyming, variant length of lines within the same poem, and a general indifference to portentous thoughts or any manner of philosophizing. Ben Jonson uses a different formal structure, but much the same basic approach:

Song: To Celia

Drink to me only with thine eyes,
And I will pledge with mine;
Or leave a kiss but in the cup,
And I'll not look for wine.
5   The thirst that from the soul doth rise
Doth ask a drink divine:
But might I of Jove's nectar sup,
I would not change for thine.

I sent thee late a rosy wreath,
10   Not so much honoring thee,
As giving it a hope, that there
It could not withered be.
But thou thereon did'st only breathe,
And sent'st it back to me;
15   Since when it grows and smells, I swear,
Not of itself, but thee.

---

3 **turn** return

Richard Lovelace resorts to quatrains, rather than to either of the external shapes thus far exhibited. But his poem too displays the same basic characteristics:

To Lucasta, Going to the Wars

Tell me not, sweet, I am unkind
That from the nunnery
Of thy chaste breast and quiet mind,
To war and arms I fly.

5   True, a new mistress now I chase,
The first foe in the field;
And with a stronger faith embrace
A sword, a horse, a shield.

Yet this inconstancy is such
10 As you too shall adore;
I could not love thee, dear, so much,
Loved I not honor more.

By the latter part of the eighteenth century the song, though distinctly a literary form and no longer intended to be sung, still retained many of the same characteristics visible in the true songs of Shakespeare:

Piping down the valleys wild
Piping songs of pleasant glee
On a cloud I saw a child,
And he laughing said to me,

5   "Pipe a song about a Lamb";
So I piped with merry cheer.
"Piper pipe that song again"—
So I piped, he wept to hear.

"Drop thy pipe thy happy pipe
10 Sing thy songs of happy cheer";
So I sung the same again
While he wept with joy to hear.

"Piper sit thee down and write
In a book that all may read"—
15 So he vanished from my sight.
And I plucked a hollow reed,

And I made a rural pen,
And I stained the water clear,
And I wrote my happy songs
20 Every child may joy to hear.

(WILLIAM BLAKE)

By the nineteenth century, however, much of the musicality had been, as it were, subdued by the combination of literate expression and the weight of years of written songs:

Rose Aylmer

Ah what avails the sceptered race,
    Ah what the form divine!
What every virtue, every grace!
    Rose Aylmer, all were thine.
5 Rose Aylmer, whom these wakeful eyes
    May weep but never see,
A night of memories and of sighs
    I consecrate to thee.

(WALTER SAVAGE LANDOR)

Songs still sang, but according to the new standard:

Music, when soft voices die,
Vibrates in the memory—
Odors, when sweet violets sicken,
Live within the sense they quicken.
5 Rose leaves, when the rose is dead,
Are heaped for the beloved's bed;
And so thy thoughts, when thou art gone,
Love itself shall slumber on.

(PERCY BYSSHE SHELLEY)

And even before the middle of the nineteenth century, a poem expressly entitled "Song," and by a poet as renowned for the musicality of his verse as Tennyson, has plainly become totally a written form:

Song

A spirit haunts the year's last hours
Dwelling amidst these yellowing bowers.
    To himself he talks;
For at eventide, listening earnestly,
5 At his work you may hear him sob and sigh
    In the walks;
    Earthward he boweth the heavy stalks
Of the moldering flowers,
    Heavily hangs the broad sunflower
10   Over its grave i' the earth so chilly;
    Heavily hangs the hollyhock,
      Heavily hangs the tiger-lily.

The air is damp, and hushed, and close,
As a sick man's room when he taketh repose
15   An hour before death;
My very heart faints and my whole soul grieves
At the moist rich smell of the rotting leaves,
    And the breath
Of the fading edges of box° beneath,
20 And the year's last rose.
    Heavily hangs the broad sunflower
      Over its grave i' the earth so chilly;
    Heavily hangs the hollyhock,
      Heavily hangs the tiger-lily.

Not even the refrain can make this singable. The song has become, willy-nilly, the lyric—and though we still use the word, "song" plainly means something utterly different. Here, for example, is a "song" by a fine and clearly lyric twentieth-century poet:

---

19 **box** hedge

Morning Song

Look, it's morning, and a little water gurgles in the tap.
I wake up waiting, because it's Sunday, and turn twice more
than usual in bed, before I rise to cereal and comic strips.
I have risen to the morning danger and feel proud,
5   and after shaving off the night's disguises, after searching
close to the bone for blood, and finding only a little,
I shall walk out bravely into the daily accident.

(ALAN DUGAN)

A poet younger still ought to make the point beyond dispute:

Nurse's Song

As though I'm fooled. That lacy body managed to forget
That I have eyes, ears; dares to spring her boyfriends on the child.
This afternoon she told me, "Dress the baby in his crochet
Dress," and smiled. Just that. Just smiled,
5   Going. She is never here. O innocence, your bathinet
Is clogged with gossip, she's a sinking ship,
Your mother. Wouldn't spoil her breasts.
I hear your deaf-numb papa fussing for his tea. Sleep, sleep,
My angel, nestled with your orange bear.
10 Scream when her lover pats your hair.

(LOUISE GLÜCK)

This too is a splendid poem, by a splendid poet—but how far we have
come, in the matter of song, from "Under the greenwood tree"! The
gain is equal to the loss, on the whole: my point is simply that a vast sea
change has occurred, and readers, like other voyagers, ought to be
aware of the particular ground under their feet.

(5) Dialogues; Monologues

Poetry has always made use of dialogue—not quite such extensive
use, of course, as fictive prose has made, but significant use nonethe-

less. And poems have for many years been written entirely in dialogue form. In medieval times, especially, the question-and-answer dialogue poem was regularly employed by schoolteachers, to help teach grammar, and by religious teachers, to help impart doctrinal knowledge. Medieval poets wrote in the dialogue form just as frequently, the two speakers being most often the soul and the body, debating their relative positions and merits. But the Virgin Mary and Joseph, or Mary and her son Jesus, or a questioner on earth and an answerer in heaven were also the speakers in such poems.

Though the poem in dialogue is a recognized genre, however, it is not a separate form: the interior shape of the poem, its logic and its movement, and usually its tone are governed by the fact of its being written in dialogue, but its external shape can be anything the poet chooses to make it. There are no applicable rules or conventions.

East London

'Twas August, and the fierce sun overhead
Smote on the squalid streets of Bethnal Green,°
And the pale weaver, through his windows seen
In Spitalfields,° looked thrice dispirited.

5 I met a preacher there I knew, and said:
"Ill and o'erworked, how fare you in this scene?"—
"Bravely!" said he; "for I of late have been
Much cheered with thoughts of Christ, *the living bread.*"

O human soul! as long as thou canst so
10 Set up a mark of everlasting light,
Above the howling senses' ebb and flow,

To cheer thee, and to right thee if thou roam—
Not with lost toil thou laborest through the night!
Thou mak'st the heaven thou hop'st indeed thy home.

(MATTHEW ARNOLD)

---

2 **Bethnal Green** industrial area in Northeast London   4 **Spitalfields** London area settled by French weavers

This is neither great poetry nor exclusively a dialogue poem. I set it out because it is a sonnet, and that fact shows as well as any comment could the absence of rules or conventions as to the external shape of dialogue poetry. Other poets, using other forms, have of course done rather better:

> Cupid as he lay among
> Roses, by a bee was stung.
> Whereupon in anger flying
> To his mother, said thus crying:
> 5 "Help! O help! your boy's a-dying!"
> "And why, my pretty lad," said she?
> Then blubbering, replied he,
> "A wingèd snake has bitten me,
> Which country people call a bee."
> 10 At which she smiled; then with her hairs
> And kisses drying up his tears:
> "Alas!" said she, "my wag! if this
> Such a pernicious torment is:
> Come, tell me then, how great's the smart
> 15 Of those thou woundest with thy dart!"

(ROBERT HERRICK)

The Bird

> What did you say to me
>   that I had not heard.
> She said she saw
>   a small bird.
>
> 5 Where was it.
>   In a tree.
> Ah, he said, I thought
>   you spoke to me.

(ROBERT CREELEY)

Expostulation and Reply

"Why, William on that old gray stone,
Thus for the length of half a day,
Why, William, sit you thus alone,
And dream your time away?

5   "Where are your books?—that light bequeathed
To beings else forlorn and blind!
Up! up! and drink the spirit breathed
From dead men to their kind.°

"You look round on your Mother Earth
10   As if she for no purpose bore you;
As if you were her first-born birth,
And none had lived before you!"

One morning thus, by Esthwaite lake,
When life was sweet, I knew not why,
15   To me my good friend Matthew spake,
And thus I made reply:

"The eye—it cannot choose but see;
We cannot bid the ear be still;
Our bodies feel, where'er they be,
20   Against or with our will.

"Nor less I deem that there are Powers
Which of themselves our minds impress;°
That we can feed this mind of ours
In a wise passiveness.

25   "Think you, 'mid all this mighty sum
Of things forever speaking,
That nothing of itself will come,
But we must still be seeking?

"—Then ask not wherefore, here, alone,
30   Conversing as I may,
I sit upon this old gray stone,
And dream my time away."

(WILLIAM WORDSWORTH)

---

8 **kind** own species   22 **impress** influence

The Attempted Rescue

I came out on the wrong
side of time and saw
the rescue party leave.
"How long must we wait?"
5   I said. "Forever. You
are too far gone to save,
too dangerous to carry off
the precipice, and frozen stiff
besides. So long. You
10 can have our brandy. That's life."

(ALAN DUGAN)

The Telephone

"When I was just as far as I could walk
From here today,
There was an hour
All still
5   When leaning with my head against a flower
I heard you talk.
Don't say I didn't, for I heard you say—
You spoke from that flower on the window sill—
Do you remember what it was you said?"

10 "First tell me what it was you thought you heard."

"Having found the flower and driven a bee away,
I leaned my head,
And holding by the stalk,
I listened and I thought I caught the word—
15 What was it? Did you call me by my name?
Or did you say—
Someone said 'Come'—I heard it as I bowed."

"I may have thought as much, but not aloud."

"Well, so I came."

(ROBERT FROST)

And she said:
> "You remember Mr. Lowell,
"He was your ambassador here?"
And I said: "That was before I arrived."
5 And she said:
> "He stomped into my bedroom. . . .
(By that time she had got on to Browning.)
". . . stomped into my bedroom. . . .
"And said: 'Do I,
10 "'I ask you, Do I
"'Care too much for society dinners?'
"And I wouldn't say that he didn't.
"Shelley used to live in this house."

She was a very old lady,
15 I never saw her again.

(EZRA POUND)

The monologue differs basically from the dialogue only in the number of speakers—one in the monologue, two (or more) in the dialogue. But there is another difference, subtle but frequently obvious. As the voice of a single person, and having no give-and-take between two (or more) characters, the monologue tends toward a greater degree of inwardness. We hear not only the voice but also the inner thoughts of the persona. One of the greatest practitioners of the genre (indeed, of both genres) was Robert Browning:

Soliloquy of the Spanish Cloister

1.
Gr-r-r—there go, my heart's abhorrence!
> Water your damned flower-pots, do!
If hate killed men, Brother Lawrence,
> God's blood, would not mine kill you!
5 What? your myrtle-bush wants trimming?
> Oh, that rose has prior claims—
Needs its leaden vase filled brimming?
> Hell dry you up with its flames!

2.

At the meal we sit together:
10   *Salve tibi!*° I must hear
Wise talk of the kind of weather,
      Sort of season, time of year:
Not a plenteous cork-crop: scarcely
      Dare we hope oak-galls, I doubt:
15 *What's the Latin name for 'parsley'?*
      What's the Greek name for Swine's Snout?

3.

Whew! We'll have our platter burnished,
      Laid with care on our own shelf!
With a fire-new spoon we're furnished,
20   And a goblet for ourself,
Rinsed like something sacrificial
      Ere 'tis fit to touch our chaps—
Marked with L. for our initial!
      (He-he! There his lily snaps!)

4.

25 *Saint*, forsooth! While brown Dolores
      Squats outside the Convent bank
With Sanchicha, telling stories,
      Steeping tresses in the tank,
Blue-black, lustrous, thick like horsehairs,
30   —Can't I see his dead eye glow,
Bright as 'twere a Barbary corsair's?
      (That is, if he'd let it show!)

5.

When he finishes refection,°
      Knife and fork he never lays
35 Cross-wise, to my recollection,
      As do I, in Jesu's praise.
I the Trinity illustrate,
      Drinking watered orange-pulp—

---

10 **salve tibi** Greetings to you! (Latin)   33 **refection** a meal.

In three sips the Arian° frustrate;
40   While he drains his at one gulp.

6.

Oh, those melons? If he's able
    We're to have a feast! so nice!
One goes to the Abbot's table,
    All of us each get a slice.
45 How go on your flowers? None double?
    Not one fruit-sort can you spy?
Strange! And I, too, at such trouble,
    Keep them close-nipped on the sly!

7.

There's a great text in Galatians,
50   Once you trip on it, entails
Twenty-nine distinct damnations,
    One's sure, if another fails:
If I trip him just a-dying,
    Sure of heaven as sure can be,
55 Spin him around and send him flying
    Off to hell, a Manichee?°

8.

Or, my scrofulous French novel
    On grey paper with blunt type!
Simply glance at it, you grovel
60   Hand and foot in Belial's gripe:°
If I double down its pages
    At the woeful sixteenth print,
When he gathers his greengages,
    Ope a sieve and slip it in't?

9.

65 Or, there's Satan! one might venture
    Pledge one's soul to him, yet leave
Such a flaw in the indenture°
    As he'd miss till, past reprieve,

---

39 **Arian** heretic who denied the doctrine of the Holy Trinity   56 **Manichee** believer in the Manichean heresy   60 **Belial's gripe** the devil's grip   67 **indenture** contract

Blasted lay that rose-acacia
70   We're so proud of! *Hy, Zy, Hine . . .*
    'St, there's vespers! *Plena gratia*
        Ave, Virgo! Gr-r-r—you swine!

The inwardness of the monologue makes it extremely attractive to contemporary poets, both those who speak in a voice resembling their own and those who reconstruct some historical voice:

The Gift

Lord, You may not recognize me
speaking for someone else.
I have a son. He is
so little, so ignorant.
5   He likes to stand
at the screen door, calling
oggie, oggie, entering
language, and sometimes
a dog will stop and come up
10 the walk, perhaps
accidentally. May he believe
this is not an accident?
At the screen
welcoming each beast
15 in love's name, Your emissary.

(LOUISE GLÜCK)

Teddy Roosevelt

stumping again it hurts by god
have travelled all around the tattooed
lady my country looking for the right
spot to raise the banner of straw some
5   watertower some windmill though my big head
aches and i miss the wax works greatly
clouds hang above old toads strange poppies
acetylene evenings seven fireflies solitude

blue pastures where a bull paws up cool soil
10 dragging my bad leg through the spirit village
seized by the women covered with sycamore leaves
as if i was the corn dog the potato man
no one knows me understands my language
the pulse of the tattooed lady is bad
15 i fear for her life i fear for her death
i would give her both if i could but i sit
here on the porch of this rainsmoke penthouse
while the music rises like mosquito smudge
through which a red sun comes rolling rolling

(DAVID YOUNG)

(6) Other Traditional Forms

I shall briefly define each form here included, and give one (and in a few instances two) examples.

(a) ballade

A four-part form, twenty-eight lines in all, composed of three octaves and a final quatrain (i.e., half an octave) known as the *envoi*. The lines can be four metrical feet in length, or five. The rhyme scheme for the octave is A B A B B C B C, the eighth and final line of the octave being repeated as a refrain in each of the octaves. The rhyme scheme for the *envoi* is less restrictive, but is usually B C B C, the last line being once again the refrain employed in the three octaves. In the strict ballade form (that is, in the original French) there are only three rhymes used throughout; the English ballade necessarily relies on greater freedom in its rhyming pattern.

The ballade of dead ladies

Tell me now in what hidden way is
    Lady Flora the lovely Roman?
Where's Hipparchia, and where is Thais,
    Neither of them the fairer woman?
5   Where is Echo, beheld of no man,

Only heard on river and mere,°—
    She whose beauty was more than human? . . .
But where are the snows of yester-year?

Where's Héloise, the learned nun,
10   For whose sake Abelard, I ween,
Lost manhood and put priesthood on?
    (From Love he won such dule° and teen!°)
    And where, I pray you, is the Queen
Who willed that Buridan should steer
15   Sewed in a sack's mouth down the Seine? . . .
But where are the snows of yester-year?

White Queen Blanche, like a queen of lilies,
    With a voice like any mermaiden—
Bertha Broadfoot, Beatrice, Alice,
20   And Ermengarde the lady of Maine,—
    And that good Joan whom Englishmen
At Rouen doomed and burned her there,—
    Mother of God, where are they then? . . .
But where are the snows of yester-year?

25 Nay, never ask this week, fair lord,
    Where they are gone, nor yet this year,
Except with this for an overword,—
    But where are the snows of yester-year?

(Dante Gabriel Rossetti, translated from the French of FRANÇOIS VILLON)

(b) limerick

A five-line form written in anapestic feet (see Chapter 6 for details), the first, second, and fifth lines being three metrical feet in length, the third and fourth lines being two metrical feet. The rhyme scheme is A A B B A. Virtually all limericks are humorous; many are bawdy.

There once was a man named Bright,
Who exceeded the speed of light,

---

6 **mere** lake   12 **dule** grief, sorrow; **teen** harm, injury

He'd go on his way
At the first light of day
And return on the previous night.

There was a young belle of Old Natchez,
Whose garments were always in patchez,
When comment arose
On the state of her clothes,
She drawled, When Ah itchez, Ah scratchez!

(OGDEN NASH)

(c) rhyme royal

A seven-line stanza, the lines being of five metrical feet, and the rhyme scheme being A B A B B C C. It tends to be used in narrative poems of some length, though it can be found in shorter poems as well.

On the Morning of Christ's Nativity: Introduction°

This is the month, and this the happy morn
Wherein the Son of Heav'ns eternal King,
Of wedded maid, and Virgin Mother born,
Our great redemption from above did bring;
5   For so the holy sages once did sing,
     That he our deadly forfeit should release,
And with his Father work us a perpetual peace.

That glorious form, that light unsufferable,
And that far-beaming blaze of majesty,
10 Wherewith he wont° at Heav'ns high council-table,
To sit the midst of Trinal unity,
He laid aside, and here with us to be,
     Forsook the courts of everlasting day,
And chose with us a darksome house of mortal clay.

15 Say Heav'nly Muse, shall not thy sacred vein°
Afford a present to the Infant God?

Introduction the rest of the poem, a hymn, is in a different form   10 **wont** was accustomed 15 **vein** writing

Hast thou no verse, no hymn, or solemn strain,
To welcome him to this his new abode,
Now while the Heav'n by the sun's team untrod,
20   Hath took no print of the approaching light,
And all the spangled host keep watch in squadrons bright?

See how from far upon the eastern road
The Star-led wizards haste with odors sweet:
O run, prevent° them with thy humble ode,
25 And lay it lowly at his blessed feet;
Have thou the honor first, thy Lord to greet,
     And join thy voice unto the Angel choir,
From out his secret altar touched with hallow'd fire.

(JOHN MILTON)

Note that in the seventh line of each stanza, here, Milton has length-
ened the line to six metrical feet.

(d) rondeau

There are two varieties, a longer rondeau of fifteen lines, divided
into three stanzas of five, four, and six lines, and a shorter rondeau of
twelve lines, divided into two stanzas of six lines each. In both varieties
there is, in the French practice, a rhyme scheme built of only two
rhymes; the English versions naturally employ a less restrictive rhyme
pattern. Also in both varieties there is a refrain; in the shorter form,
here illustrated, the refrain occurs at the end of each stanza. Further,
the refrain is made of the first word or words of the first line of the
poem. Line length is not restricted.

Kissing her hair I sat against her feet,
Wove and unwove it, wound and found it sweet,
Made fast therewith her hands, drew down her eyes,
Deep as deep flowers and dreamy like dim skies;
5 With her own tresses bound and found her fair,
     Kissing her hair.

---

24 **prevent** anticipate

Sleep were no sweeter than her face to me,
Sleep of cold sea-bloom under the cold sea;
What pain could get between my face and hers?
10   What new sweet thing would not relish worse?
Unless, perhaps, white death had kissed me there,
                    Kissing her hair?

(ALGERNON CHARLES SWINBURNE)

(e) sestina

A thirty-nine-line form, which takes its name from the fact that its structure is founded in a six-line stanza which is used six times, and ended with a triplet (or half sestet). In the French practice there is no rhyme; instead, there is a predetermined pattern according to which the words that end each line in the first stanza are also used as end words in each succeeding stanza, but in different line positions. That French practice is not strictly followed in the illustration. Considering, however, that the poet has undertaken to rhyme as well as to reemploy the end words of stanza one, the variation can be both forgiven and understood. Note that the intent of the repetition of end words is carefully preserved, no end word occurring twice in the same position in any of the stanzas. Line length is not restricted.

Sestina

I saw my soul at rest upon a day
        As the bird sleeping in the nest of night,
Among soft leaves that give the starlight way
        To touch its wings but not its leaves with light;
5   So that it knew as one in visions may,
        And knew not as men waking, of delight.

This was the measure of my soul's delight;
        It had no power of joy to fly by day,
Nor part in the large lordship of the light;
10   But in a secret moon-beholden way
Had all its will of dreams and pleasant night,
        And all the love and life that sleepers may.

But such life's triumph as men waking may
    It might not have to feed its faint delight
15 Between the stars by night and sun by day,
    Shut up with green leaves and a little light,
Because its way was as a lost star's way.
    A world's not wholly known of day or night.

All loves and dreams and sounds and gleams of night
20   Made it all music that such minstrels may,
And all they had they gave it of delight;
    But in the full face of the fire of day
What place shall be for any starry light,
    What part of heaven in all the wide sun's way?

25 Yet the soul woke not, sleeping by the way,
    Watched as a nursling of the large-eyed night,
And sought no strength nor knowledge of the day,
    Nor closer touch conclusive of delight,
Nor mightier joy nor truer than dreamers may,
30   Nor more of song than they, nor more of light.

For who sleeps once and sees the secret light
    Whereby sleep shows the soul a fairer way
Between the rise and rest of day and night,
    Shall care no more to fare as all men may,
35 But he is place of pain or of delight,
    There shall he dwell, beholding night as day.

Song, have thy day and take thy fill of light
    Before the night be fallen across thy way;
Sing while he may, man hath no long delight.

(ALGERNON CHARLES SWINBURNE)

Note that the triplet, too, employs the six end words of stanza one, using three of them as end words, three of them at any point inside each of its three lines. (Some poets like to call the triplet an *envoi*; I prefer myself to reserve that term for the ballade form.)

(f) spenserian

A nine-line form, eight lines being of five metrical feet, the last line being of six metrical feet. Although in subsequent usage the rhyme scheme is not restricted, Edmund Spenser, for whom the form is named, rhymed it A B A B B C B C C. Preeminently a stanza for poems of great length (Spenser employed it in his *The Fairy Queen*, an immense allegory which he did not live to finish), it is hard to illustrate properly except in excerpts. What follows, accordingly, is one half of Alexander Pope's delicious "imitation" of Spenser:

The Alley

In ev'ry town, where Thamis rolls his tide,
A narrow pass there is, with houses low;
Where ever and anon, the stream is eyed,
And many a boat soft sliding to and fro.
5 There oft are heard the notes of infant woe,
The short thick sob, loud scream, and shriller squawl:
How can ye, mothers, vex your children so?
Some play, some eat, some cack° against the wall,
And as they crouchen low, for bread and butter call.

10 And on the broken pavement here and there,
Doth many a stinking sprat° and herring lie;
A brandy and tobacco shop is near,
And hens, and dogs, and hogs are feeding by:
And here a sailor's jacket hangs to dry:
15 At ev'ry door are sun-burnt matrons seen,
Mending old nets to catch the scaly fry;
Now singing shrill, and scolding eft° between,
Scolds answer foul-mouthed scolds; bad neighborhood I ween.

The snappish cur (the passengers° annoy)
20 Close at my heel with yelping treble flies;
The whimp'ring girl, and hoarser-screaming boy,
Join to the yelping treble shrilling cries;

---

8 **cack** defecate   11 **sprat** small herringlike fish   17 **eft** afterward, again   19 **passengers** passersby

The scolding queen to louder notes doth rise,
And her full pipes those shrilling cries confound:
25　To her full pipes the grunting hog replies;
The grunting hogs alarm the neighbors round,
And curs, girls, boys, and scolds, in the deep bass are drowned.

(g) terza rima

A linking form, written in any number of three-line stanzas. The rhyme scheme runs A B A B C B C D C, and so on: the nonrhyming line is always the middle line of each stanza, and it determines the rhyme to be observed in the first and third lines of the next stanza, ad infinitum. In Italian, a language extremely rich in rhymes, it is a relatively simple form to follow. Dante's three-book epic *The Divine Comedy* is composed entirely in terza rima. In English it is exceedingly difficult—and virtually the only successful poem written in this form, in English, is Shelley's "Ode to the West Wind." Yet note how Shelley bends the form into something closely approximating a kind of sonnet. He has four three-line stanzas, rhymed as in the Italian, but ends each section of the poem with a rhymed couplet. The lines are each five metrical feet.

1.

O wild West Wind, thou breath of Autumn's being,
Thou, from whose unseen presence the leaves dead
Are driven, like ghosts from an enchanter fleeing,

Yellow, and black, and pale, and hectic red,
5　Pestilence-stricken multitudes: O thou,
Who chariotest to their dark wintry bed

The wingèd seeds, where they lie cold and low,
Each like a corpse within its grave, until
Thine azure sister of the Spring shall blow

10　Her clarion° o'er the dreaming earth, and fill
(Driving sweet buds like flocks to feed in air)
With living hues and odors plain and hill:

---

10 **clarion** trumpet

Wild Spirit, which art moving everywhere:
Destroyer and preserver; hear, oh, hear!

2.

15 Thou on whose stream, mid the steep sky's commotion,
Loose clouds like earth's decaying leaves are shed,
Shook from the tangled boughs of Heaven and Ocean,

Angels of rain and lightning: there are spread
On the blue surface of thine aëry surge,
20 Like the bright hair uplifted from the head

Of some fierce Maenad,° even from the dim verge
Of the horizon to the zenith's height,
The locks of the approaching storm. Thou dirge

Of the dying year, to which this closing night
25 Will be the dome of a vast sepulcher,
Vaulted with all thy congregated might

Of vapors, from whose solid atmosphere
Black rain, and fire, and hail will burst: oh, hear!

3.

Thou who didst waken from his summer dreams
30 The blue Mediterranean, where he lay,
Lulled by the coil of his crystalline streams,

Beside a pumice isle in Baiae's Bay,°
And saw in sleep old palaces and towers
Quivering within the wave's intenser day,

35 All overgrown with azure moss and flowers
So sweet, the sense faints picturing them! Thou
For whose path the Atlantic's level powers

Cleave themselves into chasms, while far below
The sea-blooms and the oozy woods which wear
40 The sapless foliage of the ocean, know

---

21 **Maenad** a frenzied, raging woman, attendant to the god Bacchus   32 **Baiae's Bay** near Naples

Thy voice, and suddenly grow gray with fear,
And tremble and despoil themselves: oh, hear!

4.

If I were a dead leaf thou mightest bear;
If I were a swift cloud to fly with thee;
45 A wave to pant beneath thy power, and share

The impulse of thy strength, only less free
Than thou, O uncontrollable! If even
I were as in my boyhood, and could be

The comrade of thy wanderings over Heaven,
50 As then, when to outstrip thy skyey speed
Scarce seem a vision; I would ne'er have striven

As thus with thee in prayer in my sore need.
Oh, lift me as a wave, a leaf, a cloud!
I fall upon the thorns of life! I bleed!

55 A heavy weight of hours has chained and bowed
One too like thee: tameless, and swift, and proud.

5.

Make me thy lyre, even as the forest is:
What if my leaves are falling like its own!
The tumult of thy mighty harmonies

60 Will take from both a deep, autumnal tone,
Sweet though in sadness. Be thou, Spirit fierce,
My spirit! Be thou me, impetuous one!

Drive my dead thoughts over the universe
Like withered leaves to quicken a new birth!
65 And, by the incantation of this verse,

Scatter, as from an unextinguished hearth
Ashes and sparks, my words among mankind!
Be through my lips to unawakened earth

The trumpet of a prophecy! O Wind,
70 If Winter comes, can Spring be far behind?

(h) triolet

An eight-line form, all in one stanza (an octave), and using only two rhymes throughout, in the pattern A B A A A B A B. There are two refrains. The first is the first line, which is repeated, verbatim, as line 4 and then again as line 7. The second refrain is line 2, which is repeated as line 8. Line length is unrestricted.

"The Child Is Father to the Man" (Wordsworth)

"The child is father to the man."
How can he be? The words are wild.
Suck any sense from that who can:
"The child is father to the man."
5   No; what the poet did write ran,
"The man is father to the child."
"The child is father to the man."
How *can* he be? The words are wild.

(GERARD MANLEY HOPKINS)

(i) villanelle

A nineteen-line form, divided into five stanzas of three lines each (triplets) and a concluding quatrain. In the French practice—followed in the first of the two illustrations here but not followed in the second—there are only two rhymes throughout. The rhyme scheme is A B A in the triplets, A B A A in the quatrain. Also in the French practice, there are two refrains. The first is the first line of the poem, which is repeated as lines 6, 12, and 18. The second refrain is line 3, which is repeated as lines 9, 15, and 19. Again, the first illustration follows the French practice exactly; the second follows it, but with some variations in wording. Line length is unrestricted.

Do not go gentle into that good night,
Old age should burn and rave at close of day;
Rage, rage against the dying of the light.

Though wise men at their end know dark is right,
5   Because their words have forked no lightning they
Do not go gentle into that good night.

Good men, the last wave by, crying how bright
Their frail deeds might have danced in a green bay,
Rage, rage against the dying of the light.

10 Wild men who caught and sang the sun in flight,
And learn, too late, they grieved it on its way,
Do not go gentle into that good night.

Grave men, near death, who see with blinding sight
Blind eyes could blaze like meteors and be gay,
15 Rage, rage against the dying of the light.

And you, my father, there on the sad height,
Curse, bless, me now with your fierce tears, I pray.
Do not go gentle into that good night.
Rage, rage against the dying of the light.

(DYLAN THOMAS)

The Waking

I wake to sleep, and take my waking slow.
I feel my fate in what I cannot fear.
I learn by going where I have to go.

We think by feeling. What is there to know?
5 I hear my being dance from ear to ear.
I wake to sleep, and take my waking slow.

Of those so close beside me, which are you?
God bless the Ground! I shall walk softly there,
And learn by going where I have to go.

10 Light takes the Tree; but who can tell us how?
The lowly worm climbs up a winding stair;
I wake to sleep, and take my waking slow.

Great Nature has another thing to do
To you and me; so take the lively air,
15 And, lovely, learn by going where to go.

This shaking keeps me steady. I should know.
What falls away is always. And is near.

I wake to sleep, and take my waking slow.
I learn by going where I have to go.

(THEODORE ROETHKE)

(7) Free Forms

Like They Say

Underneath the tree on some
soft grass I sat, I

watched two happy
woodpeckers be dis-

5   turbed by my presence. And
why not, I thought to

myself, why
not.

(ROBERT CREELEY)

This is a poem in eight lines. From a formal perspective that is the most definite statement, at least of any large significance, that can be made about its shape and structure. It breaks every even-numbered line, but not according to any established or conventional principle: these are definitely not what, earlier, I called couplets. There is no rhyme, no refrain—in short, there is nothing traditional about this as a form. That does *not* mean the poem is formless: it is not. Rather, it means that the form has been developed in good part to meet the demands of the subject, the treatment, the tone, and the other imperatives that are important to the poet. There are rhythmical structures, for example, for the poem carefully winds down into lines with fewer stresses. And there are in fact more subtle structures, ways in which sense and sound, shape and movement, come together, work together. This is frequently called organic form—that is, form which arises out of and helps dictate substance, form which is, if you will, natural rather than artificial. There are gains and there are losses: the net result, it must be emphasized, is a fine poem, light, compelling, perceptive. This is the farthest thing from anarchy.

William Carlos Williams, indeed, developed the free form into something very like a new form of its own. As in the following example, Williams came to favor a subpattern of three lines broken across the page, each indented more sharply than the other; he wove his poems out of such three-line units.

The Artist

Mr. T.
    bareheaded
        in a soiled undershirt
his hair standing out
5   on all sides
        stood on his toes
heels together
    arms gracefully
        for the moment
10 curled above his head.
    Then he whirled about
        bounded
into the air
    and with an *entrechat*
15   perfectly achieved
completed the figure.
    My mother
        taken by surprise
where she sat
20   in her invalid's chair
        was left speechless.
Bravo! she cried at last
    and clapped her hands.
        The man's wife
25 came from the kitchen:
    What goes on here? she said
        But the show was over.

Extendable to virtually any length, a poem built on such three-line units is also readily compressible into still more compact forms, as in the following "Poem," again by William Carlos Williams:

> As the cat
> climbed over
> the top of
>
> the jamcloset
> 5 first the right
> forefoot
>
> carefully
> then the hind
> stepped down
>
> 10 into the pit of
> the empty
> flowerpot.

Poets develop all sorts of formal variations: so-called "freedom" does not in any sense mean freedom from form, but only freedom to work with it.

Dream Song 77

Seedy Henry rose up shy in de world
& shaved & swung his barbells, duded Henry up
and p.a'd poor thousands of persons on topics of grand
    moment to Henry, ah to those less & none.
5 Wif a book of his in either hand
he is stript down to move on.

—Come away, Mr. Bones.

—Henry is tired of the winter,
& haircuts, & a squeamish comfy ruin-prone proud national mind,
     & Spring (in the city so called).
10 Henry likes Fall.
Hé would be prepared to live in a world of Fáll

for ever, impenitent Henry.
But the snows and summers grieve & dream;

these fierce and airy occupations, and love,
15 raved away so many of Henry's years
it is a wonder that, with in each hand
one of his own mad books and all,
ancient fires for eyes, his head full
& his heart full, he's making ready to move on.

(JOHN BERRYMAN)

It helps to know that the first book Berryman published of these
"dream songs" was seventy-seven poems in length; this was the last
poem in that first volume, which helps explain why the persona (here in
many ways identifiable with the poet) is "making ready to move on." It
would help, too, to have read those first seventy-six poems, to establish
the context in which, say, we meet "Mr. Bones" (who he?), or the
reason for the minstrel-show blackface dialect (Berryman was not
black). But my purpose here is not to explicate the poem, which is not
straightforward and, absent its context, not easy, but only to comment
on its form. What is the form? It is eighteen lines. The lines are of no
predetermined length. There are a few end words that resemble imper-
fect rhyme (*rime faible*): none/on in lines 4 and 6, all/full in lines 17
and 18. But the poem neither rhymes nor has what could be called a
rhyme scheme or pattern. With knowledge of the other poems of the
same sort, it becomes apparent that the underlying shape is three
strophes (not stanzas) of six lines each. But, once again, what *is* the
form? The answer is, simply, that it is a form invented by John Berry-
man for his own use, and which in fact he used extensively for some
hundreds of poems. I do not know of any other poet who has used the
form. Is that illegitimate? Is there something intrinsically wrong with
adjusting form and content, personally and in a distinctly craftsman-
like way, to suit what it is that one wants to say and the way in which
one wants to say it? Again, there are gains and there are losses—but
one of the losses, if it is a loss, is that of the poet's convenience, for it is
harder to create your own form than to work with one used and
perfected by hundreds of others who have gone before you. (How

many composers write symphonies today, as Beethoven and Haydn once did? How many painters paint realistic landscapes, or photographic portraits?)

George Herbert was more than prepared for that loss of convenience, three hundred and more years ago.

Heaven

O who will show me those delights on high?
     Echo.   I.
Thou Echo, thou art mortal, all men know.
     Echo.   No.
5 Wert thou not born among the trees and leaves?
     Echo.   Leaves.
And are there any leaves, that still abide?
     Echo.   Bide.
What leaves are they? impart the matter wholly.
10   *Echo.   Holy.*
Are holy leaves° the Echo then of bliss?
     Echo.   Yes.
Then tell me, what is that supreme delight?
     Echo.   Light.
15 Light to the mind: what shall the will enjoy?
     Echo.   Joy
But there are cares and business° with the pleasure?
     Echo.   Leisure.
Light, joy, and leisure: but shall they persever?
20   *Echo.   Ever.*

Other poets have experimented with echoic effects (though none more ingeniously or tellingly), but to my knowledge no poet has adopted exactly this form, with these line lengths (five metrical feet followed by two metrical feet). Do the merits of Herbert's poem depend on whether or not others have chosen to use the form he here uses? Surely not.

In short, as I have insisted from the start, our purpose in analyzing the free forms of modern poetry must be to understand them, their

---

11 **leaves** of a book as well as of a tree: i.e., the Bible   17 **business** trouble

function, their utility, their effect. The fact that they are less familiar to readers brought up on more traditional poetic fare is irrelevant to their merits or to their meaning.

(8) Concrete Poetry

Essentially, concrete poetry is a form in which shape and visual effects are more important than traditional notions of meaning.

```
silencio   silencio   silencio
silencio   silencio   silencio
silencio              silencio
silencio   silencio   silencio
silencio   silencio   silencio
```

                (EUGEN GOMRINGER)

"Silencio" is the Spanish word for "silence." The reiteration of that word is coupled with a vacant center—a silence—around which the words are grouped. That reiteration and that visual patterning *is* the poem.

There are more possibilities to concrete poetry than Gomringer's work shows; because many of those possibilities are very visual indeed I cannot demonstrate them. But here is a concrete poem that does more of what we have come to expect poetry to do:

```
            it
it          is              here
            little
            it
it          is              little
            here
            it
it          was             here
            little
it          is              lost
```

                (IAN HAMILTON FINLAY)

Playful, but not unserious, concrete poetry has plain limitations. But who doesn't? New ways of looking at structure, coupled with new ways of looking at meaning, cannot in the long run be anything but beneficial—for both the writers and the readers of poetry. We need to be wary of our natural distrust of the new and the different.

METRICS

MUSICALITY AND METRICS are not the same thing, the former having to do with larger issues of rhythm, word groupings, word choice, and so on, and the latter having to do only with conventional patterning of lines. English being what is known as an accentual language, rather than (like French or Spanish) a syllabic language, the metric of English is and has always been accentual in nature. Our first metric, that of the body of poetry known either as Anglo Saxon or Old English, is in fact heavily accentual. The Old English line was based on a stress-count principle, linked with a slightly less prominent but nevertheless deeply important alliterative practice. A typical Old English poem, with the unusual spellings modernized, is the nine-line "Caedmon's Hymn":

> *N*u shulon *h*eriyean   *h*eofonriches *w*eard,
> *m*eotudes *m*eahte   and his *m*ody*th*ank,
> *w*eork *w*uldorfaeder,   swa he *w*undra ye*hw*aes,
> *e*che *d*rihten,   *or* on*t*ealde.
> 5 He *a*erest *sh*eop   *eo*rthan *b*earnum
> *H*eofon to *h*rofe,   *h*alig *sh*yippend;
> tha *m*iddan*y*eard   *m*onkunnes *w*eard,
> *e*che *d*rihten,   *a*efter *t*eode
> *f*irum *f*oldan,   *f*rea ael*m*ihtig.

I have italicized the stressed consonants and vowels (all vowels were considered to alliterate with all other vowels). Without going into detail—for the Old English prosodic rules are relevant only to Old English and, in part, to some late alliterative poems like *Sir Gawain and the Green Knight* and *Piers Plowman*—the presence of four stresses per line, but either two or three alliterations per line, should be clear. In translation the poem reads:

> Now sing the glory of God, the King
> of Heaven, our Father's power and His perfect
> Labor, the world's conception, worked
> In miracles as eternity's Lord made
> 5   The beginning. First the heavens were formed as a roof
> For men, and then the holy Creator,
> Eternal Lord and protector of souls,
> Shaped our earth, prepared our home,
> The almighty Master, our Prince, our God.

> (translated from the Old English by BURTON RAFFEL)

The basic nature of English has not (and could not have) changed, in the relatively brief period of its existence. (Old English dates from roughly A.D. 700 to roughly 1100; Middle English dates from roughly 1100 to roughly 1500; and everything after 1500 is known as Modern English—or, to us, simply English.) But two powerful forces, both connected to the same political event, the Norman Conquest of 1066, have accelerated the normal processes of linguistic adaptation and have to some degree brought English closer to its neighbor across the English Channel, French. The first force involved was the substitution of French for English as the vehicle of commerce, the law courts, the royal court, and society generally, during the period up to about 1400. This left English as more or less a "peasant" language, free to evolve largely without the restraining influences of society's cultured conventions. The second force was the proximity of French and of French literary culture, leading eventually to a vast influx of loan words drawn from French and to a significant and long-lasting influence of French metrical practice. The result was, in effect, a sort of "compromise" between the two metrical traditions, the original Old English and the French. The work of Geoffrey Chaucer, who did not originate but who did perfect and popularize this amalgamation, best and most completely illustrates what might be called, in his name, the Chaucerian compromise:

> Whán that Ápril with his shówrĕs soote
> Thĕ dróughte ŏf March hāth pérced tŏ thĕ roote,
> Ānd bathĕd évĕry veíne ĭn swich licóur,
> Ŏf which vértŭ ĕngéndrĕd ĭs thĕ flówr;
> 5 Whán Zĕphýrŭs eek wĭth his sweetĕ breeth
> Ĭnspírĕd háth ĭn évĕry hólt ānd heeth
> Thĕ téndrĕ cróppĕs, ănd thĕ yónge sónnĕ
> Háth ĭn the Rám his hálvĕ cóurs yrónnĕ,
> Ānd smálĕ fówlĕs makĕn melōdyĕ
> 10 Thāt slepĕn ăl thĕ night wĭth ópĕn yĕ—
> Sŏ príkĕth hém Nátŭre ĭn hĭr córagĕs—
> Thānne lóngĕn folk tŏ góon ŏn pílgrímagĕs,
> Ănd pálmĕres fŏr tŏ séekĕn straungĕ stróndĕs
> Tŏ férnĕ hálwĕs, cóuthe ĭn sóndry lóndĕs;
> 15 Ănd spécially frŏm évĕry shírĕs éndĕ
> Ŏf Éngelónd tŏ Cántĕrbury they wéndĕ,
> Thĕ hóly blísfŭl mártyre fór tŏ seekĕ
> Thāt hém hăth hólpĕn whăn that they wĕre sékĕ.

I have marked the unstressed (or weak) syllables with ˘, and the stressed syllables with ´ —but the significant thing is that this Middle English sample, unlike the previous sample from Old English, required me to mark *all* the syllables, stressed and unstressed alike. Unstressed syllables do not matter in Old English prosody; they matter a great deal in the poetry of the Chaucerian compromise, and later, because the prosody has become partly stress and partly syllabic. The basic unit in Old English poetry is the stressed syllable; the basic unit in poetry of the Chaucerian compromise is the foot, composed usually of one unstressed and of one stressed syllable.

Let me set out a rough prose translation of the passage quoted above, lineated to match Chaucer's poetry, and then move on to discuss the foot, its meaning and use, in greater detail.

> When April with his sweet showers
> Has pierced to the root the drought of March,

And bathed every [plant-]vein in such a liquid,
By means of which "virtue" [power] flowers are engendered;
5   When the west wind too, with his sweet breath,
Has created [caused to grow] in every wood and field
The tender sprouts, and the young [from an astronomical stand-
     point] sun
Has run half his course in the constellation of Aries [the Ram],
And small birds make melodies,
10 [Birds] who sleep all night with open eyes—
So Nature stirs them in their hearts—
Then people long to go on pilgrimages,
And [really dedicated] pilgrims to seek strange shores
[And] distant shrines, known in various countries;
15 And especially from every shire's end
Of England they come to Canterbury,
To seek the holy blissful martyr [St. Thomas à Becket],
Who helped them when they were sick.

A metrical foot can be defined, for English poetry, as one stressed syllable and the number of unstressed syllables, from zero to as many as four, that cluster about that stressed syllable. No foot has more than one stressed syllable, which is easy enough to understand. But: it must also be understood (a) that in English poetry stress is relative stress, rather than absolute stress, and (b) that stress is established, for metrical purposes, only within the foot. This does not mean that we need pronounce a line differently once we understand its scansion (i.e., its metrical analysis). In well-written poetry there may be some minor discrepancies between the meter and the natural reading pattern, but those discrepancies should not be serious—or, by definition, we are not dealing with well-written metrical verse.

Ŏ, whát ā rógue aňd péasănt sláve aṁ Í!

This familiar line from Shakespeare's *Hamlet* has five stresses; it therefore has five feet. Each of the five feet in this line begins with an unstressed syllable and concludes with a stressed syllable. Notice that neither punctuation nor word division has any effect on metrical feet: there is a comma in the middle of the first foot, and there might just as well be a semicolon, or a colon, or a period. With a very few exceptions, punctuation is simply immaterial to scansion. Notice too that the first syllable of the word "peasant" is stressed and is in the third metrical foot, but the second syllable is unstressed and is in the fourth metrical foot.

But this is all more definite and certain than we really can be. Metrical analysis is not totally scientific, nor is it constant from age to age. How do we know, for example, that Shakespeare did not intend the first syllable to be stressed, in this line, and the second to be unstressed—in which case, plainly, the punctuation becomes of some significance, though still not controlling?

Ó, whãt ã rógue ãnd péasãnt sláve ãm Í!

The answer is that we do not know: this second possible scansion, differing in its analysis of the first foot of the line, is completely plausible. And absent any solid, objective indication from any other source (syntax, rhyme, meaning), when we cannot decide between two possible scansions we must simply admit that certainty is unavailable. But note that "possible" is not quite so open-ended as it might sound; there are governing rules as to what is and is not possible, metrically.

Consider, for a moment, the next-to-last word in the line, "am." I have marked it—and this *is* certain—as unstressed. But the third word in the line, "a," and probably the second half of the sixth word, "peasant," receive less stress, in any natural pronunciation of the line. True, but irrelevant—for natural stress within the line is not the sort of stress metrical stress is. Metrical stress, again, is (a) stress within a particular foot, and (b) relative to whatever other syllables happen also to be inside that particular foot. In the fifth foot, the other syllable is "I," and though "I" may not receive so heavy a natural reading stress as, say, "rogue," or "slave," this too is irrelevant. The only choice is between the syllables inside the particular foot—and the natural pronunciation makes it clear that "I" takes a slightly larger, slightly heavier stress than does "am." It need not be much of a difference; the very slightest amount will do—and in cases where no real decision can be made, there is a convention which solves the problem for us.

[two metrical feet omitted] Sad task, yět árgŭmént
Nŏt léss bŭt móre hĕroĭc thăn thĕ wráth
Ŏf stérn Āchíllĕs ŏn hĭs fóe pŭrsued . . .

(JOHN MILTON, *Paradise Lost*, Book IX, lines 13–15)

This is essentially the same metrical pattern as the Shakespeare line, discussed a moment ago: five metrical feet, each with an unstressed and a stressed syllable. I have, however, not marked the first two words, "sad task." There is in fact absolutely no objective reason to stress one of these words over the other. Plainly, they belong in the same foot, so one *must* be stressed over the other. How are we to decide? The convention dictates that the controlling pattern of the other feet must be considered to have been followed in these otherwise unresolvable feet too. The other feet are all in the pattern which starts with an unstressed syllable and proceeds to a stressed one. *Voilà!* We will therefore agree, quietly but with all the authority of tradition behind us, that we will consider (*not* pronounce: simply consider *for metrical purposes*) these two words to be an unstressed syllable followed by a stressed one.

There are four possible feet, in English metrics, as follows:

- ˘´ = iambic
- ´˘ = trochaic
- ˘˘´ = anapestic
- ´˘˘ = dactyllic

There are, in theory, no limits to the length of metrical lines; in practice, eight feet is pretty much the absolute maximum. The conventional names for the various line lengths are as follows:

one foot	=	monometer
two feet	=	dimeter
three feet	=	trimeter
four feet	=	tetrameter
five feet	=	pentameter
six feet	=	hexameter
seven feet	=	septameter
eight feet	=	octameter

These are Greek-derived names, because Latin poetry took lessons from the Greeks, and because English poets took their first lessons from the Latins. They may seem somewhat fearsome, at first, but they quickly become matters of easy custom—and, in truth, are they really any more fearsome than, say, quark and charm and gluon and muon? any more fearsome than bytes and their computer-language colleagues? Virtually every profession has its specific and accepted terms; these are the ones that poetry—a profession as much as any other—has adopted. If we all want to know what we mean when we say anything about metrics, we need to all use the same words.

Some meters (i.e., patterns of metrical feet) are more common than are others. English is, for better or worse, basically an iambic language. Pick up any passage from the nearest newspaper, the nearest prose book; listen to any conversation. We tend to fall into rough but clearly apparent iambics, whether we like it or not (or know it or not). Poetry is no better and no worse than the language it is written in: English poetry too is overwhelmingly iambic. For all practical purposes, indeed, it is so overwhelmingly iambic that iambic and, in the nineteenth century (and in forms like the limerick), anapestic are really the only metrical patterns we will find at work. Dactyllic is very rare indeed; trochaic is not quite so rare, but rare enough so that it is nearly impossible to find a line, let alone a poem, written in unadulterated trochaic meter. Even when one tries, consciously and hard, to keep a poem (or a line) in trochaic, so strong is the iambic nature of the language that, inevitably, the trochaic degenerates into iambic.

> Who shall doubt, Donne, where° I a poet be,
> When I dare send my epigrams to thee?
> That so alone canst judge, so alone dost make;
> And, in thy censures, evenly dost take
> 5 As free simplicity to disavow
> As thou hast best authority t'allow.
> Read all I send, and if I find but one
> Marked by thy hand, and with the better stone°,
> My title's sealed. Those that for claps° do write,

---

1 **where** whether   8 **stone** an uncertain reference, perhaps to a Greek custom of recording good luck and bad luck by depositing in a jar stones of different colors   9 **claps** applause

10　Lĕt púnĭes',° pórtĕrs', plăyĕrs'° prăise dĕlíght,
　　Añd, tíll thĕy búrst, thĕir bácks lĭke ássĕs lóad:
　　Ă mán shŏuld séĕk grĕat glŏrȳ, ănd nŏt bróad.

(BEN JONSON)

The first two feet in the first line are clearly trochaic; thereafter, inevitably, the poem slides back into iambic. Trochaic inversions (so called because a trochee—that is, a single trochaic foot—is simply an iamb—or single iambic foot—reversed) are among the most common variations, in English metrical practice. We see such inversions in the first foot of line 8 and the third foot of line 9. Variety is the spice of metrics, too; no good poet writes perfectly regular meter.

There is another important convention illustrated in this Jonson poem. Consider how I have scanned line 3. The first "so" is marked as an unstressed syllable; the second "so" is somehow amalgamated with the unstressed syllable that follows it, both together being counted—but *only* for metrical purposes: in reading the poem aloud one should sound the second "so" exactly as one does the first—as if they were only a single unstressed syllable, instead of two such syllables. What accounts for this strange proceeding? I am tempted to say, poetic desperation, but the true answer is that this, like "sad task," is a convention—that is, a generally agreed-upon device, invented by and used by poets to save themselves from metrical embarrassment. It is the apostrophe which signals the convention. Jonson frequently needed such help: witness the fifth foot of line 6, where he relies on it once again. Poets are not supposed to lean too heavily on *any* convention; it is a sign of poetic incapability, almost as bad as strict metrical regularity.

Notice, once more, that metrical feet are indifferent to word division, to punctuation, and the like.

Notice, also, the fourth foot in the last line, where "and," almost as weakly stressed a word as English has available, is nevertheless given metrical (relative) stress, because it is in the same metrical foot as the exceedingly weakly stressed second syllable of "glory." This too is something that poets are not supposed to place excessive reliance

---

10 **punies** small people, people of no importance; **players** actors (of low social standing)

upon: Jonson is rather too often on the edge of metrical embarrassment, here and elsewhere.

A Forsaken Garden

In a coign of the cliff between lowland and highland,
  At the sea-down's edge between windward and lee,
Walled round with rocks as an inland island,
  The ghost of a garden fronts the sea.
5   A girdle of brushwood and thorn encloses
  The steep square slope of the blossomless bed
Where the weeds that grew green from the graves of its roses
  Now lie dead.

(ALGERNON CHARLES SWINBURNE)

Just as trochaic inevitably slides into iambic, so too does anapestic. Swinburne is notoriously fond of the anapestic meter—but a simple body count shows that there are thirty feet in this stanza, of which seventeen are anapestic, or just under 57 percent. That is hardly overwhelming, though it is significant. Twelve feet are iambic, and the remaining foot, namely the first foot of the last line, is quite simply anomalous—that is, it does not fit any pattern, being a stressed syllable without any unstressed syllable before or after it. The second foot of that final line is clearly iambic—and we are then left with the anomalous (irregular, abnormal) first foot. These things happen, in poetry as elsewhere.

Notice in the first foot of line 3 and the second foot of line 6 the metrical convention at work, as earlier identified in the passage from Milton's *Paradise Lost*.

Notice, finally, how strangely like the Old English alliterative pattern is the alliteration in the Swinburne stanza just discussed.

Carrion Comfort

Not, I'll not, carrion comfort, Despair, not feast on thee;
Not untwist—slack they may be—these last strands of man
In me or, most weary, cry *I can no more*. I can;

Can something, hope, wish day come, not choose not to be.
5 But ah, but O thou terrible, why wouldst thou rude° on me
Thy wring-world right foot rock? lay a lionlimb against me? scan
With darksome devouring eyes my bruisèd bones? and fan,
O in turns of tempest, me heaped there; me frantic to avoid thee and
    flee?

Why? That my chaff might fly; my grain lie, sheer and clear.
10 Nay in all that toil, that coil, since (seems) I kissed the rod,
Hand rather, my heart lo! lapped strength, stole joy, would laugh,
    chéer.
Cheer whom though? The hero whose heaven-handling flung me,
    fóot tród
Me? or me that fought him? O which one? is it each one? That night,
    that year
Of now done darkness I wretch lay wrestling with (my God!) my
    God.

(GERARD MANLEY HOPKINS)

I have not marked this poem for scansion purposes; the markings you
see were made by the poet, who wrote this poem in 1885. It is a
sonnet—or, rather, it is a sonnet as Hopkins reinterpreted that form.
There are fourteen lines, there are rhymes, there is an octave and there
is a sestet. But what has happened to the meter? Nothing I have said
thus far will be of any assistance: Hopkins—like Walt Whitman,
roughly his contemporary—helped begin what has turned out to be a
major revolution in poetry. As a Jesuit, and as an Englishman, Hop-
kins was unwilling to simply jettison the Chaucerian compromise.
Instead, he developed what he called "sprung rhythm," which amounts
to almost but not quite jettisoning iambic pentameter in favor of a line
of any number of syllables (line 8 has eighteen, here, and lines 6 and 12
each have fifteen) but of five stresses only. It is an uncomfortable and
unrealistic attempt to preserve something, at least, of the older system.
Whitman's approach has turned out to be far more workable, and is
what twentieth-century poets have by and large employed, when they
chose not to write in Chaucerian compromise metric.

---

5 **rude** roughly

When I heard the learn'd astronomer,
When the proofs, the figures, were ranged in columns before me,
When I was shown the charts and diagrams, to add, divide, and
    measure them,
When I sitting heard the astronomer where he lectured with much
    applause in the lecture-room,
5 How soon unaccountable I became tired and sick,
Till rising and gliding out I wander'd off by myself,
In the mystical moist night-air, and from time to time,
Look'd up in perfect silence at the stars.

(WALT WHITMAN)

Rhyme has gone by the board; so too has anything even vaguely resembling the metric of the Chaucerian compromise. There is no way that this poem can be made to "scan," in the traditional sense of that word. It is musical, it is rhythmical, but its music and its rhythms are what we have come to call "free verse."

There is another approach, more theoretical than practical, to rhymeless poetry that is not traditionally metrical. Known as syllabic metrics, this sort of poetry organizes its lines according to the number of syllables contained therein. No reference is—in theory—made to the number of stresses or to any other prosodic indicator. The trouble is that, English being an accentual language, there is in practice no way for a reader (or speaker) of the language to actually hear or in any way take note of syllable count. And what this means is that no matter how real syllabic metrics may be to those who employ them, they can have no reality to readers or to listeners. Indeed, unless they are warned that a poem employs syllabic metrics, the reader or listener is more likely than not to be unable to perceive any such prosodic system. This is a linguistic rather than a poetic fact: it is impossible for any utterance in English *not* to be governed by the rise and fall of stressed and unstressed syllables. Let me repeat: this is not a matter that can be debated, nor is it a matter of syllabics being merely difficult. Syllabics are literally impossible in English, poetry being no more exempt from basic linguistic rules than is any other artifact of language.

In spite of these indisputable facts, there are, and probably will continue to be, poets who insist that their verse is governed by what they call syllabic metrics. They can point to their poems and count the syllables—and indeed, once alerted to the game, one can find the proper syllable count. Again, the rub is that the syllable count does not govern the verse: no matter how sensitive your ear, you cannot hear syllabics, you cannot in any way be aware of their sound or their music, and they cannot influence—much less govern—the musical organization of any line written in our language. It is a bit like a hidden puzzle: it may be there, in one sense, but unless you know in advance that it *is* there, you will not discover it, and even once you discover it, it will not make any difference in how you read or understand the line. The writers of syllabic verse may be content with a pattern which achieves literally nothing, but the English language denies them anything more significant.

Modern poetry which does not employ traditional metrics—there is of course a good deal of modern poetry which continues to employ the prosody of the Chaucerian compromise—is overwhelmingly cast in post-Whitmanian modes. The chief difference between Whitman's free verse and that employed in our time is that Whitman end-stops each line. That is, he comes to a halt of some duration at the end of each line. Modern *vers libre* (free verse) makes extensive and free use of enjambment—that is, the end of a line is not marked for a halt, but moves directly and immediately into the beginning of the line that follows. Here are two examples, in the first of which there are three enjambments in lines 1–5, and in the second of which there is enjambment throughout:

Twilights

The big stones of the cistern behind the barn
Are soaked in whitewash.
My grandmother's face is a small maple leaf
Pressed in a secret box.
5   Locusts are climbing down into the dark green crevices
Of my childhood. Latches click softly in the trees. Your hair is
gray.

The arbors of the cities are withered.
Far off, the shopping centers empty and darken.

A red shadow of steel mills.

(JAMES WRIGHT)

Continuum

Some beetle trilling
its midnight utterance.

Voice of the scarabee,
dungroller,
5   working survivor . . .

I recall how each year
returning from voyages, flights
over sundown snowpeaks,
cities crouched over darkening lakes,
10   hamlets of wood and smoke,
I find
     the same blind face upturned to the light
     and singing
     the one song,

15   the same weed managing
     its brood of minute stars
     in the cracked flagstone.

(DENISE LEVERTOV)

And feeling can run high, between the adherents to the traditional metrical scheme and those who follow Whitman. It has been running high for a very long time, as the following poem by Edgar Lee Masters shows:

Petit, the Poet

Seeds in a dry pod, tick, tick, tick,
Tick, tick, tick, like mites° in a quarrel—
Faint iambics that the full breeze wakens—
But the pine tree makes a symphony thereof.
5   Triolets, villanelles, rondels, rondeaus.
Ballades by the score with the same old thought:

---

2 **mites** tiny biting insects of the spider family

The snows and the roses of yesterday are vanished;
And what is love but a rose that fades?
Life all around me here in the village:
10   Tragedy, comedy, valor and truth,
Courage, constancy, heroism, failure—
All in the loom, and, oh, what patterns!
Woodlands, meadows, streams and rivers—
Blind to all of it all my life long.
15   Triolets, villanelles, rondels, rondeaus,
Seeds in a dry pod, tick, tick, tick,
Tick, tick, tick, what little iambics,
While Homer and Whitman roared in the pines!

Petit, of course, is the word used in French to describe someone or something physically small.

The stance of the other side, adhering firmly to tradition, is nicely put by Stephen Spender—not surprisingly, a British poet—in the following poem:

Statistics

Lady, you think too much of speeds,
    Pulleys and cranes swing in your mind;
    The Woolworth Tower has made you blind
To Egypt and the pyramids.

5   Too much impressed by motor-cars
    You have a false historic sense.
    But I, perplexed at God's expense
Of electricity on stars,

From Brighton pier shall weigh the seas,
10   And count the sands along the shore:
    Despise all moderns, thinking more
Of Shakespeare and Praxiteles.°

The comments of T. S. Eliot, a magnificent critic as well as a poet, are perhaps the best way of resolving—by not resolving—the dispute.

---

12 **Praxiteles** ancient Greek sculptor, fl. ca. 350 B.C.

Writing in 1917, he declared roundly that *"vers libre* [free verse] does not exist . . . it is a battle-cry of freedom, and there is no freedom in art. And as the so-called *vers libre* which is good is anything but 'free,' it can better be defended under some other label." On the other hand, he demands, why insist on formal traditional scansion, which "tells us very little"? There is, he insists, "no reason why, within the single line, there should be any repetition; why there should not be lines (as there are) divisible only into feet of different type"—which would, to be sure, destroy the traditional notions of metrical patterning. As to rhyme, he adds that "it is possible that excessive devotion to rhyme has thickened the modern ear. The rejection of rhyme is not a leap at facility; on the contrary, it imposes a much severer strain upon the language." As to formal patterns, too, he notes that "the decay of intricate formal patterns has nothing to do with the advent of *vers libre*. It had set in long before." He concludes, accordingly, that "the division between Conservative Verse and *vers libre* does not exist, for there is only good verse, bad verse, and chaos." He rephrased this, even more pithily, twenty-five years later, saying "no verse is free for the man who wants to do a good job." (He noted, in an aside, that "I have never been able to retain the names of feet and meters, or to pay the proper respect to the accepted rules of scansion.")

AUTHOR INDEX

POEM INDEX

SUBJECT INDEX

Poets and poems represented in this book are here indexed, rather than in the two finding lists which precede this Index, *only* when they are mentioned or discussed in passing. Poems quoted, and discussion of those poems, may be located via the finding lists, either by title or under the author's name.